Life Above Zero

Making mindset manageable, health holistic, spirituality science, and life liberating!

By

Lauren Kerr

Bachelor Psychology, Honours
International Life Coach + NLP practitioner

LIVING LIFE ABOVE ZERO; MAKING MINDSET MANAGEABLE, HEALTH HOLISTIC, SPIRITUALITY SCIENCE, AND LIFE LIBERATING!
Copyright 2020 by **LAUREN KERR**

All rights reserved. No part of this book may be used or reproduced in any manner whatsoever without written permission from **LAUREN KERR**, except as provided by Australia copyright law or in the case of brief quotations embodied in articles and reviews.

The scanning, uploading and distribution of this book via the Internet or via any other means without the permission of the publisher is illegal and punishable by law.

Please purchase only authorised electronic editions and do not participate in or encourage electronic piracy of copyrighted materials. Your support of the author's rights is sincerely appreciated.

Printed in Australia
ISBN: 978-0-6487280-3-0 (sc)
ISBN: 978-0-6487280-4-7 (e)

First Printing: 2020

"This book will equip you with the practical skills and mindset, backed with the psychology, research and statistics to help you unlock the code to success, in your life, relationships, and career. (With some positive, warm and fuzzy vibes thrown in, sprinkled with tough love)."

" Lauren gets it - 'Life Above Zero' is how Lauren shows up in all areas of life, it's a testimony of how understanding and mastering your inner world changes your outer world and the lives of everyone you touch! There is so much wisdom and lessons in these pages I have learnt later in life as a woman, mum, friend, business owner and wife that I wish I could have gifted to a younger version of me. I can't wait for this book to be passed onto friends, sisters and daughters to empower them with the self belief, self worth and skills to nourish their mental health and go after what they want in life - unlocking health, wealth AND abundance!"

LOREN LAHAV,
International Speaker, Coach and Author

" These days, I'm all about embracing my 'flawsome' so Lauren's willingness to get real, raw and vulnerable and talk about the not so pretty parts of life and business is something that I both appreciate - and applaud. I believe it's really important for us to be encouraging more open, honest discussions surrounding mental health, self sabotage, the fear of rejection, failure and our need for non stop comparison. My mission is all about empowering women so I'm keen for women of any age and stage in their lives to deep dive into this book to explore mindset and understand their psychology so that they have the tools to become the very best version of themselves."

ASHY BINES,
Co-Founder and Creative Director of the Ashy Bines Group

"After mentoring and coaching people in business for the last 10 around years I know that anyone from any walk of life can be successful but you need to master and strengthen the character traits of grit, vision, persistence, passion, delayed gratification and resilience to break free from mediocrity. I love that in this book Lauren teaches you how to master your mindset so you can break through your comfort zones and self limiting beliefs in order to uplevel and create a life and business you're proud of. 'Life Above Zero', isn't wishy washy or woo woo, Lauren is direct and provides simple, applicable steps in order to make long term changes and take control back of your life and future."

FRAZER BROOKES,
Business Coach, Author and Speaker

CONTENTS

Chapter 1: What is Life Above Zero? — 13

Chapter 2: Before You Move Forward You Need to Let Go — 31

Chapter 3: Who Am I? — 45

Chapter 4: You Can't Hit a Target Without a Focus — 67

Chapter 5: Self-Sabotage; What Stops Us from Taking the Action — 85

Chapter 6: Passion and Perseverance; The Secret Sauce — 109

Chapter 7: Owning All Parts of You — 127

Chapter 8: Enjoy the Journey — 141

Chapter 9: Playing Small Doesn't Serve the World — 167

Chapter 10: Feel the Fear and Do it Anyway — 187

Chapter 11: It's Ok to Not Be Ok — 209

Chapter 12: Manifest and Show Up — 235

Chapter 13: How You Do Something is How You Do Everything — 259

Chapter 14: Living with Intention; Choose to Thrive, Not Just Survive — 273

Chapter 15: Playing Above the Line — 297

Chapter 16: Your Personal Formula — 313

Chapter 17: Do the Best You Can with What You Can, as Long as You Can — 325

Introduction

I want to start by thanking all my teachers and mentors. A special thank you to my biggest teachers – my beautiful parents. Thank you for giving me the biggest and best gift I will ever receive, unconditional love. Because of you, I know how to give love, but I also know how to receive it. Because you believed in me, I have believed in myself enough to live my mission, and because of you, I can inspire others to live their Life Above Zero, too.

I am grateful for every person who has crossed my path and enjoyed a little slice of my experience in this beautiful world. And for those who have either taught me a lesson, been a mirror to reflect my own bullshit, or held a safe space for me to fall over and pick myself up again. I am a committed student of life. I am a result of the people I talk to, the books and studies I have read, degrees and courses I have completed, and universities and conferences I have attended.

Do you ever feel you read books and attend conferences and they are all saying the same thing but in a different way? That is because leaders leverage off ideas and resources, and success leaves clues. You can't skip the awkward learning curve, but you can definitely shorten it by learning from those who have gone before you. Unlike what some bad ass may have advised you, rules are not made to be broken. Follow them!

There are universal laws you follow if you want success! For example, if you want to be healthy, move and eat well, right? If you want to have money, spend less than you save or create. Do you want to be successful in business? Celebrate small wins with gratitude and persistence.

This is the code to unlocking success in your lives, relationships, and careers. Stand on the shoulders of giants; the student always out does the teacher! Nothing in this book is original - these ideas and concepts have been passed down for thousands of years and are the universal laws that govern all the life around us. I am fortunate enough to have stood on the shoulders of giants, so this is my gift from them, to you.

*"I not only use all the brains that I have,
but all I can borrow."*

WOODROW WILSON

CHAPTER ONE

What is Life Above Zero?

WHAT IS LIFE ABOVE ZERO?

I am so thrilled to have you here and I trust the universe has an intention for you, ensuring this book crossed your path for a reason. Before I freak you out and you pop this book back or return it to your friend (who reads way too many self-help books), yes, I'm a massive believer in universal laws; one being the law of attraction.

If that is not something that also aligns with your beliefs or you think that is all a little too 'woo-woo', we have a whole book yet to change your mind. Please know this isn't just another self-help book that promises you all your wildest dreams will be served on a silver platter if you think about it often enough.

Instead, this book will equip you with the practical skills and mindset, backed with the psychology, research and statistics to help you unlock the code to success in your life, relationships, and career. With some positive, warm and fuzzy vibes thrown in, sprinkled with tough love.

You're probably wondering, *what is "Life Above Zero" and how do I live it?*

Well, first, I need your commitment to be real and raw with yourself. Whatever comes up for you in this book, know you will only get out what you put in. It's hard when someone expects you to open up and trust them if you don't know a little about them, so, let me go first.

I've always felt like I had a mission in this world. I learned early on in my teenage years to let go, trust my gut, and follow the pull. There is so much research about this you will get to find out about later in the book (I told you there was lots of juicy stuff in store for you).

My gut instinct has pulled me in so many directions over the years. Different education and courses, different jobs, different romantic relationships, social circles and friendships, and even different countries. My biggest tug from my gut was when I was seventeen. I felt the pull towards the sunshine, towards new experiences, new depths and new lessons.

Ironically, the pull towards it all was so strong, you would be forgiven for thinking I was running away from something – but that wasn't quite the case. I was being pulled away from so much unconditional love and support, pretty much everything I've ever known. Away from my comfort zone, my beautiful, loving family. (Mum, Dad, two younger brothers, and my pug, Jellybean). My high school boyfriend who I thought I would be with forever. My friendships, and that town on the river that had been my playground and a haven for seventeen years. Everything.

If I'm honest, reflecting now (and I think even secretly I knew it back then), I *was* running away from something. Running away from the fear of mediocrity. I had been with my high school boyfriend for nearly four years. We were head over heels for each other (ahh, first love). I *thought* I saw how the rest of my life would pan out. Easy. Predictable. Simple. Our own little fairy tale. (Oh God, how naïve was I?)

He was a year older. He had gotten into a university in Canberra. And the plan was: he would have a gap year while I was finishing year twelve and then I would follow him to Canberra (because I would hate being apart). We would adventure and conquer life together and live happily ever after with a couple of kids somewhere close to our families. We were both simple people who found fulfilment in the small stuff and had similar values. This plan seemed common when you fall in love in a small town.

I have always looked up to my parents. I love the marriage they have; I love the family they've created and safe haven they designed for me and my brothers, especially when I knew that one in two marriages ended in divorce.

They are teenage sweethearts and had been together since my mum was fourteen (not without their rocky patches - no marriage is immune to them). I just wanted that, and I honestly thought I could have easily had that.

I knew what marriage gave my mum; the connection, the love, the belonging, the security (both emotionally and financially), shared memories, shared laughs, shared tears and shared pains. I knew it took hard work, commitment, mutual respect, patience and compromise.

I was lucky to have, and still have, a close relationship with my mum. She is my best friend. Mum was open with me early on and would try to pass on her wisdom so I could make the best decisions, saving me from some of that teenage heartache. That is what all mums try to do in the best way they know how.

If you are a gen Y baby like me – chat to the older women in your life and ask about the values and expectations of women in that era. Women could go to a university and pursue their passion and careers. Whether it be consciously from their family and friends or unconsciously communicated and reinforced via magazines, books and movies at the time, one thing was certain. It was more widely and traditionally expected that women would follow their partners' business pursuits and be the homemaker.

Sure, there were some brave and courageous women who broke out from that mould (like many still do today – and girlfriend, I salute you) but that was a compromise my mum made. She loved my dad so much she abandoned her dreams and her career to be with him and accommodate his (not that he ever asked her to do that, but it's crazy what we do for love!)

> Holding onto something so tightly in fear of losing it is only an attempt to demonstrate ownership of it

I guess, for me, as much as I loved my boyfriend and the future we planned together, the fear of the compromise I had to make to fulfil that "white picket fence" dream scared the shit out of me. That word beamed down on me again "mediocrity."

Risking that life together was scary, and man, was the journey that followed a painful, but beautiful one. Risking my independence, adventuring, exploring, and pursuing my own career was scary, but I knew the pain of regret would have cut me so much deeper. If it was meant to be, it would be.

Holding onto something so tightly in fear of losing it is only an attempt to demonstrate ownership of it. Let it go and if it finds its way back to you, it is yours, it always has been, and it always will be.

Looking back now I realise how arrogant it was of me to use that word - **'mediocrity'**. I now know life takes guts. Courage. Hard work. Magic. Not that it was mediocre. Destiny had a different path for me. Also, it turns out I was too selfish to compromise. I am embarrassed to admit it, but this is exactly what I want to encourage you to do as you read this book.

Be open to recognising the not so pretty parts of yourself and courageous enough to own them. There is nothing wrong with staying in your hometown and living out your fairy tale. I guess I just wanted something different. Not more. Not less. Just different.

Leaving probably was one of the hardest, yet most powerful decisions I have ever made, and it drastically changed the direction of my entire life.

Moments like these are called "pivots." Moments in your life; one event, one person or one decision changes everything.

> Moments like these are called "pivots."
>
> Moments in your life;
>
> one event, one person or one decision changes everything.

I am committed to consciously creating a life I love. I refuse to believe life is happening to us, instead it is happening for us. You're in the driver's seat. Get involved and have your say in the creation process – the life you currently have is a direct reflection of the decisions you've previously made. Want a better or different life? *Make better or different choices*. It's as easy or as hard as that. (Sorry, but I warned you there was no silver platter service here).

I made a decision, and I busted my little butt off studying in year twelve. I am not naturally 'smart', but this girl has 'grit' (another thing I will teach you about later in chapter six). I got a scholarship upon my graduation to study Psychology at Griffith University.

The first in my family to go to university, I moved as soon as I turned

Universal Assignments

When you reflect on your life, what are some pivot points that changed the trajectory of your life or the path you were travelling down (whether you perceive it to be negative or positive)? Was it a person, an event or a decision?

eighteen to the sunny Gold Coast in Australia. My new playground to explore. A new lifestyle, new friends, new education and the famous Cavill Ave. High heels. Hot nights. Vodka (the cheap stuff). Dance floor. More Vodka. Uh oh. Toilet. Vomit. Repeat.

This was enough excitement in itself. Being just eighteen and a girl who loves to dance all night! I tried to mend my broken heart so with that, too, came the excitement of new boys.

By the way, if you're heart-broken and wanting to try that life: I don't recommend it. Save yourself the awkward and embarrassing walks of shame and know the only way to put a broken heart back together is by doing the work and learning to love yourself first. There is no quick fix, you can't find someone to do that for you, but I promise more on that later, too.

So... why Psychology?

I have always been passionate about helping others and wanted to leave a positive impact on the world to ensure my life would not be lived in vain. That I served others, left a legacy behind, and the world was happier, better, more educated, connected and accepting because of my presence.

Health is holistic and is just as much about the mind and soul as it is about the physical body. There is power in learning how to understand and control our mindset, instead of allowing our mindset to control us.

I loved deep and meaningful conversations; I was that awkward person at a party who wouldn't say too much, but once I had you in a corner, I would pull out the random, deep, personal, and thought-provoking questions. I hated small talk and still do!

I loved understanding people, their decisions, and their lives, and would listen without judgement to let them know they were enough, and I would fall in love with strangers' imperfections. Seriously, don't you wish others could see themselves the way you see them?

> Health is holistic and is just as much about the mind and soul as it is about the physical body

I was eager to understand myself and others, and why we do the random things we do. There had to be some method to all the madness! My psychology degree sparked a curiosity for life. Pretty much everything there on after really derived from lessons and opportunities that arose from immersing myself in learning and education, in all of its forms.

Fast forward a few years, a few too many late nights, way too many hangovers, lots of bar jobs and promotional modelling work (which paid my bills through uni), overseas trips between uni semesters, and a uni exchange where I lived in Hawaii. Throw in a few more boys I had no inclination of ever emotionally opening myself up to and Voila! I wrote a thesis 'Moderating Body Language Effects on Task Performance'.

I graduated my Bachelor of Psychology with Honours! I guess the university chewed me up and spat me out. All starry-eyed and optimistic about the future, I had no idea what I wanted to do. Despite the seventeen years straight of schooling, I didn't feel like I was genuinely prepared for the 'real world'.

I didn't have much practical experience; most kids from my era (unlike our parents) were encouraged to go to a university. (I guess their mums must have got in their ear, too, and passed on those lessons). The reality was/is, there are way too many of us who are over qualified with not enough jobs.

So many graduates are taking positions they don't need their degree or the $40,000 HECS debt to do. Then they apply for jobs only to be told they don't have enough experience.

It was a super frustrating time and I know I talk on behalf of a lot of Generation Y when I say this, and I don't think it gets spoken enough about. I wasn't one hundred percent sure I wanted to work in the research field or as a clinical psychologist. So I wasn't sold on adding a few more tens of thousands of dollars to my HECS debt to do a further two years of study.

I was excited and eager to get experience and start applying all the knowledge that had been brewing in my brain. For nearly two decades I had been herded through classrooms like sheep, spoken at, and told to revise notes. I hoped I could remember enough of all the pretty highlighted headings and dot points I'd scribbled all over my summary pages to regurgitate it on the exam paper to score myself a high distinction. Or just a pass – as I remember my university pals saying, "Ps get degrees".

Isn't that how the western school system works? Throw in some fun, too, for those who survived unscathed from that time. Unless you are socially awkward and your self-esteem hit an all-time low because you had buck teeth before you got your braces. But more on that in chapter seven.

In all seriousness, I knew the Positive Psychology Field called to me, which was something I got a taste for in my degree.

When Positive Psychology was introduced to me in a class, it was explained that, traditionally, when you go see a psychologist, they often ask "what's wrong?" As though something needs to be wrong with a focus on disease or ill mental health. Therefore, energy, support, research, and direction have to be given to get you back to the baseline of zero. Which was in essence, a state of mediocrity and normality.

What is normal these days anyway? That is often open to perception and interpretation even with the application of objective tools like a DSM (The Diagnostic and Statistical Manual of Mental Disorders). In contrast, positive psychology was about asking questions like "what's right?" Focusing on strengths, building on that, and leveraging on all the things you do well to have more of it in your life.

That was where the theory and term "Life Above Zero" came from. It resonated so much with my personal experience, my view on life, my passions. It soon become my personal and professional mission to inspire others to create and live their own Life Above Zero. And I would do so by living my message, educating, empowering, and showing others how I did it.

There is more than mediocrity, there is more than the baseline or the bare minimum. There is soaring, there is exceeding, there is abundance, there is Life Above Zero, and everyone deserves to live it.

At the time, Positive Psychology was a relatively new realm popular in Europe. However, it was only recently gaining awareness in Australia with emerging research (with the help of quantum physics) depicting positive psychology practices and theories. These were more effective in helping build a rapport with clients and making meaningful changes.

In Australia, the only Master's program in Positive Psychology offered at the time was in Melbourne and I wasn't ready to give up my Gold Coast lifestyle. Thirsty for some experience in a job that was emotionally

"Look around you and look inside you.
How many people do you think are settling?
I will tell you: A hell of a lot of people.
People are settling every day into okay
relationships and okay jobs and an okay life.
And do you know why?
Because okay is comfortable.
Okay pays the bills, gives you a warm bed at night
and allows one to go out with co-workers on a Friday
evening to enjoy happy hour.
But do you know what okay is not?
Okay isn't thrilling, it isn't passion; it isn't the reason you
get up every day;
it isn't the reason you go to bed late
and wake up early.
Okay is not the reason you risk absolutely everything
you have for the smallest chance that something amazing
could happen."

ANON

rewarding, I was successful in receiving a position in the Queensland Government's competitive graduate scheme where I got a job working in Child Protection and Safety.

> There is more than mediocrity,
>
> there is more than the baseline
>
> or the bare minimum.

For the purpose of not glorifying my story, I can't forget to tell you that was after my plan A fell through. I had my heart set on being a psychologist in the Army. I applied and went through a series of tests and interviews but didn't pass my medical because of cancer cells on my cervix. (Another story for another chapter).

At the time, I was disheartened and frustrated but sometimes doors are closed in your face because they are not meant for you. The universe (or God, whatever you perceive him/her to be) knows you better than you know yourself and has a better plan in store for you. I now know this to be true.

After all this, not only was my degree and high distinctions not enough, I had to enter a competitive graduate program to finally land my first full-time job. Complete with a two to three hour commute every day. Woo hoo! This is the holy grail, isn't it?

No more juggling three to four casual jobs. No more working until four a.m. in skimpy bartending outfits. And no more missing out on the weekends!

So lucky! Instead, I will work forty to fifty hours a week (plus unpaid overtime) for the next fifty years of my life. I'll commute ten to fifteen hours a week, compete with my colleagues for positions higher up the corporate ladder. Be an emotional punching bag for my clients who refuse to take responsibility for their shit. And, if I'm lucky, I will get every second Christmas off to visit my family (only if my twenty days annual leave is approved). I hit the jackpot!

Okay, okay, I will put my serious hat on again. It was an exciting time to be working for the Queensland Government and, in particular, Child

Protection. It had just implemented a new Collaborative Assessment and Planning framework that was changing the way authorities were working with and strengthening families to protect children. I loved it.

I was in my element and delved right into the tools, research and practices based in the foundations and theory of positive psychology. In the graduate scheme they gave me a budget I could invest in my personal development. I used it to enrol (yet again more education. I know, I am crazy) and study around full-time work to get my life coaching certificate. I became an International Accredited Life and Wellness Coach and NLP (Neurolinguistics Programming) Practitioner.

I found working with the families on my case load that my life coaching skills become one of my biggest assets in assisting families and developing a rapport with them. I am so thankful for my colleges and the leaders in management during the years I worked in child protection.

Working in this area and system is such a hard job. I have faith our country's children in care are in good hands because of the leaders in management who continue to show up, day in and day out. They fight for what's right, not what's easy; for a child's right to be loved, supported, accepted and protected.

I learned so much about myself, about humanity, about working in a team and what working in a corporate ladder looks like. With all the red tape and work place politics that comes with it, the job took its toll on my ability to live my life and I struggled to leave work at work.

I got frustrated with the fact I couldn't help everyone. I had to admit I couldn't change the world. I wanted to work with people who voluntarily wanted help to be happier and healthier, not because the court ordered them to do so. I lost my sparkle, my hope and my belief in humanity. I lost my own genuine lust and zest for life and all the beautiful, small things that make it so special.

I decided to, once again, trust my gut. This time it pulled me towards opening my life coaching business, which I called (I'm sure you could guess by now) 'Life Above Zero'. This is where all the pieces of the puzzle came together. I am not airy-fairy; my head is not up in the clouds. Working in Child Protection made sure I was grounded in the reality of humanity. Being confronted daily with high-risk cases and circumstances made me very aware of the highs and lows in life, the differences in opportunities and experiences. This grounds me yet does not jade me.

I now mentor thousands of women around the world to live a life of health, wealth and abundance with one-on-one life and wellness coaching. I run workshops, business mentoring, and wealth creation program "Babes in Business" and a Podcast "Babes Talking Business." I am genuine, transparent, and honest. In this book, I do not want to sugarcoat my words or only show the best bits of life. I want to challenge you and your perspective on hard and unpleasant feelings of losing loved ones, the uncertainty of new beginnings, failures, disappointments, ending relationships, being stuck in a rut, and feeling lost. The stuff that nobody writes books about.

I want to demonstrate and teach you how to face those difficult times with a holistic and mindful approach so you can learn how to get the most out of life by practicing gratitude. My intention for this book is to teach, coach, and empower you with life skills to lead a balanced, fulfilling life, with meaningful relationships, a rewarding career, and maintain your holistic health.

I would love for you to look back on where you have come from with acceptance and gratitude. That idea may sound like swallowing razor blades now, I know, but get back to me at the end about this. Trusting the process, looking for and loving the lessons along the way, understanding and even better *managing* your emotions and mindset. Working out what makes you happy (like really happy) and creating more room for those things and those people in your life.

Use this book to share love and light. A resource, a coach, a friend, some inspiration you can always turn to – to regain focus, gain momentum, to pick yourself up, and to hear validation. A polite reminder that you are worthy. There is Life Above Zero, and you deserve to live it.

Life Above Zero encompasses a holistic view of living and wellbeing, acknowledging there is more than not being sick, not being sad, and not having anything to complain about. Yes, those are things to be grateful for, but are you truly grateful for them?

Does your soul ooze gratitude for the energy you have to freely devote to the things you deem important? Are you even aware of what values are important to you? Are you surrounded by friends, but still feel alone? When you hear your loved ones speak, are you being present and listening

"So many people live with unhappy circumstances and yet will not take the initiative to change their situation because they are conditioned to live a life of security, conformity and conservatism. All of which may appear to give one peace of mind, but in reality, nothing is more dangerous to the adventurous spirit within a man than a secure future. The very basic core of a man's living spirit is his passion for adventure. The joy of life comes from our encounters with new experiences, and hence there is no greater joy than to have an endlessly changing horizon, for each day to have a new and different sun."

INTO THE WILD

to what they have to say?

Connection. Purpose. Intention. There is more to life than coasting through it. And there is more to life than being "just okay." There are reasons to wake up every day and feel enthusiastic with a genuine lust for life. There is a Life Above Zero. You don't need a lot of money or the perfect body, you don't need a lot of friends or the perfect partner, and you don't need a lot of attention.

All you need is your perspective challenged, broadened, and heard. I hope with each of the chapters you read; you can grow and learn something new. I hope something I say resonates with your soul and you slowly start to live deliberately, a Life Above Zero.

It seems every day life's treadmill pressures us to run faster and faster just to keep up. We live in an age where we consume information, food and media at a breakneck pace, with so many influences dictating to us what is important, forcing expectations upon us of the person we have to be.

We have every minute of our scheduled days packed with errands, tasks and chores. We rush from one place to the next and we rush to get ready in the morning. Then we rush to get to work on time just to rush in completing the tasks expected of us before we then rush home to meet our next obligation. And then we prepare ourselves for our next rushed day.

Life is increasingly competitive. Too many of us become dependent upon adrenalin to keep us running. We access adrenalin on demand: tea, coffee, alcohol, cigarettes, sugar. These mimic the effects of the real thing, however, ironically can lead to 'burn out', where we feel stressed and unhappy instead of fuelled and energised.

Many of us feel overwhelmed because of our fast-paced lives, leading to an alarming spike in diagnosed depression and anxiety in our society. I cannot tell you all life's secrets. I can't change your entire life today. What I can do is promise to volunteer personal experiences, education, tools, strategies and research. This will help you start each day with intention, purpose and gratitude, and the skills to help you on the days where you wake up and struggle to find those things.

You may not have the time to make big changes yet. That's OK, however, with this book choose to honour yourself and your worth. If you can only commit to small steps, start there. Your journey starts with you taking that first small step. Honour your time, honour your health, and honour your soul longing for purpose.

Try to sit with your thoughts and complete the little tasks here for you. (I like to call them universal assignments). Look inside yourself for *genuine* energy. The biggest source of energy is enthusiasm and a lust for life. When you reduce stress there is less need for adrenalin. Now that you know a little more about me and my intention for this book, I would love to know: *what brought you here?*

Universal Assignments

What brought you here?
What is your intention?
What are you hoping
to get out of this book?

CHAPTER TWO

Before You Move Forward You Need to Let Go

Life Above Zero is all about creating a life you love, moving forward, and living a life in alignment with your values, having clarity of what's important to you, and making more room for it. I think it's important to know that, before you can move forward, acknowledge where you currently are.

For most of us, consciously taking the time and space to do that scares the shit out of us. It is confronting because, more often than not, there is a large discrepancy between where we are and where we want to be. Or where we are and where we thought we would be or realising the expectations of where you believed you should be.

When you make the space and take the time to acknowledge where you currently are in your life, in your relationships, in your finances, and in your career, for most of us, we find something is holding us back. Whether it be a past wrong, a missed opportunity, or a previous relationship we are holding on to. To move forward, you need to let go.

Remember at the start of this book where I encouraged you to be brave, to be real and raw with yourself? I bet as you read the above paragraph someone came to mind, right? Perhaps someone who has previously hurt you or you are constantly seeking approval and validation from?

Don't worry, your secret is safe with me. But let's work with that; remember when I explained you will get out of this book what you put in? Unfortunately, pain does not discriminate. It affects us all; the elderly, children, men, women, the rich, and the poor.

Every race in every country, in every town or city or village is subject to

*"That's the thing about pain.
It demands to be felt."*

JOHN GREEN, *THE FAULT IN OUR STARS*

pain. The pain of stubbing a toe, the pain of a broken bone, or a split lip. Then, there is a different kind of pain, which is not tangible, not as obvious to others as a sling or bruise.

More often than not, it's not the pain that's the issue, it is how we deal with it. Girls get it over and done with. Generally, we accept the fairer sex, women, talk about when they're in emotional pain. Women cry, talk, cry some more and analyse their broken relationships from every single angle so they can resolve it.

What are you holding onto?

For this exercise, let's talk about the breakdown of romantic relationships. Research has identified women fall in love faster. Ironically, they also get over relationships faster than their male counterparts.

Sorry guys, but you suck at moving on. Men, at the end of a relationship, revert to wearing a façade. Men will say they're okay and genuinely believe that for some time. They will distract themselves with anything they can get their hands on. Mates, alcohol, sports, gym, work, and casual sex for a few months.

This is partly why the suicide rate is higher amongst men. Eventually, when their façade weakens, their pain creeps up and surprises them. Finding themselves facing a failed relationship will push a man to one of two conclusions:

1) Man realises he really is happier without Sally. He goes about his business and meets Jill.
2) Man realises he really isn't ok. He realises he's made a mistake and, usually by this time, Sally has moved on and is now dating Jack.

Welcome to the club! Failed relationships. We all have them.

Gen Y, we've come up with a brilliant foolproof plan for moving on:

You explained to them how you felt and the need for the clean break. Because we are all mature adults who can handle talking about emotions, right?

You cut them out of your life. Let's be honest, you blocked them on Facebook and stopped following them on Instagram but are using your best

*"Resentment is like drinking poison
and hoping it will kill your enemies."*

NELSON MANDELA

friend's account to stalk them.

You are moving forward with your life. Well, you're trying to and are hoping whoever you've left behind is seeing all your fabulous Instagram posts about how well you're doing without them.

Just stop. What you're doing is not working. These are all appropriate and relevant steps and congratulations for being decisive enough to walk away from anything that no longer serves you, grows you, or makes you happy. However, as much as I would like to tell you you're on your way, I am sorry to say you are not.

The crazy Facebook stalking and forced smile in your Instagram selfie isn't fooling anyone, including yourself. The "buts," "what ifs" and "I should haves" are making you crazy. It's a slow process, but you will get there. First, we need to explore your thinking.

The reason people have trouble letting go of relationships are usually the huge questions "why" and "what if." Generally, there is still resentment or disbelief how one party fell short of the other's expectations, or because there is unfinished business.

Resentment. Let it go. As the famous Nelson Mandela states, "Resentment is like drinking poison and then hoping it will kill your enemies." Wasting energy hating another person is not doing you any favours. If they hurt you, why are you the one who is being punished feeling all this hate and heavy feelings?

If they haven't been bothered enough to address and solve the situation, you allowing them to consume your energy is not affecting them. You lie awake thinking of your situation, and they are sleeping just fine. The only thing you are doing is closing yourself off from all the gifts the universe is trying to give to you, if only you were present. Allow your past to make you better, not bitter.

Frustration is just misplaced expectations

Expectations. Expect things only of yourself, that way you cannot be disappointed. Frustration is just misplaced expectations. A wise woman (my beautiful mother) once told me not to place my own expectations onto someone else. The old saying "treating others how you would like to be treated" still stands during the breakdown of a relationship.

"People are often unreasonable, irrational,
and self-centred.
Forgive them anyway.
If you are kind, people may accuse
you of selfish, ulterior motives.
Be kind anyway.
If you are successful, you will
win some unfaithful friends and
some genuine enemies.
Succeed anyway.
If you are honest and sincere,
people may deceive you.
Be honest and sincere anyway.
What you spend years creating,
others could destroy overnight.
Create anyway.
If you find serenity and happiness,
some may be jealous.
Be happy anyway.
The good you do today will often be forgotten.
Do good anyway.
Give the best you have, and it will never be enough.
Give your best anyway.
In the final analysis, it is between you and God.
It was never between you and them anyway."

MOTHER TERESA

I know you don't want to but give your best anyway. Unfortunately, there are no rules or textbook dictating each role in a relationship and there certainly aren't any rules during the ending of a relationship. You have to just learn and move forward. At least next time you'll allocate your energies accordingly.

It's not all about you. I know it's tough to believe, but generally, a relationship that has broken down affects both of you. Try to be mindful of how the other person feels; just because things have ended between you does not make them a bad person. Maybe they were brought up with different family values, maybe their culture doesn't hold the same beliefs or meaning, maybe they have been hurt before and you are just witnessing their carefully critiqued coping mechanism.

If there is honestly nothing more you can do to fix the situation, you've taken ownership of your part in the breakdown. All you can do is acknowledge you did all you were willing to at the time; you were the best person you could be. Understand it happened and dwelling on it, reliving it, ruminating on every little detail won't change anything.

Forgive them,

not because they deserve it,

but because you do.

You only prevent yourself from closing a chapter and getting closer to your Life Above Zero. Let go of the negative energy. Let go of the hate. And let go of the heavy burden. Forgive them, not because they deserve it, but because you do.

But What If?

"But what if I had…?" You've done all you can. So, the unfinished business. The "what if?"

What if what? This is one I hear repeatedly. Insert your excuse: timing, priorities, work, travelling, etc. If you were to be brutally honest with yourself, if you both truly wanted the relationship to work, you would both be fighting for it now!

Write down every reason you're telling yourself is the excuse for the prolonged letting go. Once you have written them all down, imagine each of those excuses being as you want them to be. For example, if one thing you're telling yourself is: "What if I spent more time with his family/friends?"

Imagine yourself wiping that excuse out and picture spending more time with his family and friends, really envision it. How do you feel now? I am confident you still won't feel ready to commit or try mending that relationship again. That's because, yes, you like them, you like the comfort you find in them, they were part of your journey and that chapter of your life, but it's not enough. It's not enough for you now, the person you've grown into or the direction you're wanting to pursue. Be honest to yourself. You like them, or maybe they like you, but not enough.

Getting Closure

Closure. It's something so many women yearn for and I swear so many men would benefit from it, were it socially acceptable for men to talk about feelings. (We are closer than any other generation when it comes to men and their feelings. Generation Y, give yourself a pat on the back).

This is such a powerful step for moving forward. You need to have already sat and made peace with your thoughts and acknowledged your feelings. Once you have explored your feelings, I am sure you will have some questions. Why did they hurt me? Did I do something wrong? Did they not understand me?

After the chaos has cleared and you can muster up the courage to talk to the other party without your heart dropping to your stomach or breaking down into tears, ask them those questions. Ask for some honest feedback. Maybe it was you, maybe it was them. There is no such thing as failure in life, only lessons, and that includes relationships, too. Learn from past mistakes. Grow. Live. Love. BUT IT'S NOT THAT EASY!

It will get easier. I know there's probably many of you reading this thinking, *yes, if only it was that easy*. Or maybe you have tried all the above and still can't let go. That's okay. You got burnt. Bad. But as cliché as it sounds, you can't have the rainbow without the rain. Would you rather have loved and lost than to never know what it felt like to love and be loved in return?

Here is a sneaky psychology trick to help; you are in charge of your thoughts and with that, you can control your reality.

STEP 1:
Challenge your schemas. Sorry about the jargon, schemas are mental representations you create based on information provided by life experience then stored in your memory. For example, I say summer and your schemas you have stored from your experiences of summer are triggered so you automatically think of sun, heat, beach, bikinis, ice-cream, etc.

Now think of all the schemas that are automatically triggered when you think of them. All the feelings that may come flooding back. Now all the things they may have done to upset you, intentional or not, tie it up in a parcel in your memory. That's one schema. Throw it away. It happened. It hurt. It left you with a scar, but you grew from it.

STEP 2:
Now, think of all the positive schemas: the good memories, the innocence, the smiles, the laughter, the belonging, the friendship. Don't tie that up. Scatter them in a mental scrapbook with bright, vibrant stick-it notes, like little reminders of the fun. When you think of them, when you hear their name, when a song comes on that reminds you of them, look back at your mental scrapbook of all the great memories and smile. Allow this to be your triggered schemas.

Never, ever regret something that once made you smile. You can't just wake up one morning and not love someone anymore. And if you can it wasn't love. Acknowledge and give yourself permission to admit you loved them, you will always love them, but you're no longer in love with them.

Take ownership for your part of the breakdown,

but nothing more and nothing less.

We love, we learn, and we live.

It's time to let go

Radiate positive energy, be grateful for your time with them and hope wherever they are they are happy, just as you deserve to be happy, and finally let them go. Sometimes it is a passed wrong, a painful relationship breakdown, or expectations that fell short holding you back.

For the purpose of this chapter, I focused on relationship being a romantic one, but the same strategies and mindset work and apply for all relationships. As for many people, it is not a romantic relationship holding you back. It can be a relationship breakdown with a parent, a respected elder, sibling, colleague, business partner, or child that you're unclear with, that keeps coming up for you and causing you pain.

The same strategies and psychology, such as practicing empathy, forgiveness, and gratitude apply. Take ownership for your part of the breakdown, but nothing more and nothing less. We love, we learn, and we live.

Universal Lesson

Name the person you're holding on to. It is like a monster under the bed. It is scary, but when you shine the torch on that little bugger it can no longer creep up on you because you're aware of it. What questions do you have? What do you need to know for closure? What are the "what ifs" you're telling yourself? What part of the breakdown do you need to take responsibility for? What are you forgiving them for? What are you letting go?

CHAPTER THREE

Who Am I?

When you're feeling like you are lost or in a rut, or even an overwhelming feeling like life is pulling you in lots of different directions, sometimes it's not what is holding you back that is preventing you from moving forward. Sometimes it's because you're not even quite sure what you should be moving towards; what would give you that fulfilment, what would be enough, what or who would give you that happiness that you're chasing?

So often, so many people I talk to have this feeling like they are settling for a life, relationship or career less than the one they know they are capable of having, doing or being. They feel underwhelmed and are not living life lit up. They're not living life on their terms, not waking up with enthusiasm, or passion or that fire in their belly.

They get stuck in a routine where they're doing the same mundane things over and over again – they've been doing it for years. Somewhere along the way, they forgot what they wanted to do, be, see when they "grew up" and all the magic and infinite possibilities that surrounds them.

They stop dreaming and paying attention to the things that light up their life. Instead, they stay loyal to the things that demand their time and energy. Things like emails, bills, expectations, mortgages, school runs, the commute, getting to work on time, finish at five, rush to make tea, clean the house, and do the groceries. Then they get to the top of the 'to do' list before we do the week all over again.

There is a growing body of scientific research that suggests we are all

"Insanity is doing the same thing over and over again and expecting different results."

ALBERT EINSTEIN

caught in a powerful psychological trap, a vicious cycle in which the more we try to find happiness, the more we suffer. In the fast-paced western world, most of us look like ducks on water. On the surface, we are trying to pretend we are cool, calm, and collected and as if we have our shit together. But beneath the surface, our legs are paddling like crazy just to keep our heads above water.

We now have this crazy thing called social media. Not only are we beating ourselves up because we are falling short of the expectations we are placing on ourselves in this forever racing, demanding world, but we are also comparing our lives to others' highlight reels and feeling even worse.

We have friends posting on Instagram what their partner did for them, and magazines feeding us what we have to look like to be desirable. TV advertisements manipulating us to believe we need to own materialistic objects to be happy. Government policies and traditional schooling forcing us to conform to a lifestyle and belief we need to "work" five days a week, 365 days a year to deserve a couple of weeks' break. Society selling us the concept of having a career, your own home, and settling down with kids of your own is the epitome of happiness.

Why is it then we have an increasing amount of middle-aged, middle class women suffering from depression and anxiety? They have followed the recipe book for a fulfilled and happy life to the T, then found themselves full of despair and confusion when they don't feel as ecstatic as they were told they would be. Did they pour in ¾ cup too much of having fun?

What is happening is, somewhere along the way, we forget what used to light us up as kids. What we naturally enjoyed doing and would spend our energy and time freely immersing ourselves in, when our only concern was whether we "felt like doing it." Our lives were dictated purely by what we wanted, and we enjoyed before we had someone else dictate what we should/have to be doing with our time, energy and money.

> Each and everyone one of us has
>
> our very own values system

"And every day, the world will drag you by the hand, yelling, 'This is important! And this is important! And this is important! You need to worry about this! And this! And this!' And each day, it is up to you to yank your hand back, put it on your heart and say, 'No. This is what is important.'"

ANON

That is what is happening now. Instead of having parents telling us what we have to do or should do, we also have social media, society, magazines, books and TV shows dictating what is and isn't important. (Although some of us may still have that. Consider yourself lucky if your parents are still around or love you enough to care).

Sometimes we take on other people's values because we think that's what will make us happy, instead of remembering each and everyone one of us has our very own values system. This is your recipe for happiness and success in your lives, careers and relationships.

For example, let's say you follow a girl on Instagram who posts all these photos of her travelling the world for work. You get jealous and feel like you're not successful because you fall short of that.

When you get honest with yourself, you realise that wouldn't make *you* happy because you're a homebody. You like your space, you like having a routine and a small intimate friendship circle. Changing rooms, cities, and having to put yourself out of your comfort zone to meet new people constantly would give you anxiety. All you would want to do is be back in your cute little apartment with a cup of tea with your partner and your dog.

Or, let's say you have somebody who has lots of money and with that, they go shopping all the time, live in a mansion in the city and live a lavish lifestyle. They are always talking about the latest fashions and you catch yourself wishing you had that, feeling like you're not good enough.

When you get really honest with yourself you know you hate shopping, hate being indoors. You would be more comfortable and find more enjoyment wearing the same denim shorts and bikinis every weekend and spending your days basking in the sunshine with your favourite book. Although that lifestyle is impressive, and I am sure she's worked really hard to create that, it wouldn't make *you* happy at all.

What if, let's say, you have a friend who is a complete socialite and spends most weekends at parties with all the "who's who." They have a big social media following, and big social networks and you feel alone, like you're not important and it taunts you, making you feel like you don't have friends. But if you're honest with yourself, maybe you reflect and remember you hate big social gatherings, you hate small talk, and you hate gossip. You would get more fulfilment catching up with an old/new friend for a beer and having in-depth conversation and laughing about the last big life mistake you made or epic parenting failure.

Maybe large social settings make you anxious or awkward. Whatever it is, you *know* if you were at that party you wouldn't have fun because that is not who *you* are or what makes *you* happy.

In saying this, though, pay attention to the things others may be doing that make you feel jealous or envious. Those feelings, too, serve a propose. They can be a clue of what you wish you had, or something of important value to you that provides you with joy and fulfilment you're currently neglecting, or not prioritising or pursuing.

But, this is the problem. So many people can talk all day about what's wrong in the world, what they don't want, what they don't like, what they aren't happy with. (Whether that is in a job, in a relationship in their life, or in themselves). Yet they can't articulate or feel comfortable talking about what makes them happy and what lights them up!

If you don't know how to make yourself happy, how do you expect someone else to?

If you don't take the time to reflect or ask yourself these questions, and you don't know the answers, can you really be that surprised you're not living your life above zero? That you feel like you're in a rut, or not fulfilled? If you don't know how to make yourself happy, how do you expect someone else to?

The secret formula for happiness is living life in alignment to your values, respecting and making time for the things important to *you* and light *you* up. When you're living your values, that's when you get that genuine, organic feeling of enthusiasm and zest for life, and you're waking up and living life with intention and purpose.

It doesn't mean you don't have bad or sad days because everything in life comes in duality, but you have fulfilment in overcoming those challenges and triumphs with a sense of transcendence.

So who are you, really?

My question for you, is, who are you? What do you stand for? What's important to you? What lights you up? If you honestly don't know, there are lots of ways to figure it out. What do you spend most of your free time doing or thinking about? What do you spend most of your money on? What surrounds you in your home?

Where are you most happy? If money was unlimited, what would you do with your time on this planet? There are some great resources, quizzes and surveys you can do online that can help you identify your values. My favourite is Dr. D. Martini's free test, which you can do here: **https://drdemartini.com/values/**

Once you have identified your five top values, my favourite strategy, and tool to help me live my life aligned is a mission statement. If you're unsure what a mission statement is, Google it. (That is the answer to everything these days, isn't it? Hallelujah for Uncle Google!)

A mission statement is something that even big companies have that outlines their goals and their values. A mission statement is also something you can use as an individual to help you get clear on what your mission is, what your goals are, and what is important to you!

The point of a mission statement is to write down the things applicable to the type of person you want to be or grow into. For example, when you were younger, let's say you had an idol you looked up to like Batman, or someone in business or in life that you inspired to be more like. Let's use Queen B, Beyoncé.

Maybe when you were stuck at a crossroads, feeling overwhelmed, or unsure of your next move you might ask, "If I was as fearless and confident as Beyoncé, what would she do right now?" You can replace Beyoncé with the person you may naturally look up to, whether it's a friend, a business mentor or your parents.

This is a great, empowering question that can help unlock possibilities and ideas outside your conditioned way of thinking and cultured lens you see the world through. But it can also set up unrealistic expectations of yourself because, let's be honest. You're not Beyoncé!

You have your own zone of genius and values, which would consequently mean your next move would be different if you want to make the best decision for your vision, mission and happiness. Instead,

Universal Lesson

Let's get clear on what is important to you. What are your top five values?

you can ask yourself: what would the best version of me do right now, or, in an ideal world, how would I love to consciously respond to this?

And this is where your mission statement comes in, helping you consciously make decisions to help you realign with the things important to you. It will help guide you when you feel lost or at a crossroads, or even help redirect you when you stray from your values and find yourself in a rut. It highlights what you need to prioritise and make time and space for in your life to get that fulfilment and zest back!

So, how do you write a mission statement?

For each of your values, write a paragraph for how the best version of you would honour that value and how that value would show up and be implemented in your life. Remember, when you write it, it's not who you are now as we are not perfect (none of us are). It is the ideal version of you, how you want to show up in the world, for your partner, for your friends, for your kids, for your colleagues, and employees.

It will be how you want to be remembered at your funeral, who you want to see and be proud of when you look at yourself in the mirror. Once you have written it, you can pop it on your mirror, in your diary, in the note section of your phone, or in the car's glove box. Somewhere you can easily access it when you need reassurance. When you need advice, you can listen to the wise words and get direction from the best version of you to ensure you continue to live your life aligned, with purpose, with intention, and integrity.

> Put your hand on your heart and read your mission statement to take control of your time and energy.

When you find yourself at a crossroads, when you feel lost and you're not sure where to go from here, you can let go. Maybe you feel overwhelmed and like life is tugging you in a million different directions saying, "this is important, and this is important," you can let go. Put your

"Peace. It does not mean to be in a place where there is no noise, trouble or hard work. It means to be in the midst of these things and still be calm in your heart."

ANON

hand on your heart and read your mission statement to take control of your time and energy.

Remind yourself these things are important to me, not the rest of the world because, remember, that is their recipe for success and fulfilment, not yours. Ask yourself, in the perfect world, if I could control the situation how would I ideally like to respond? Because guess what? You do! Bad shit happens to good people every single day, but we have control over how we respond. So that's a great opportunity to use your mission statement and think consciously and live intentionally.

I wrote my first mission statement when I was nineteen and, every year, I critique it and review it. (Life is fluid, experiences mould and change our view of the world and our values), but it has remained in my diary ever since. Every time I feel lost or conflicted, I come back to it and I check in with myself. This is to ensure I am living life in alignment with my goals, who I want to be, what I stand for, and what is important to me.

For the purpose of helping you create your own, I will share with you the first mission statement I ever wrote, which has evolved from there. Please do not compare yours to mine and don't copy it. As I explained earlier, that's why so many people are so lost and confused, they take on others' values as their own.

"Independence/individuality/autonomy: I will always be honest to myself; feel, see, and speak my truth, however, never force my values onto anyone else. I will always remain humble, open-minded, and refrain from ignorance, being tolerant and grateful for difference.

Friendship and family: I will always strive to invest, understand, and nurture my relationships in my inner and outer worlds. Allowing the past to make me better rather than bitter, learning to forgive as I aim to not only see the best, but bring out the best in others, by inspiring and motivating. I will love fearlessly and wholly and be loved in return.

New experiences and learning: I will lead an abundant life full of diversity and compassion. I will get involved and try everything once and wholeheartedly,

*"The longer I live, the more I realise
the impact of attitude on life.
Attitude, to me, is more important than facts. It is more important than the past, than education, than money, more important than circumstances, than failures, than successes, than what other people think, say, or do. It is more important than appearance, giftedness, or skill. It will make or break a company, a church or a home. The remarkable thing is we have the choice every day regarding the attitude we will embrace for that day. We cannot change our past, we cannot change the fact people will act in a certain way. We cannot change the inevitable. The only thing we can do is play on the one string we have, and that is our attitude. I am convinced that life is 10% what happens to me and 90% how I react to it. And so it is with you.
We are in charge of our attitudes."*

CHARLES R. SWINDOLL

allowing myself time and opportunities for mistakes and learning. I will never be afraid to become vulnerable, allowing myself to be affected by all the beauty around me. Taking it all in with gratitude, feeling it, and giving it love. I'll commit 100%, promising to never settle for mediocrity or anything less than a life I am capable of living.

Inner peace: despite always being active and involved, I will always give myself time to take a step back and reflect. To ensure I am aware of what it is I am doing, and I align my behaviour with my beliefs. I refuse to become a slave to society and its expectations. I will question the purity of my intentions and ensure they are not dictated by social constructs such as money, status or fashion. I will be motivated not manipulated.

Health and happiness: I will stay in tune with my body, leading a balanced life committing to healthy eating and regular exercise restricting large amounts of things and people that cause self-harm. I will know and indulge in a healthy dose of what makes me happy; dancing, eating, and running."

A mission statement is one strategy I use to keep me aligned because life happens, we are not perfect; we have off days. Like you go to the gym and work on building muscle, you need to show up every day and lift the weights to strengthen your mindset; it's a muscle too.

Some weights for your mindset gym

Some other "weights" I use to help with my mindset are vision boards. I know I warned you earlier in the book I am a massive believer in the law of attraction. I promise you I will share with you the quantum psychics and research behind it later.

Like I explained earlier in this chapter, somewhere along the way we stopped dreaming and believing in the infinite possibilities. We started settling, thinking smaller, thinking safer and about what is practical, what is the norm and is accepted. We start believing we are less deserving and stop believing in ourselves.

> You need to show up every day and lift the weights to strengthen your mindset; it's a muscle too.

We succumb to the mind numbing routines and expectations of those around us who have also settled, which absolutely kills our creative outlet. We consume media and utter bullshit, spend way too much of our time online and on TV watching people live their lives rather than staying in our own lane and focusing on creating ours—a life we love!

It hinders our ability to think outside the box and outside of what we know and see in our conditioned lives, so we stop doing more, we stop striving; we stop thinking bigger and playing harder. Vision boards are a great way to get you out of your funk, to push pass the self-limiting beliefs and what you perceive is "realistic" or "the norm" and start stepping into your wildest dreams.

Your only limit is your imagination. Find and put together images of where you want to go, how you want to feel, where you want to live, who you want to be with, any affirmations or quotes that ring true for you. A little psychology trick for you: when you're creating your vision board, tap into all your senses by getting really clear on what you would see, feel, hear, smell, and taste.

This is also an NLP technique (Neurolinguistic programming) because your brain doesn't know the difference between physically doing something and just imagining you're doing it. It still creates the same psychological and physiological responses such as increased heart rate, tears coming down your face, gratitude, excitement, sweat, salivation, anxiety, muscle tension, etc.

That is why you will see a lot of coaches who use visualisation, especially Olympians in sports using mental rehearsal because your body has the same response to going over something in your head and actually physically doing it.

If you have a vision board of all the things you want to do, see, feel, and be, it can really talk to all your senses. Some people even put together a slide show where they can incorporate music for this exact purpose of intensifying the sensual experience. It can ignite that fire, really exciting you, taking you out of your current reality, and making you feel and experience something greater.

Make it a habit to connect and look at your vision board every day. This is so powerful for creating the motivation you need to get the action done to reach your goals. Just thinking about it isn't enough, sorry. Use this to help you be consistent, to remind you of why you are showing up for yourself on the hard days. And why you need to persist through the challenges (because, girlfriend, there will be lots of them!)

When you have negative nellies who feel uncomfortable by your goals who get in your head doubting it's achievable – you have proof! (They are honestly just fearful you will outshine them; just your typical case of tall poppy syndrome). The fact you can find a picture of it means it can be done. If you can think it, you can achieve it!

Once you get clear on your values, you're able to live in accordance to them and experience a sense of alignment. Even in times where you find yourself standing by yourself, you will find comfort in the fact you're living in accordance to your truth with integrity.

I love researcher Brené Brown's definition of integrity; it fits so well with the overall message of living a Life Above Zero. "Choosing courage over comfort. Choosing right over what is fun, fast or easy. And choosing to practice your values rather than simply professing them."

This motivation is so powerful because it is intrinsic, meaning you are being motivated by what is important to you; your values, your goals, your mission, your vision and your purpose, rather than extrinsically motivated. For example, doing something because your boss, your partner, your parent, or society told you you had to, or you should.

No one likes being told what to do, that is why we have detention, we have divorce, and we have jail. When you don't take the time to get to know who you really are and what values you stand for, or you ignore or suppress them, you experience a phenomenon psychologists have found called "cognitive dissonance."

Psychologist Leon Festinger proposed the theory of cognitive

"True belonging is the spiritual practice of believing in and belonging to yourself so deeply that you can share your most authentic self with the world and find sacredness in both being part of something and standing alone in the wilderness. True belonging doesn't require you to change who you are; it requires you to be who you are."

BRENÉ BROWN

dissonance centred on how people try to reach internal consistency. He suggested people have an inner need to ensure their beliefs and behaviours are consistent. Inconsistent or conflicting beliefs lead to disharmony, which people strive to avoid.

Consequently, the term "cognitive dissonance" is used to describe the feelings of discomfort that result from holding two conflicting beliefs. When there is an inconsistency between beliefs and behaviours, something must change to eliminate or reduce the dissonance. Just as hunger leads toward activity oriented toward hunger reduction, cognitive dissonance is a motivation that will inspire people to change their behaviours to align with their values. To consciously or unconsciously deny, abandon, or suppress their values to convince themselves to believe they are being congruent and living with integrity and alignment.

> Choosing courage over comfort.

> Choosing right over what is fun, fast or easy.

This is what many people believe could trigger the onset of depression, living in accordance to someone else's value system rather than being passionate and lit up about their own unique mission and zone of genius. We can reduce Cognitive Dissonance in one of three ways:

1) Change one or more of the attitudes, behaviour, beliefs, etc., to make the relationship between the two elements a consistent one. When one of the dissonant elements is a behaviour, the individual can change or eliminate the behaviour. However, this mode of dissonance reduction frequently presents problems for people as it is often difficult for people to change well-learned behavioural responses (e.g., giving up smoking).

2) Acquire new information that outweighs the dissonant beliefs. For example, thinking smoking causes lung cancer will cause dissonance if a person smokes. However, new information such as "research has not proved definitely that smoking causes lung cancer" may reduce the dissonance.

3) Reduce the importance of the cognitions (i.e., beliefs, attitudes). A

person could convince themselves it is better to "live for today" than to "save for tomorrow." In other words, he could tell himself a short life filled with smoking and sensual pleasures is better than a long life devoid of such joys. In this way, he would decrease the importance of the dissonant cognition (smoking is bad for one's health).

> Mismatches between your beliefs and your actions can lead to feelings of discomfort and depression, but such feelings can sometimes lead to change

Notice that dissonance theory does not state these modes of dissonance reduction will work, only that individuals in a state of cognitive dissonance will take steps to reduce the extent of their dissonance. Cognitive dissonance plays a role in many value judgments, decisions and evaluations.

Realising how conflicting beliefs impact the decision-making process is a great way to improve your ability to make faster and more accurate choices that align with your values. Mismatches between your beliefs and your actions can lead to feelings of discomfort and depression, but such feelings can sometimes lead to change, growth and happiness.

In some instances, you might rationalise away the conflict, but in some cases, you might change either your beliefs or your behaviour to make the two consistent and realign with your values.

Writing a letter from my future self is another "weight" I use to help condition my mindset. (Not to mention it is a lot of fun!) It may sound corny, but pretend you fast forward in time to a date in six months, one year, two years, five years, or ten years' time. Envision where you would love to be in your life, career, relationships with others, yourself, where you are living, who you're living with, what you're doing for wealth creation, what you're doing with your time, etc.

Then, pretend you are writing a letter to yourself from that date. Same technique goes as the mission statement. Try to engage all the senses; where are you sitting as you write the letter, what can you see, smell, taste, hear, and describe what life looks like and what the journey has been like up to that point.

Pop a date on it (for example, if you imagined yourself in a year's time, that is the date you write on the letter and you get to read it in a year's time). It is like a time capsule, and like the vision board, a great strategy to get you thinking bigger, doing more, helping more, and being more.

Personally, it's my favourite strategy to do on New Year's. I love reflecting on the year I had with gratitude, reading the letter I wrote myself a year ago and co-creating what I want to manifest and attract in the next twelve months as well. So, who are you? Who do you want to be? Who do you need to become to attract/attain the life you want to live?

If you're not currently there yet, what are some values you need to work on and use to navigate life at the moment? You can be anyone you want to be. It is about that consistent effort every day and realising where you may not be showing up as you want to in the world. Or noticing some traits you need to strengthen or values you need to prioritise.

The techniques, such as the mission statement, vision board and letter to your future self all have awareness in common. You need to know what is important to you and what it is you want in life. If you can learn how to identify it and articulate it, that is the hardest bit done.

The universe will conspire and work in strange and magical ways to deliver it to you. If you don't know what you want, you can't be angry, bitter, or disappointed when it doesn't deliver because you didn't know what you wanted to order off the menu in the first place. Take some time to reflect, get in tune, and rediscover yourself and what lights you up!

Think about where you want to be in 5 years' time, the future letter could be one month, six months, whenever you like. Have fun with it. Articulate to the universe what you want, get clear on who you want to be, use some of these strategies to manifest these things.

They don't just turn up on your doorstep because you think about them. That is not what I am saying at all (and I promised you at the start this was not one of those books that promised you the world). Knowing what you want and who you are, are the first steps to taking control of your time, your energy, and knowing where to invest it consciously so you live with intention and purpose.

Universal Lesson

Use some of these strategies to self-reflect or go soul searching to find what your top five values are. And how the ideal you, or the best version of you you would love to be, would incorporate that into your life every single day.

CHAPTER FOUR

You Can't Hit a Target Without a Focus

Okay, so now you've had the time and space to think, to make peace with your past, and reflect with gratitude, not spite. To become aware and conscious of who you are and what's important to you. Now it's time to move forward creating your Life Above Zero now you are clear on the foundations you're building on!

Often, when I am coaching clients, the reason they are feeling stagnant or stuck can usually be narrowed down to three things:

1) They haven't let go of something/someone and it's preventing them from having peace. They become so blinded by the pain and resentment, they fail to see all the beauty, magic, miracles, and the joy in the small things around them.

2) They are not aware of who they are, what makes them happy, and what they stand for, so they are getting frustrated and confused by where life keeps taking them. But, they haven't popped a destination in their GPS or at least given the driver (God, the universe, quantum physics, humanity, autonomy – whatever faith you believe in) any directions!

3) They haven't anything to look forward to. They are going through the ebbs and flows of life without setting a goal, without having something to push and strive for, something to aim or work towards or count down to. Like a kid counting down for Christmas, we all have that fun-loving, excited child in all of us. Feed it! Play with it! Just because we may get grey hairs and sun spots does not mean we have to get old and boring. Make

"You can't hit the target without a focus."
LAUREN KERR

life fun, set yourself some goals, which will give you some direction so you don't feel like you're stuck in the same spot for too long.

Setting your goals and intentions isn't just something you do when you want to lose weight on New Year's. Goal setting is one of the most powerful researched tools for creating success, both in business, health and life! What I love most about them is they also allow you the time to reflect on how far you have come. And the opportunity to ask yourself where it is you are going, where it is you want to be, and, ultimately, who do you want to be?

I know life can get full (I am conscious not to use the word "busy." There is nothing glorified about being busy. It tells me you don't manage your time well or prioritise the things you love most, including yourself, with self-care). It can be a struggle for most to find some quiet time alone to set your goals, but goals are dreams with legs.

I am a big fan and advocate of goal setting. If I was to show you my goals and dreams I wrote down since finishing high school. It is as though I was telling or forecasting my future! Everything I wanted the universe has delivered. Sometimes in a different shape or form to what I had in mind. But I have learned to trust the process because sometimes the universe knows me and what would make me happy and fulfilled better than I do!

I would love to think I made these dreams come true, but I know setting those goals were essential in getting me to where I wanted. Goals provide you with direction and purpose. If you know what you want, what you are working towards, and what is important to you. This can help guide you in every decision you make. It will provide clarity when you find yourself at a crossroad and empower you with motivation and direction when you find yourself lost. Here are some tips to help you make and stick to goals:

Before you start, remember it's about you.

You need to ignore what everyone else is doing and achieving. Your life is about breaking your own limits and outgrowing yourself to live your best life. You are not in competition with anyone else. Plan to out-do your past, not other people. The first thing you will need to do is get yourself in the right head space. The first time you do this, find yourself a big chunk of time in one of the upcoming days to sit down and inspire yourself. A day where you don't have to rush off or have a time limit on where you have to be so you can give yourself permission to slow down, tune in, and dream big. Depending on what floats your boat, you may like to sit on the beach, bask in the sunshine with a pen and notebook. Or you could sit down on the couch with a yummy candle burning, a cup of green tea, listening to the rain. Or maybe in bed in your PJs, wrapped up in your pillow castle, with your incense burning and Angus and Julia Stone softly, yet sweetly, serenading you through your speakers.

A balanced life reflects balanced goals.

When you are setting your goals make sure they reflect your values. An easy way to ensure this is by listing your five top values you identified in the earlier chapter, the aspects of your life you prioritise over others. They don't need to be in order. For example, health, happiness, family, career, finances. Then, for each value, make sure you have a corresponding goal whether it be a big change or maintaining your current efforts. This ensures one goal does not consume all your energy, causing you to neglect other areas of life that are also important to you. This way, you now have a written commitment to hold yourself accountable to approach your life with a holistic and mindful approach. If you need help setting goals for each value, ask yourself the following questions to help inspire you and get the creative juices flowing: What do I want to do? Who do I want to be? What do I want to see? What do I want to have? What do I want to learn and experience?

> When your goals don't give you energy from within, that's a great warning sign they are being imposed on you from the outside.

Go through each goal and vision you've just written. You may have a few different ones for each value, and that's fine, as long as you have at least one for each of your top values. If a goal you have written doesn't excite you or scare you, you don't feel that tug or pull in your gut, then that is a good indication your values may have changed.

Go back to the values exercise and check for yourself. Remember, your values can be fluid and are reactive to life experiences. When your goals don't give you energy from within, that's a great warning sign they are being imposed on you from the outside. Whether it is something you feel you should do, have to do, or are expected to do, and when, you won't stick to that goal.

You won't persevere when things get tough and you will lose interest. Your goal will quickly become a chore or an obligation. That is not what goal setting it about. It is fun; it helps you think bigger, play bigger, and work harder!

Once you're certain your goals are intrinsically motivating, you will go through each one using the S.M.A.R.T. formula. Work through one goal at a time and take them through this process.

Your goals have to be "SMART", which means: Specific, Measurable, Achievable, Results Based and Time Based.

SPECIFIC:

Be specific, for example: "My partner and I want to buy our first property this year. One for us to live in, where we can continue to enjoy our current lifestyle.

A two-bedroom, two-bathroom apartment, two car spaces, and lots of natural light in a small apartment block with body corporate fees no higher than $50 a week. And in a 5km radius from our work places so we can continue to walk to work, I can go for my morning walks on the beach, and we go out for dinners after work."

MEASURABLE:

The best way to do this is to break it down into smaller, achievable goals.

Example: "We know the apartment we want is worth around $440,000 on the market at the moment. We need to save a 10% deposit, which is $44,000. Our aim is to have this saved in two years' time. We have worked out that it will be $22,000 a year which is $1833 a month, $458 a week.

For us to save this deposit in twenty-four months, we need to save 10% of our weekly pay check and set up an automatic transfer to a "do not touch" savings account. There are no exceptions and WE WILL NOT touch this account until we are ready to withdraw our deposit.

"Vision without execution is hallucination."
THOMAS EDISON

ACHIEVABLE:

Your goals should challenge and stretch you a little to make you work harder, but make sure they are realistic. "My Partner and I sat down, looked at our weekly budget and worked out what our expenses come to and how much our cost of living is including a dinner here and there and gifts for loved ones.

We have worked out that putting an additional 10% of our weekly income away each week is a stretch. It is doable as long as we prepare our lunches for work each week instead of spending $20 a day each on lunch and coffee."

Example of what NOT to write: "We think 10% saved each week is reasonable, and it still leaves us money to live on so we will see how it goes and make it work." This type of thinking will just set you up to fail. Do not wing it! If you fail to prepare and ensure you are clear with your goals and not have an action plan to get you there, be prepared to fail.

RESULTS BASED:

Get clear on how you will tangibly measure your goal process and completion. Example: "I will measure and track my progress every quarter of the financial year to ensure I am on track. In September, December, March, and June we will ensure we are saving $5500 each quarter to be on track for our financial goals.

I have created a Google document where we can track our savings, reflect, and see if there are even other avenues or costs we can cut out to help us get to our goal sooner. We have achieved this goal when we have saved $44,000 in our "do not touch" savings account."

Also, if you have a goal you're a little unsure of or is really stretching and challenging you to achieve it, write down the obstacles and the benefits of eventually overcoming them, and achieving this goal. If you pre-frame that, you won't be as surprised when the challenges pop up and less likely to throw in the towel when it gets tough. Because you expected and planned for that and got honest with yourself about what it would take and what you would sacrifice, you will be better prepared.

Example: "We will probably miss out on a few expensive and fun outings with friends such as holidays and weekend getaways. We'll have to be organised to prepare our lunches each week, but when we have 2/3 of our house deposit, we can start the fun part. Shopping for apartments, going to open homes, and getting new items for our new home."

TIME BASED:

Remember what it felt like the night before an assignment was due before the summer break? Five coffees deep, and thriving off adrenalin at the thought of having three whole months in the sun with your besties going on road trips and to festivals?

Well, same thing; give yourself a sense of urgency and a good timeframe. Anyone can save for a house deposit in four or five years' time, but why not make it sooner? This will make you FOCUS on your goals, stay excited, and help you stay on track. Make your dreams real as soon as possible!

This fun, little planning and goal setting activity will have you feeling inspired, motivated, and focused. It works by attracting those things in life. The wildest ideas you thought never possible and making them an absolute reality. You can use these goal strategies weekly to help you focus and live with intention, monthly, quarterly, or even yearly, from anything from health and wellness, to finance, career, travel, and relationship goals.

I love using my goal setting also as an opportunity to reflect. Reflect on your year; what did you learn? What made you happy? What worked? What will you do differently next year? Remember, there is no such thing as failure, only feedback.

This strategy and way of thinking will help you in strengthening and practicing your mindfulness and gratitude. When you set goals in alignment with your values and they're intrinsically motivating, you will pursue them with "flow" instead of "force." Flow is not some woo-woo or hippy word, either; it is another psychology phenomenon.

Achieve goals with Flow instead of Force

Do you remember that moment when creativity and productivity sprung from your mind, smoothly? According to positive psychology cofounder, Mihaly Csíkszentmihályi, this state is called "flow" and it is an important contributor to creativity and wellbeing.

The experience of flow is universal, and it has been reported to occur

"The most important decision about your goals is not what you're willing to do to achieve them, but what you are willing to give up."

DAVE RAMSEY

across different classes, genders, ages, cultures, and it can be experienced in many types of activities. If you've ever heard someone describe a time when their performance excelled and they used the term being "in the zone", what they're describing is an experience of flow.

It occurs when your skill level and the challenge at hand are equal. Psychologist Mihaly Csíkszentmihályi was a prisoner during World War II. From witnessing the pain and suffering from many people around him during this time, he developed a curiosity about happiness and being content with life.

He observed how many people were unable to live a life of contentment after their jobs, homes, security, etc., were taken from them during the war. After the war, he read philosophy and took an interest in art and religion to seek an answer to the question, what creates a life worth living?

Eventually, he stumbled upon psychology whilst at a ski resort in Switzerland. He attended a lecture by Carl Jung, who talked about the traumatised psyches of the European people after World War II. He was so intrigued; he started to read Jung's work, and eventually took an interest in psychology, which led him to the United States to pursue psychology. What he really wanted was to study the roots of happiness.

With Csíkszentmihályi, studies led him to conclude happiness is an internal state of being, not an external one. His popular book, *Flow: The Psychology of Optimal Experience* is based on the premise happiness levels can be shifted through introducing more "flow."

Happiness is not a rigid state that can't be changed. On the contrary, happiness takes a committed effort to be manifested. After the baseline set point, there is a percentage of happiness every individual has the responsibility to take control of. He believes flow is crucial to creating genuine happiness.

Through much research, Csíkszentmihályi began to understand people were most creative, productive, and often happiest when they are in this state of flow. He interviewed athletes, musicians, artists, etc., because he wanted to know when they experienced the most optimal performance levels.

He was also interested in finding out how they felt during these experiences. He developed the term 'flow state' because many of the people he interviewed described their optimal states of performance as

"The best moments in our lives are not the passive, receptive, relaxing times… The best moments usually occur if a person's body or mind is stretched to its limits in a voluntary effort to accomplish something difficult and worthwhile."

MIHALY CSÍKSZENTMIHÁLYI

instances when their work "flowed out of them without much effort."

Csíkszentmihályi aimed to discover what piqued creativity, especially in the workplace, and how creativity lead to more productivity. He also determined flow is not only essential to a productive employee, but it is imperative for a contented one as well. In his own words, flow is: "A state in which people are so involved in an activity that nothing else seems to matter; the experience is so enjoyable that people will continue to do it, even at great cost, for the sheer sake of doing it."

What exactly is flow?

Imagine for a moment you are running a race. Your attention is focused on the movements of your body, the power of your muscles, the force of your lungs, and the feel of the street beneath your feet. You are living in the moment, utterly absorbed in the present activity. Time seems to fall away. You are tired, but you barely notice.

According to positive psychologist Csíkszentmihályi, what you are experiencing in that moment is known as "flow" - a state of complete immersion in an activity. He describes the mental state of flow as "being completely involved in an activity for its own sake. The ego falls away. Time flies. Every action, movement, and thought follows inevitably from the previous one, like playing jazz. Your whole being is involved, and you're using your skills to the utmost."

Flow experiences can occur in different ways for different people. Some might experience flow while engaging in a sport such as skiing, tennis or soccer. For me, I have always been able to find it in dancing or running (and only recently, in writing this book). Others might have such an experience while engaged in an activity such as painting or drawing.

According to Csíkszentmihályi, there are ten factors that accompany the experience of flow. While many of these components may be present, it is unnecessary to experience all of them for flow to occur:

- Clear goals that, while challenging, are still attainable.
- Strong concentration and focused attention.
- The activity is intrinsically rewarding.
- Feelings of serenity; a loss of feelings of self-consciousness.

- Timelessness; a distorted sense of time; feeling so focused on the present that you lose track of time passing.
- Immediate feedback.
- Knowing the task is doable; a balance between skill level and the challenge presented.
- Feelings of personal control over the situation and the outcome.
- Lack of awareness of physical needs.
- Complete focus on the activity itself.

So, what can you do to increase your chances of achieving 'flow'? Flow is likely to occur when you face a task that has clear goals requiring specific responses. A game of chess is a good example of when a flow state might occur. For the duration of a competition, the player has very specific goals and responses, allowing attention to be focused entirely on the game during the period of play.

"Flow also happens when a person's skills are fully involved in overcoming a challenge that is just about manageable, so it acts as a magnet for learning new skills and increasing challenges," Csíkszentmihályi explains. "If challenges are too low, one gets back to flow by increasing them. If challenges are too great, one can return to the flow state by learning new skills."

> "If challenges are too low, one gets back to flow by increasing them. If challenges are too great, one can return to the flow state by learning new skills."

While flow experiences can happen as part of everyday life, there are also important practical applications in various areas including education, sports and the workplace.

EXAMPLES OF FLOW IN EDUCATION

Csíkszentmihályi suggested over-learning a skill or concept can help people experience flow. Another critical concept in his theory is the idea of slightly extending oneself beyond one's current ability level. This slight stretching of one's current skills can help the individual experience flow.

EXAMPLES OF FLOW IN SPORTS

Just like in educational settings, engaging in a challenging athletic activity that is doable but presents a slight stretching of one's abilities is a good way to achieve flow. Sometimes described by being "in the zone", reaching this state of flow allows an athlete to experience a loss of self-consciousness and a sense of complete mastery of the performance.

EXAMPLES OF FLOW IN THE WORKPLACE

Flow can also occur when workers are engaged in tasks where they can focus entirely on the project at hand. For example, a writer might experience this while working on a novel or a graphic designer might achieve flow while working on a website illustration.

Besides making activities more enjoyable, flow also has several advantages. Flow can lead to improved performance. Researchers have found flow can enhance performance in a wide variety of areas including teaching, learning, athletics, and artistic creativity; flow can also lead to further learning and skill development.

Because the act of achieving flow indicates a substantial mastery of a certain skill, the individual must continually seek new challenges and information to maintain this state. It becomes apparent with psychologists' research that it is important not only for your success, improvement, and achievement of goals. To firstly set them and do so clearly!

But, also, for your happiness to experience enjoyment and a sense of purpose and direction by you setting your own challenges. Goals that intrinsically inspire you to deliberately create and put yourself in situations that stretch you and constantly challenge you to grow, evolve, and reach your full potential.

This is why in the SMART formula above I encouraged you to set goals that are achievable but also inspire yourself to stretch yourself too, so you can experience 'flow'. (I am deliberate to use the word 'inspire' instead of 'motivate' because inspire implies you are intrinsically motivated to achieve the goals because you placed that demand on yourself. This is rather than the demand being imposed on you externally, which would simply 'motivate' you. And motivation is like weeing your pants; it makes you feel all warm and fuzzy but disappears quickly).

As you can see from the diagram below, research has found your goals need to stretch your current skill level to create and experience 'flow'. However, it needs to still be achievable otherwise you can create anxiety. Likewise, if a goal is too easy, you create boredom. This is why so many people who don't have goals feel like they're just going through the motions of life feeling underwhelmed, stagnant, and in a rut without that natural zest and enthusiasm for life. They are missing that 'flow'.

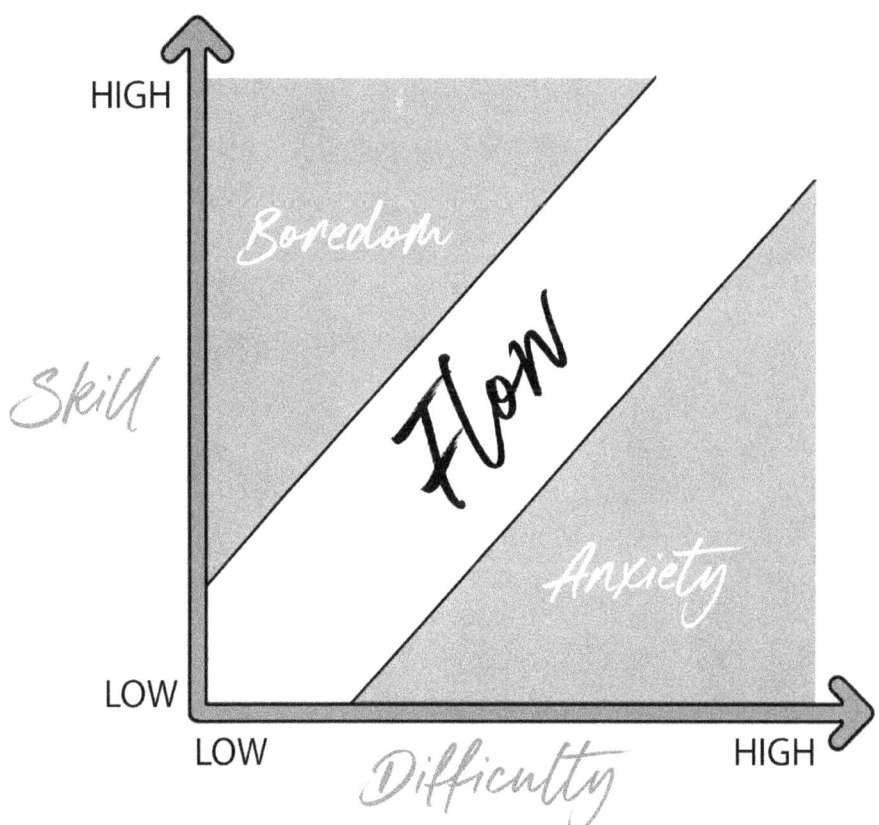

"Happiness takes a committed effort to be manifested."

MIHALY CSÍKSZENTMIHÁLYI

CHAPTER FIVE

Self-Sabotage; What Stops Us from Taking the Action

I promised you this was a self-help book *without* the bullshit. Just because you write what you want on paper and set some goals doesn't mean they will magically manifest. You have to work for them; like I said, goals without action are hallucinations.

But I stand by that articulating what you want is the hardest part. You just have to decide and 100% commit instead of wasting half of your energy umming and ahhing, going back and forth. You will free 100% of your resources to spend on working towards your goals instead.

So many of us have goals, yet do nothing to work towards them. Failed New Year's resolutions are a great example. This is because change is hard. Let me show you and explain to you why change is so hard and why so many people fail to stick to their New Year's resolutions, so you can smash your own goals for the year. (Then life, once you get the hang of it).

First off, please know it is not you! It's not that you're lazy. It's not that you're just one of those people who start things and can never finish things. That is a cop out! It is not your personality. It is because change is hard for everyone. Here is psychology for you; your brain is hardwired to take the most convenient route to anywhere, the shortcut, the quickest, easy way with no resistance.

If you could live on a toilet, sleep, shit, and get food brought to you, you would be really happy! Unfortunately, that doesn't raise your kids or pay your bills so you can afford to put a roof over your head, food on the table, or afford the servant to bring your food on the toilet!

That is why we have stereotypes, heuristics, and make judgments about other people. A heuristic is a mental shortcut that allows you to solve problems and make judgments quickly and efficiently. These strategies shorten decision-making time and allow your brain to function without constantly stopping to think about your next course of action.

> If you want to be someone different, experience something different, you need to do something different and think something different.

Heuristics are helpful in many situations, but they can also lead to cognitive biases, which I promise to tell you about in another chapter. Most people, at some point in their life (mostly around New Year's), set goals; whether they be life, health, wellness, relationship, financial, or business. Yet most people will abandon them before the year is through, or even before they have the chance to fail them. They don't even try!

Let me tell you why that is and how you can prevent that from happening so you aren't one of the phonies who say "new year, new me" and remain the same person you were last year; running the same mundane rat race routine, moaning about the same shit, telling yourself the same bullshit excuses. If you want to be someone different, experience something different, you need to do something different and think something different.

The sad truth is, for change to occur, the pain of staying where we are must be greater than the pain of growing. For most people, as much as they moan about their health, their relationships, their job, etc., the reason they are not making a change is that they like wallowing in their own shit! It's familiar there! It's easier, more comfortable, and less painful than the pain of growing because change is not easy, it takes effort; it takes persistence and requires commitment.

> Change can be disruptive, it can be uncomfortable, and unfamiliar.

That is why so many people wait for shit to happen, they wait for the straw that breaks the camel's back before they do something. They wait to lose a loved one or have a health crises before they invest in their health. Or they wait until they fall pregnant or go through a separation before they look into creating another stream of income. Or they wait for someone they know to die young to realise life is just too freaking short. They are wasting theirs not doing things that light them up or they are worrying about petty shit that, in the larger scheme of things, really does not matter.

Change can be disruptive, it can be uncomfortable, and unfamiliar. Ask yourself, is the thought of being stagnant and stuck in a rut, between where you are and where you would like to be, more enjoyable? These are three things I find prevents most people from achieving their goals, or better yet, even taking that first step.

If you recognise them and understand how they work, you will limit your ability to self-sabotage your goals. Because you and I know, the only thing stopping you from achieving them is the bullshit excuse you keep telling yourself as to why you can't have them.

You are chasing someone else goals!

People set goals on what they think will make them happy or they think will make them successful rather than getting clear on what makes them happy and what their definition of 'success' is. So, like I explained in the previous chapter, get clear on your values, make sure your goals align with them. They intrinsically motivate you and are not influenced or manipulated by fashion, status or money.

We give up when our goals aren't easy!

It is like we dream these big goals; we get clear on what we want, what we want to strive for, what would make us happy, and then we find out it is hard, and it will 'take work'. Then we decide our goals and dreams are no longer important, we neglect our 'why' and give up!

It's like we say we want to grow and get taller, then we complain when we get growing pains! It's not you, it's not that you're lazy, it's not your personality. And it's not that you're one of those people who start things and can never finish them. Like I said earlier, all those excuses are just that. Excuses! They are a cop out!

Change is hard for *everyone!* So you need to pre-frame this. Acknowledge your goals, pre-frame right now that yes, it will take work! So when you experience your first challenge, you're not surprised and say, "Oh, I didn't realise this would be this hard and take so much effort, I can't do it." Or "I won't do it."

A powerful, little psychological pre-frame you can use is all those things you're telling yourself you can't be, have, achieve, or become. You need to replace your "I can't" in those sentences to "I won't." I bet you feel like a spoiled little child throwing a tanty now, don't you? Because the truth is you can. But you're choosing to give up or put it in the 'too hard' basket and you won't commit to make it work or chip away at it consistently until you achieve it.

No one will come up to you and say, "You know that dream job you want where you work four hours a week from the Bahamas with your six-figure salary, here you go. It is all yours!" Or, "You know that dream man you're looking for, the 6 ft., tanned, muscly, blue-eyed, rich, kind, humble, well-travelled, educated, with no kids, history or baggage? Well, he is at the door and he said he is madly in love with you."

Or, "you know that body you want? Twenty kg lighter, tanned and toned, vibrant and healthy with no sun damage, stretch marks, cellulite, or wrinkles? You can have mine. Easily solved!" Whether your goals are financial, about career, relationships or health, they won't happen unless you show up and work for them, sorry. Sure, the universe can work its magic, but you have also got to do your part.

There is a great tool called the change Matrix, which you can use to help you pre-frame your goals. I used to use this tool when I was working with families in child protection who needed to make meaningful changes to address child protection concerns. This was so children could be reunified after child protection orders had been taken or be kept safely in the home to prevent children being removed.

These were serious changes, whether it be domestic violence, sexual abuse, substance misuse. There was a lot at stake, so obviously I didn't want to set them up to fail. This task was a great tool which allowed parents and families to get honest with themselves and the department on what it

Universal Assignment:

If change happened, the worst that could happen	If change happened, the best that could happen
If no change happened, the worst that could happen	If no change happened, the best that could happen

would take and what was at stake.

In the same way, I don't want to set you up for fail. I would love for you to do this exercise and be really transparent with yourself about what the road will look like to achieve your goals.

After doing this tool yourself, I *know* you will realise the sacrifices, the amount of work, time, energy (and even finances) it will take to achieve your goals. But I also know you will find there is always so much more to gain than you ever have to lose.

The change matrix is a great way to be transparent with yourself and pre-frame your goals.

Most days you won't feel like doing it!

I will take that excuse you have saved for your rainy day and squish it right now! I already know and I am pre-framing you'll probably use that excuse one hundred times this year. And for each one of your goals and action step you put together, I can promise you, most days YOU WILL NOT FEEL LIKE DOING IT! "I don't feel like getting out of my warm bed at 5:30am and going to gym." "I don't feel like picking the salad sandwich over the donut." "I don't feel like picking the green tea over the coffee." "I don't feel like spending a couple of hours working on my side hustle tonight after I finish work instead of relaxing on the couch and watching the latest episode of the Bachelor." "I don't feel like studying Saturday instead of going to the beach." "I don't feel like being a good partner and investing in my relationship and compromising. I want to be selfish." "I don't feel like being an understanding parent and being patient with the kids. I just want to scream."

> The difference between the people who do the work and the people who don't is they separate feelings from action.

Do you honestly think anyone 'feels' like doing those things compared to other things they could do? No. But the difference between the people who do

"Embrace the suck. It is the work that isn't fun, the in-between stuff that nobody sees – that is going to make all your dreams come true."

MEL ROBBINS

the work and the people who don't is they separate feelings from action. For example, let's say you have a health goal, your alarm goes off 5:30am to go to the gym. This is where the struggle first starts, and you need to take that first bit of action.

It's not even the gym bit that you're struggling with, it's even before that! It's deciding whether you'll snooze the alarm or get up. You're already self-sabotaging and doubting whether you should take action. The question isn't if I should go or if I can, because I know I should. I know I have two legs and a car downstairs that will get me there, the real question is, do I feel like it?

Whatever your goal is and the action you need to take to get there, often it is your feelings that stop you. Whatever your goals are, if you find yourself battling feelings of lethargy, anxiety or self-doubt, know that most days you can't control how you feel. *But* you can choose how you *act* and, funnily enough, once you act it will change how you feel. Trust me!

For an example, do you feel sluggish first thing in morning and have to drag yourself to the gym or for a walk? Do you feel energetic after going for the workout or walk? Or have you felt unsure in business or work and were doubting yourself before pitching a sale or giving a presentation, but afterwards, felt confident and were so happy you put yourself out of your comfort zone?

> Doubt takes you out of action,
>
> but action takes you out of doubt

Doubt takes you out of action, but action takes you out of doubt; you need to separate your feelings from action. Acknowledge and admit you don't feel like doing it but consciously decide you will do it anyway because of the reasons you listed in your change quadrant. You know what it will cost, but you also know what it will pay!

Embrace the suck - Choose your shit sandwich!
I also want to pre-frame for you there will be parts of your goal or dream destination you won't enjoy! But that's what gets you where you want

to be, and everything in life comes in duality. For example, as much as Olympians love the hype and competition of the Olympics, the travel and recognition, do you honestly think they love getting up at 4am every day the four years in-between to train?

Do you think rock stars who travel the world, have millions of admiring fans, fortune, and fame enjoy the fact they can't duck into their corner store on the weekends in their tracksuit with no make-up on without a paparazzi in their face?

Or the fact they can't make a little mistake like the rest of us humans without being scrutinised and bullied in the media? I love helping others and inspiring others to live their Life Above Zero, but I dislike having to be on social media. I dislike networking events and having to put myself out there and speak in front of hundreds, and sometimes even thousands of people. It scares the shit out of me and zaps all my energy!

I would much rather sit in my safe, comfortable bubble and conserve all my energy. But I also know being an introvert working in an extrovert industry I need to put my big-girl, business boss babe pants on and do those things because my mission is bigger than me. And the only way to serve the many is to do things I don't necessarily enjoy.

I'm so passionate about my vision. I'm passionate about my message, and if I don't get out here and find ten minutes of courage and share with you what I'm about or what I'm up to. I can't expect people who really need to hear my message, or people who are really stuck, or whoever I could be resonating with out there, to find me.

Just like a fireman puts on his uniform for work to get done what he needs to for work to serve and help others, I am sure he doesn't wear it around at home or in his down time. Similarly, if you are in a corporate job, I'm sure most of you don't sit there on your weekends wearing your tailored skirt, or maybe your suit jacket. Am I right? It's something you put on to get your business done.

Likewise, for me, I embrace the suck and do things that do not feel natural for me. I put on my 'extrovert jacket' to best do my job so I can continue to do the thousand other things I love and enjoy about my work. There are so many introverts working in extrovert roles and you don't have to be an extrovert to work with large groups of people. It just takes ten seconds of courage and committing to and understanding there are parts of certain roles, goals, and destinations you will not enjoy, but that does not mean it is not for you.

This world is so much bigger than you and me, and if you have a business, if you've got a vision, it is so much bigger than you. Understanding that helps you do the scary, sucky things you may rather not do. In saying that, when things get challenging, when there are things you don't enjoy or don't want to do, remember it is part of your journey. This gets you to where you want to be or become who it is you want to become. Connecting to your 'why' is a great way to embrace the suck!

When I am mentoring women in business, one of the first things I get them to do is an exercise where they take the time and create the space to reflect on their why. Why did they say yes to starting their own business? What is their intention and vision for their business? What do they want their business to be, look like and provide for themselves, loved ones, future and legacy they leave behind?

Business, just like life, is not all sunshine and rainbows. Life gets full, life pulls you in lots of different directions. There are people who don't share the same values as you who will tear and beat you down and you can quite easily lose your way, your goals, vision, mission, and purpose. Which is why the fail rate in start-up businesses is so freaking high, with one in two businesses failing in the first twelve months.

That is why it is so important to have a strong 'why' and remind yourself by connecting with it every damn day! Know why you're busting your butt fourteen hours a day. Know why you're sacrificing your weekends with friends and working on getting that start-up off the ground. And know why, despite the fact you received ten no's today, you will go start another conversation to find that one person who needs the service or product you have in your hands. Know why after putting the kids to bed you will stay up until midnight working on your side hustle even though you're exhausted and would rather be in bed.

Have a why that will make you cry! When you have a why bigger than your excuses, you will find it easier to be consistent, embrace the suck, and show up for yourself even on the bad days because it's exactly that. You're doing this for you and what you can create for your family, your future, and the people in the world you can serve from stepping into your zone of genius.

> Having a strong 'why' can give you the ability to call on psychological and physical power you never knew you had within you.

There is a science behind having a strong why. It helps you tolerate short-term pain for long-term satisfaction. Research has found by having photographs of their loved ones, it gave soldiers the strength to live and face another day. It gave them hope and a reason to not give up knowing they had another reality outside all the pain and heartbreak they were witnessing. There was an abundance of love, light and laughter waiting for them on the other side of the suck.

Paramedics and nurses remind patients of their loved ones when they are fighting their own painful and emotional crises to remind them to not give up. To keep fighting because they have so many reasons why they still need to be here in the world. Having a strong 'why' can give you the ability to call on psychological and physical power you never knew you had within you.

Another quick tool you can use when you have to embrace the suck and 'don't feel like it' is Mel Robbins' 'five-second rule'. Because, let's be honest, that is all of us at least once every day. She's written a book on it, so go check it out if you want to understand the research and psychology behind it. It is a great metacognition trick which allows you to outsmart your brain and beat it at its own game.

Remember when I explained earlier, your brain is wired to want to just wallow in its own shit and take the path of least resistance? When you know you need to or should do something that will get you closer to your goal, but your brain is resisting? Shut up the thousand excuses it is muttering in your head and interrupt the inner noise with a countdown: 5, 4, 3, 2, 1- GO!

It's crazy how powerful this trick is! I double-dare you to give it a go. Don't wait for you to feel like doing it until you take the action. I know despite most people's best intentions to make each year their best year, most people quickly lose their momentum with their energy being spent on various other commitments when routine sets back in after holiday season.

Seeing those New Year Resolutions the whole year through

Holiday season seems to be the time people realise they are unhappy when they are dreading to return to their day job to work another fifty-two weeks to earn another holiday. So they set new business or career goals. Or, over the break, they have spent enough time with their loved ones who reflect the baggage they have been carrying around and they can't hide their shit anymore. That is the kick up the butt they need to set new wellness, relationship and personal development goals.

I know the reality many of us are familiar with after holiday season is coming into the new year with some new health goals after binging a little too much on the festive food and alcohol. I am guessing you have been there once or twice, too?

Despite the realisation we may be unhappy with where we currently are and may even decide we need to do something about it, it is also around February people get stuck back into work. They're getting the kids settled back into school and transporting them to their daily sporting commitments. Those new year resolutions and the goals we set for ourselves and the things we decided were important get neglected. Instead, our time and energy are spent like that duck on water trying to stay afloat rather than consciously deciding and being in charge of where we want to spend our money, energy and time.

Here are some secrets on how to keep the motivation to see those goals or resolutions through. Whatever your goals are, the best way to ensure you have the commitment and dedication to keep working at them is asking yourself, where is the motivation coming from?

You will find that fire and focus is easier to maintain when the goals you are setting are intrinsically motivated. You want them; you are willing to work and make sacrifices for them because YOU want it. If you are setting a goal because someone else is telling you to or because society expects you to, you can bet when you're faced with your first hurdle you will struggle to source the energy and desire to jump.

*"When a child is learning how to walk
and falls down fifty times, we never think
to ourselves, 'maybe walking isn't for them.'"*
ANON

Goals are fun.

They are not a chore or a way to beat yourself up. They are an opportunity to articulate to the universe what you want to hold yourself accountable and will take steps to get there. That fire and passion will drive you no matter what obstacles you face because you genuinely and organically wake up each day yearning for it.

Goals (it doesn't matter how big or small) help give our lives purpose and meaning. If you are feeling like you are stuck in a rut, set a small goal to help you get up and moving in 'flow'. Hold yourself accountable right from the beginning when you are setting your goals. Don't rely on anything you don't have power over.

> If you are feeling like you are stuck in a rut, set a small goal to help you get up and moving in 'flow'.

This is your goal, no one else's. You are responsible for achieving it. If you make excuses or blame others, it was never your goal to begin with. Hiccups and hurdles are part of the process. You set out to achieve YOUR goal, so remember, these are not failures, only feedback. What will you try next or do differently?

Just Start. Trust me, setting the goal is the hardest part because you have had to sit down and really ask yourself what it is you truly want, what you are willing to sacrifice and work hard for. As Nike says, "just do it!" You don't have to see the whole staircase, just the first step.

Positive self-talk is important at all times; however, it is even more crucial with goals. If you let your doubt and self-limiting beliefs dominate your thought processes, they will become your reality. You CAN do this, you are WORTHY of this, you WILL do this!

Visualise it!

Visualisation is a technique used by many sporting and life coaches. It derives from Neurolinguistic Programming. Visualise yourself doing it, achieving it. How do you feel? What do you see, hear, and smell? Who do you tell? What are you wearing?

Who is there to share the moment with you and celebrate? Visualising makes it all more real as your brain builds stronger neurological connections as it cannot discriminate between real and imagined experiences. It produces the same hormones, neurological responses and feelings regardless, allowing you to tune in and refuel that fire regularly. It reminds you of that satisfaction waiting at the end of all the hard work and on the other side of those challenges.

Write it here, there, and everywhere!

Repetition, constantly put it out into the universe, have little cues everywhere reminding you what you are doing it all for. Whether it be a picture of your dream holiday on the fridge or your body at its fittest as your phone background. Have your goal written at the front of your diary or on your bathroom mirror, have it set as your alarm in the mornings, etc.

Another handy tip is having your goals as your passwords! These days, with technology, we have to enter them a few times each day, why not use these opportunities to refuel your motivation and commitment?

Like-minded friends!

Surround yourself with like-minded friends, friends who also have goals and aspirations of their own; people who encourage you, empower you and support you. It is true, your vibe attracts your tribe! More on this later, too, I promise!

Get Help!

This goal is still YOUR goal. The destination at the end doesn't change, however, sometimes a problem shared is a problem halved. Whether it be outsourcing some work so you can focus on some bigger goals or seeking a mentor or life coach to help refuel your ambition.

Celebrate small wins!

In the previous chapter regarding goal setting, we advised big goals should be broken into smaller ones. This is done to help keep you motivated, to make the bigger goal more real and achievable. Use the smaller goals to track your progress and celebrate each victory! Celebrate your ambition, your commitment!

You are doing it! You Go Glen Coco, you GO! Be careful though. There is a difference between celebrating a small win and trying to encourage behaviour and create habits. "Classical conditioning" is a psychological phenomenon discovered by the famous Psychologist, Ivan Pavlov, where he reinforced dogs' behaviour with food.

The dogs associated the sound of the food bell with food and soon were conditioned to salivate every time they heard the bell regardless whether food was also present simply because of the repetition of the sequence of events. They learned to anticipate food would come paired with the sound of the bell.

Rewarding yourself works great when celebrating small wins but can backfire if you're trying to create a habit. You are unconsciously teaching and conditioning yourself that you will only do one thing on the premise and anticipation you will get something for it. This goes for you, too, parents, if you're trying to create some habits with your kids.

For example, let's say you tell yourself that you can treat yourself to some trashy reality TV if you go to bed early. Soon enough, you learn to associate going to bed with watching trashy reality TV. So now, regardless of what time you go to bed, you have conditioned yourself to get in the habit of watching TV anyway. This totally undermines the habit formation process and now you're no longer enjoying the payoff of more sleep with an earlier bedtime, which was your initial goal. You're self-sabotaging it by using a treat to create a habit.

The Progress Principle: give up your deadline.

Science proves that focusing on daily progress, not achieving big goals, boosts your ability to get things done and creates momentum. Every day, focus on taking even one step closer to your goals. Ask yourself: what is something I can do to today, even if it is small. What will get you closer to

X than you were yesterday? Then make that your focus. Big goals are just made up of lots of little goals.

Get re-inspired!

Like happiness, like energy. You can't expect to be feeling high levels of motivation and excitement 24/7. You have to work at it and refuel that fire. Now and then, look for inspiration to keep that drive, whether it be from reading blogs, books, movies, podcasts, documentaries, conferences, or networking events and talking to others.

The world is filled with amazing people with amazing stories. Don't get so caught up in your journey you forget to notice the ambition surrounding you. This helps ground you. PLEASE NOTE: this does not mean comparing your lives to others on social media, so you feel inferior!

It is about acknowledging we are all different people on different paths, and genuinely being happy, inspired, and learning from others' success (and failures). Use other people's achievements to inspire you of what is possible.

> Use other people's achievements to inspire you of what is possible.

Let's talk about willpower

We all have a finite source of will power. If you were a university student, did you ever notice that usually you were pretty good at adult life? You kept your apartment clean, yourself well groomed, and didn't eat too much crap? But then comes the week before exams, you cram, and something strange happens. Your apartment looks like a-bomb's hit it. You can't remember the last nutritious meal you ate. A packet of chips and some lollies for dinner somehow become appropriate and you haven't gone to a gym class or washed your hair all week.

Don't worry, you're not alone! Research has found during study week, students' hygienic practices hit an all-time low, and health and wellness habits get neglected. Despite the fact we have a short amount of time to

"Don't try and tell me that hungry is not an emotion because I feel that shit in my soul."

ANON

remember all our summaries, ironically, we are more likely to decide it is the perfect opportunity to spend some of that precious time to randomly go shopping and buy on impulse. Sound familiar?

It is a phenomenon research has found not only in university students, but in any circumstance when we are working consciously towards a goal. We need to allocate much of our psychological willpower and self-control to stay focused and on task to complete it.

Roy F. Baumeister, a social psychologist, found we only have one source of willpower. If we exhaust it all pursuing one goal, we become fatigued and have little self-control left to achieve other ones. Ever noticed you go through phases where you focus on health or business goals but struggle to do both at once?

> Pick one and commit to it every day for thirty days
>
> so it becomes a habit
>
> and no longer a question of willpower.

You may even recognise this with your health goals alone. Have you ever tried to go cold turkey and decided you would quit smoking and alcohol, go to the gym every day, and cut out all junk and processed foods? How did it go? I bet you failed miserably, am I right?

It isn't because you failed, it's because you set yourself up to fail because you don't have enough willpower to pull all that off at the same time. No one does. You only have a finite source of willpower to exercise, so you need to focus on making one change at a time. Then make it a habit so it no longer is a question of willpower, it is just something you do every day.

That is when you can then move onto the next goal. It's all about making small but sustainable, healthy lifestyle choices. Do you recall a time when your mum or dad had to prompt you to clean your teeth every morning and night even though you didn't want to? If you don't, I bet your parents do. They would remind you and make you do it.

Now, as an adult, I bet you don't think twice about it. You don't have to kick and scream and get your butt dragged to the bathroom. It is part of your daily habits and routine you have been doing for years. Think of this anytime you're struggling with a goal. Don't try to slay them all at once. Pick one and commit to it every day for thirty days so it becomes a habit and no longer a question of willpower. Then you free your willpower up to move on and work on the next goal.

FUN FACT:
Hangry (getting angry and unable to think or focus properly because you're hungry) is a real thing! Willpower is fuelled by our energy sources – sleep and glucose. When we deplete our energy stores we experience willpower fatigue and less self-control.

Women, did you know that this phenomenon occurs when we are on our period? When we are menstruating, our bodies are directing extra energy to our ovaries to create baby-making magic! During this time, because of more organs consuming our energy stores than usual, we experience a fatigue in willpower and subsequent self-control.

Do you notice (or men, do you notice this in your partners, sisters or daughters) when you are on your period, you lack the self-control you usually have to say no to naughty treats? You buy things you don't need on impulse? Or even being moody and snapping at your kids or spouse when you usually have the self-control to bite your tongue?

A similar phenomenon is called 'decision fatigue', which refers to the deteriorating quality of the decisions you make after a long session of decision-making. In a research study published by the National Academy of Sciences, psychologists examined the factors that impact whether a judge approves a criminal for parole.

The researchers examined 1112 judicial rulings over a ten-month period. A parole board judge made all the rulings and determined whether to allow the criminal's release from prison on parole. In some cases, the criminal was asking not for a release, but a change in parole terms.

You would assume factors like the crime committed or the particular laws that were broken influenced the judge, but the researchers found exactly the opposite. The choices made by the judge were impacted by all types of things that shouldn't have an effect in the courtroom.

Most notably, the time of day. At the beginning of the day, the judge was likely to give a favourable ruling about sixty-five percent of the time.

However, as the morning wore on and the judge became drained from making more decisions, the likelihood of a criminal getting a favourable ruling steadily dropped to zero.

After taking a lunch break, however, the judge would return to the courtroom refreshed and the likelihood of a favourable ruling would immediately jump back up to sixty-five percent. And then, as the hours moved on, the percentage of favourable rulings would fall back down to zero by the end of the day.

This trend held true for over 1100 cases. It didn't matter what the crime was murder, rape, theft, or embezzlement. A criminal was much more likely to get a favourable response if their parole hearing was scheduled in the morning (or immediately after a food break) than if it was scheduled near the end of a long session!

As I explained earlier, your willpower is like a muscle, and similar to the muscles in your body, willpower can get fatigued when you use it repeatedly. Every time you make a decision, it's like doing another rep in the gym. And similar to how your muscles get tired at the end of a workout, the strength of your willpower fades as you make more decisions.

Have you ever noticed brides planning their wedding are so picky and selective at the start and by the end, they say to caterers, the groom or the bridal party to pick one themselves? Or, even after you have a long day at work of making decisions and exercising your willpower to be polite to colleagues and bosses, when your partner asks you what you what for dinner, do you snap at them? Or do you find it hard to decide and just settle for the easiest option?

Similarly, major politicians and businessmen such as Former US President Barack Obama, Steve Jobs and Mark Zuckerberg have reduced their everyday clothing down to one or two of the same suits. This limited the number of decisions they had to make in a day to decrease their decision fatigue and free up their mental energy to make more important decisions!

I don't know about you, but my biggest take away from this research is eat first! Don't make any decisions when you're hungry, including the grocery shopping. I need some serious self-control in the lolly isle on an empty stomach! Oh, and make your most important decisions first, before your mental muscle gets tired.

If there was the most important court case in the world, when would you want the judge to hear it? Based on the research above, I would suggest first thing in the morning. You would want the judge and jury's best attention, energy, and focus to go toward the decisions that were most important.

The same thing goes for your work and life. What's the most important thing for you right now? Is it eating healthier? Is it building your business? Is it writing that book you have brewing inside of you? Is it learning to manage stress and relax? Whatever it is for you, put your best energy toward it.

If you have to wake up thirty minutes earlier, then do that. Start your day by working on the most important thing in your life. This is why I am a lover and advocate of morning rituals and routines to set your day up for success! If you don't have a good morning routine, I recommend you get your hands on Hal Elrod's, *The Miracle Morning*. You can thank me later.

If you can understand these psychological triggers for self-sabotage, you'll learn how to identify them. When you catch that negative self-talk, talking you out of your goals and your dreams, you will know how to call it on its shit and beat your brain at its own game.

Lastly with goal setting, make sure you put the time aside to reflect! Breaking your goals into smaller ones also allows you the opportunity to reflect. Reflect on where you have come from, how far you have come, who and what helped you, what you have learned, and how you have grown. This exercise helps to strengthen your gratitude and mindfulness.

Reassess! I can't say it enough. For your goals to be effective, they really need to intrinsically motivate you. When you are regularly reflecting, ask yourself:

Is it pleasurable?

If the answer is No, ask yourself -

Is it still worth the sacrifices?

If the answer to both questions is no, then it is time to reassess. Don't be hard on yourself; people change, life changes. Changing or choosing not to pursue certain goals does not mean you have failed.

Sometimes our values change because of our experiences and growth. If you fail to reassess your goals frequently, your goals may no longer reflect your values, beliefs, or who you are. So, Dream Big, Aim High, and Have Fun. Go get them babe!

: CHAPTER SIX

Passion and Perseverance: The Secret Sauce

REMEMBER THAT- who PERSON GAVE UP?
Neither does anyone else.

What is success? What does success mean to you? I'm sure most of you suddenly have an answer that pops into your head, because we all have different perspectives and views on what "success" is. Ultimately, that will be a direct reflection of your values.

When I say, "Think of someone you know who is successful", I know some of you, if not most of you, already have someone who pops into mind. It might be somebody you look up to in business. It might be somebody you look up to in sports, in life, in parenting, in relationships, or maybe travel.

Whatever it is, that is important to you, I'm sure. Did you think of someone? Do you hold someone in your head as somebody you aspire to be like? If I was to then ask you, "What do you think it took for them to achieve success?" Are you one of those people who instinctively believes and assumes they have achieved that level of success because they're naturally talented? That they inherited it, or it was a matter of being at the right place at the right time?

Do you catch yourself saying things like, "they were born with it," "they always had that natural skill," "yeah, but I'm not outgoing like them," "they are an extrovert," "they are smart," "I'm not tech savvy," etc.? I know personally, at school, when there were people who were really successful at a sport, people would often say, "Oh, they're just good at everything." Or when people did really well at exams, you would often hear others say, "yeah, but they're just smart."

I hate that… for so many reasons.

Universal Assignment:

Who is that person you thought of as being successful? What about them do you consider "successful"? What does "Success" mean to you?

Sorry, but that's absolute bullshit. Even research has proven that. You might reflect now and look at the people who you perceived to be successful, and yes, they might have some natural ability or something that comes in the mix. Just like a recipe, it might be that ingredient some people believe you need to make the perfect brownie. But your nan knows that secret ingredient you can add instead that makes her brownies the best you've ever had!

That secret ingredient is called Grit! Research has found natural ability doesn't mean shit. Yep, you heard it first here, folks! If you look back, I am sure you can think of those people who were successful at school, but just having that natural ability alone to learn and pick up a skill doesn't get them anywhere.

That's why you see so many people who you may look back on and remember having such high expectations of because of this "natural ability". Yet, ten years after school you're surprised they didn't live up to their potential. Does someone come to mind for you?

I know so many kids who were naturally smart and aced all their tests without having to study (the lucky shits), yet they turned out later in life to be the stoners with no ambition or drive. Don't lie, I know you know them, too. There is untapped potential because natural ability isn't enough. That is not and never will be enough for success.

Research has found the biggest predictor of success in every area of life is a trait called "grit." What I love most about this is grit isn't a natural ability. It's not that someone is naturally smart, naturally outgoing. Success isn't born. You're not born with success. You're born with potential.

To tap into that potential, you need to work on building a character trait called "grit." Grit is passion matched with perseverance. What I love about this is that anybody can have grit. This is why I hate that tendency that people assume others are successful because they're born with natural talent or they're just good at something.

> You're not born with success.

> You're born with potential

That's really unfair for the person who achieved those things because you're dismissing all the hard work they did to get there. Consider the amount of times they failed yet picked themselves up and tried again when most people gave up. You're saying that was "just luck" or "you were just born with it."

You're dismissing the fact you didn't see how hard they studied after school. You didn't see how hard they studied in their free periods when their friends wagged. Do you think sporting athletes competing at the Olympics are "just born with it"?

You didn't see how many weekends they sacrificed to train. Instead of going out and having drunken, late nights with friends, they were missing lots of those magical moments most other teenagers/young adults have.

First, you dismiss all the effort, the perseverance, and how many times they got themselves back up after they fell down; how they had to believe in themselves when no one else did. And when they had to seek support when their loved ones told them they were crazy, and their goals weren't realistic.

You dismiss the people in business who may have invested so much money and time in other projects and have lost it all before they had their breakthrough. You've dismissed all the amounts of time, money, and weekends they spent on personal development to get to where they are. You're dismissing their effort.

Second, you're doing yourself a massive disservice because you're telling yourself, "I can't have that/ achieve that/ create that because I wasn't born with it." That is bullshit. It's perseverance and passion that can get you anything you want. You can have it. Everything they have, you can have. Anything they are, you can be.

I catch people so often, whether it's my business coaching, or it's my life coaching, or even in my job when I was working in child protection, where they looked at other people and they thought, *"Oh, I can't do that. I can't be that. I can't have that. I can't feel like that."* (Instagram and social media are the worse for feeding that comparison game).

Why? Why can't you have that? You can have everything you want. It's not about ability. It comes down to passion and perseverance. A question for you is, how bad do you want it, and how hard are you willing to work for it? Because it' won't come easy.

Those people you might see successful on your Instagram or your

"The only thing I see that is distinctively different about me is that: I'm not afraid to die on a treadmill. I will not be outworked, period. You might have more talent than me, you might be smarter, you might be sexier. But if we get on the treadmill together, there's two things: You're getting off first or I'm going to die. It's really that simple."

WILL SMITH

Facebook are people you just see getting recognised in public for what they do in private. Don't doubt the amount of times they've fallen down before they got there and the amount of times they had to pick themselves up. Or the amount of times they didn't believe they could do it.

It's about perseverance. Success is when people fall down and they get up, and they get up, and they get up, and they get up again. If you have that mentality, there's no way you can't be successful because you'll never give up until you get there. So, I wanted to just crack that myth for you.

If you are one of those people comparing yourself to others, and one of those bullshit excuses coming up is, "I can't be that because I wasn't born like that, or I wasn't born with that ability." Bullshit! I will not let you wallow in your pity party holding onto that security blanket.

Anyone can have Grit, and even better, anybody can strengthen it. You can strengthen grit in two ways. One is called growth mindset, or fixed mindset. People who have a fixed mindset is that mindset I was just telling you about, where their conditioned way of thinking is, *I can't have that. I'm always like this. I always fail. I'm never successful. I always fall down. Nobody believes in me. I have no time.*

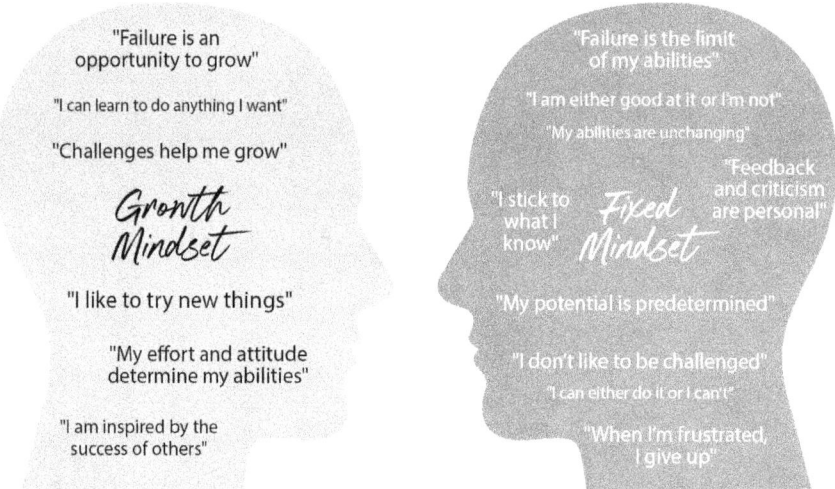

And you're right. If you think like that, you can't do it. But a growth mindset is when you fall down and you ask yourself better questions; *What can I do better? How can I be better? How can I learn from this? How am I a better person because of this? How can I help others because of this? How can I find more time? How can I make this work? How can I learn to do that or*

*"Working hard for something
we don't care about is called stress.
Working hard for something
we love is called passion."*

ANON

get better at that? If I was to ask someone who had already achieved this, what would they advise me to do? How would the best version of me respond to this?

It's about growth. This "natural ability" is one myth I want to squash and leave right here. You can do and achieve anything you set your mind to, but how many times are you willing to get up when you fail or fall?

Another myth I would love to squash for you is balance. People on their pursuit for success feel like, to get there, they will have balance. They will have this perfect amount of time set aside for their relationships, this amount of time for their exercise, this amount of time for their work, this amount of time for their sleep, this amount of time for their play.

Balance is a luxury.

So, until you get to where you want to get,

please don't dismiss your goals.

Sorry, but balance is a luxury. In pursuing success, if you want something, you won't get balance in the beginning. Think of, once again, Olympic athletes. They are a great example because I think most of you can imagine and understand the effort they put in to pursue their goals and aspirations. Do you think they have balance to get where they are?

Do you think they sit there and think, *Oh, I have already exercised for two hours today; I will watch some TV,* or, *I haven't had any time today to talk with my friends; I'll ditch training today and go have lunch with my gfs?* Balance is a luxury. So, until you get to where you want to get, please don't dismiss your goals. Don't abandon your mission, give up on your dreams, or think the journey isn't for you just because you don't have balance.

You will have to work hard, but there is a difference between "working hard" and "hard work." There will be days where your life is out of whack, days where you feel like there's more work and less play. If you want an above-average life, it will take an above-average effort and a season of strategic imbalance.

There are many people I know and come across in my work who define their success when they finally retire on the six to seven-figure income. They'll go on multiple holidays, and work on their own terms, when they like and from where they like. I honestly believe anyone can create that; however, the dream is free, but the hustle is sold separately.

It is the work that isn't fun, that nobody sees, and no one wants to do what will make your dreams come true. We are living in the era of self-indulgence; we are the Brat Pack, gen Y, who want everything, and we want it now! But we get frustrated when we don't get what we want like spoiled little kids throwing a tantrum, claiming it's not fair.

We feed ourselves all these woo-woo affirmations like "if it feels good, do it, and if it doesn't, then don't." Because of that we are losing the value and understanding of what it means to work hard, have a great work ethic, discipline, and delay gratification.

In an era where we are all chasing quick fixes and online businesses are making people believe in overnight successes, too many give up on their goals the moment they realise it takes work.

Purely in the space of business, 300,000 people every week are starting a home-based business, at a time where daycare is more than most mums' wages. Where mums are being forced back to work before they are ready because they don't have maternity leave and are missing magical moments with loved ones. People want to travel but don't have enough recreational leave. People are losing their jobs and being made redundant because online businesses, technology, and machines can do things better than they can. Side hustles are becoming extremely common.

Despite the need to create multiple streams of income, financial security, and flexible working conditions, too many people are more loyal to their boss than they are to their dreams. They have a why, a mission, a purpose, yet their dreams can be bought for a stable pay check.

So many people I stumble across in business will easily and happily show up at 9am every day and work until 5pm, five days a week for their boss, but won't commit to consistently showing up for themselves. Too many people don't have the patience to build a business as a side hustle for four years, yet they have the patience to work on someone else's dreams for forty.

Too many people don't have the patience to build a business.

> as a side hustle for four years, yet they have the patience
>
> to work on someone else's dreams for forty.

It takes work... lots of it. But it also takes determination, will power, persistence, grit, vision, a lot of ten seconds of courage to constantly commit to pushing yourself out of your comfort zone to grow yourself, not just in business, but every aspect of life. In the 1960s, a Stanford professor named Walter Mischel did one of my favourite psychological studies ever called the "Marshmallow Experiment."

Mischel and his team tested hundreds of children, most of them around the ages of four and five years old. The experiment began by bringing each child into a private room, sitting them down in a chair, and placing a marshmallow on the table in front of them.

The researcher told the child he would leave the room and if the child did not eat the marshmallow while he was away, then they would be rewarded with a second marshmallow. However, if the child ate the first one before the researcher came back, then they would not get a second marshmallow.

The choice was simple: one treat right now (instant gratification) or two treats later (delay gratification). The researcher left the room for fifteen minutes. As you can imagine, the footage of the children waiting alone in the room was rather entertaining. Some kids jumped up and ate the first marshmallow as soon as the researcher closed the door.

Others wiggled and bounced and scooted in their chairs as they tried to restrain themselves, but eventually gave in to temptation a few minutes later. And finally, a few of the children managed to wait the entire time. Published in 1972, this popular study's results that came years later is what made the Marshmallow Experiment so famous and replicated time and time again - the Power of Delayed Gratification.

As the years rolled on and the children grew up, the researchers conducted longitudinal studies where they would follow up and they tracked each child's progress in several areas. The children willing to delay gratification and waited to receive the second marshmallow ended up having higher SAT scores. They had lower levels of substance abuse,

"Courage doesn't always roar. Sometimes courage is the quiet voice at the end of the day saying, I will try again tomorrow."

ANON

lower likelihood of obesity, better responses to stress, better social skills as reported by their parents, and generally, better scores in a range of other life measures.

The researchers followed each child for over forty years and, repeatedly, the group who waited patiently for the second marshmallow succeeded in whatever capacity they were measuring. In other words, this series of experiments proved the ability to delay gratification was critical for success in life and revealed what we now believe to be one of the most important characteristics for success in health, work, and life.

Being passionate about what you do, not being distracted by new shiny objects, and the willingness to stick with it and commit for the long haul even when it gets ugly. That is the secret sauce for success in your lives, relationships, and careers. But in saying that, I really wanted to let you know the pursuit of your goals doesn't have to be this brutal slog either. It doesn't mean you run yourself on empty.

I like using the analogy for people who are visual, to think of a cup. In your start-up phase when you're hustling towards a goal, whether it's in business, financial, study, relationships, or sports, you will have times where life is so full and you're close to running on empty, to think of your cup.

When your cup is getting full, you need to have the self-regulation skills and self-awareness to prompt yourself and think, *Okay. I've done so many hours this week. I'm tired. I'm getting cranky. I'm not passionate about this. My cup is about to overflow. I will make sure I get out in the sunshine today and spend some quality time with my partner.*

That's what it's about. It's about regulating and checking how full your cup is. It can be something as simple as if you're sitting there and you've been studying for three hours and you're agitated. It's not fun and you decide *stuff it, that's it. This is just not meant for me. I'm not meant to be successful.*

That is not it at all! Instead, you could say, *Okay. my cup is nearly full. I'm agitated. I've been looking at this same screen for three hours. I will go out. I will go for a walk. I will clear my head. I will get in the right mind space. Then I will come back.*

"Passion for your work is a little bit of discovery followed by a lot of development then a lifetime of deepening."

ANON

> If you get tired, learn to rest, not quit
>
> Almost anything will work again
>
> if you unplug it for a minute or two, especially you.

If you get tired, learn to rest, not quit. Almost anything will work again if you unplug it for a minute or two, especially you. If you're a visual person, think of it like a see-saw; if you're waiting for it to balance, you will be waiting forever. Maybe when you're successful (whatever you defined that to be), whether it is when you've got that time freedom, you've created that lifestyle, you've got money freedom, you have conquered those goals; you have that ability, or you've mastered those skills, maybe then you'll have balance.

But until then, balance is a luxury. Don't think just because your time is out of whack or you're putting more in than you currently see coming out, that it's not for you. That is not what success is about. It's about persistence and it's about knowing what you want and being fearless pursuing anything that sets your soul on fire.

Instead of thinking of that see-saw, think of a cup. When your cup is getting full and you feel yourself overflowing, prompt yourself. Self-regulate. Have that self-awareness to do something for you. It's a strategic dance of ebbs and flows. I couldn't move on without having a little chapter of tough love. I know for so many of you, even though you've made it to this point, you will still abandon ship in pursuit of your goals because of believing someone is better or more talented than you. And because your goal is consuming other areas of your life.

Anything worth having won't be easy, otherwise we would all have it, and just know it's not forever. It takes a certain mindset, like a muscle you need to train every day to look for lessons. Have faith in the process, and trust everything is on the way, not *in* the way, and fall in love with the journey instead of being fixated on the destination.

If you give up today, what if that breakthrough happened tomorrow? What if you preserved one more day? What if this challenge is the lesson that teaches you and prepares you for that next level?

I really needed to squish these myths about the bullshit excuses people are feeding themselves on why they can't be who they want and why they can't do what they want to do. You can have and you can be anything that you want. Like I said, it comes down to grit; passion mixed with perseverance is the secret sauce.

If you're not passionate about something, get out there and try different things. Interest discovery is triggered by interactions with the outside world. You can't predict with certainty what will capture your attention and what won't. Likewise, you can't will yourself to like things, either.

Without experimenting you can't work out what interests will stick and what won't, so get out there! Your calling may be serendipitous, but without getting out of your comfort zone, trying new things, and following what's enjoyable, you won't find that thing that lights you up with purpose and passion.

P.S. And because I'm a realist and I don't like to sugarcoat things, please be mindful that just because you love something doesn't mean you will be great at it. Whether it's a sport or business idea, it's about work, study and practice.

That's the secret sauce to cracking the code and doing something you love every day for work. Try new things until you find "it", then pair that passion with perseverance and you, my friend, will have something most people spend their whole life searching for.

CHAPTER SEVEN

Owning All Parts of You

Owning all parts of you. I don't know about you, but I have never met "the perfect person" or stumbled across the "perfect body, job or relationship." There have been adults in my childhood I looked up to, just to grow up and realise they don't have their shit together, they never really knew what they were doing. They were just big kids themselves, winging it, doing the best they could with what they had, and learning along the way.

There were relationships and marriages I aspired to have, just to get close enough to realise they had the same cracks other people had, they had just glued it back together. My heroes, my mentors, my idols, my parents… they aren't perfect. But they are whole; they are human; they have strengths, and they have weaknesses.

I think that is something that really needs to be understood. In pursuing the perfect relationship, job, body, health, life, inner peace, that doesn't mean you don't have the un-pretty parts, the uneasy parts, or the imperfect parts. Success, fulfilment, and true happiness transpires when you recognise, own, and love all parts of yourself, which allows you to love and accept others, too.

What is confidence?

I once was asked to talk to some high school students about confidence. To be honest, I wasn't quite sure how to start. I put myself in their shoes back in high school and asked myself how relevant confidence was to me back then at that age. What did I wish future me could go back and say to my high school self? How could I help myself become a more confident person later in life, and why would I even want to? What is confidence, anyway? Can you see it? feel it? Touch it?

I am not sure how many of you guys are Lil Wayne fans. (I admit I am that girl who listens to gangster rap on way home from yoga and the farmers markets). Instantly, I thought of his lyrics *"confidence is a stain they can't wipe off."* For me, that implied confidence is something you gain from experience and lessons. It is something that can't be taken away from you once you develop it. It is like a badge you earn from not giving up when the going gets tough or shying away from the hard stuff and coming out the other side.

I wasn't sure how using some gangster lyrics would sit in justifying my argument, so like most of us geniuses living in the 21st century, I turned to Google. Google quickly informed me: Confidence is *"the feeling or belief that one can have faith in or rely on someone or something."*

With that definition in mind and putting my interpretation on it, I asked myself, what did I want my high school self to know that would give me the faith or the ability to rely and believe in myself and others? Honestly, if I could go back, I would want to warn high school Lauren to be wary, to not confuse arrogance for confidence.

Confidence isn't about walking into a room with your nose in the air thinking you are better than everyone else. It's about walking into a room and not having to compare yourself to anyone in the first place. Stay humble. For me, confidence is about acknowledging and knowing your weaknesses and accepting yourself anyway.

It's about self-love, it's about owning your short comings, owning your wonky nose, buck teeth, and not letting anyone else make you feel bad about yourself or doubt yourself. I really wish I could go back and give my thirteen-year-old self a cuddle because the bullying definitely took its toll on me back then.

> Confidence isn't about walking into a room with your nose in the air

thinking you are better than everyone else.

I wish I knew then what I know now and how nasty people are really just unhappy people looking for love, but that is all part of the journey. Confidence isn't about being better than someone else, but trying to be a better person than the person you were yesterday.

Looking back on high school me, I wish I could go back and give myself a big hug and reassure myself it was OK. Because confidence is easier said than done, it is hard not to let others' words and actions cause you to doubt yourself and question your self-worth. Especially when there are people we perceive to be "bullies" placed in your path.

Have you ever been bullied? Whether it was as a child by other kids on the playground who didn't really understand the ramifications and long-term effects their thoughtless actions and words would have on you? Or later on in life in the workplace, or even in a relationship as a form of domestic abuse?

It happens to most of us at some point in our life. It is a form of power and control where someone who feels inferior, insecure, or unhappy in themselves tries to gain or assert power by manipulation or using hurtful words or spiteful actions to bring you down and lift themselves up.

In year seven I got bullied. I got called "Bucky" and they put chewy in my hair on the school bus. I had buckteeth before my parents were so selfless and bought me braces even though they weren't in the financial position to do so. I am forever grateful for the million things they did for me and my younger brothers.

It didn't just happen on my 13th birthday, but numerous times, to a point where I was traumatised and refused to get on the school bus. My parents forced me to hold my head up high and get back on the bus. Not without following the bus all the way to school in a car behind to give those bullies who were five years older than me some serious stink eyes... My parents are so bad ass, haha!

Future me would love to go back and remind high school me that those bullies' behaviour had nothing to do with whom I was as a person. And that braces could fix my teeth, but they were stuck with that ugly personality. As cliché as it sounds, your mum and dad were right, bullies are just jealous.

Their lives were unhappy, and they weren't getting the love and support they craved so they needed to bring me down to get that from their peers, ironic, hey? I will talk more about this in the next chapter in case I have lost you here. It reflected those bullies' reality, not mine.

At the end of the day, they had to do nasty things and say nasty things to make themselves feel better about themselves. I don't know about you guys, but that's not something I would be proud of or someone I would want to be. I was upset and hurt, however, I could go to bed and be proud of myself.

I was confident I was a kind person. I was proud of the way I spoke to others. I was proud of how I treated others and how I treated myself, always trying my best, and those are things that lead to confidence. I can always rely on and have faith in me, because I know I will do the right thing by myself and others around me.

I would be lying if I said I did this all the time, because we are all human. We aren't perfect (despite how much we wish we were). We make mistakes, and that's ok. The important thing is not to be so proud and arrogant you can't apologise for making a mistake, for treating someone badly. You always have a chance to right past wrongs and be confident in who you are and what you stand for.

So, confidence. How we can apply it? How do we become it?

There are a few tricks you can do things that make you feel better about yourself. Girls, for example, we may wear make-up (although you don't need it, but I get it. When we feel good, we do good). We might buy new clothes, get our hair done.

How do you present yourself to the world? Do you have pride in how you dress, talk, the messages you convey? Do you practice becoming better at the things you want to excel at? Do you compete and put yourself in situations where you can have the opportunity for small wins to build your confidence?

All these things can lead to a better sense of self-worth. The more you value yourself and your capabilities, the more valuable you feel. This creates the effect of naturally holding your head up high, since you have higher self-esteem and are proud of who you are, what you do, and what you stand for.

The more confidence you have (meaning the more you accept, own, and love all parts of yourself), the more happiness and enjoyment you will find within yourself, in your relationships and in life. In positive psychology we also refer to this term as Self-Actualisation.

> The more confidence you have the more happiness and enjoyment you will find within yourself, in your relationships and in your life.

Self-actualisation is the final stage of development in Abraham Maslow's hierarchy of needs. This stage occurs when a person can take full advantage of his or her talents while still being mindful of his or her limitations. The term is also used colloquially to refer to an enlightened maturity characterised by the achievement of goals, acceptance of oneself, and an ability to self-assess in a realistic and positive way.

When you accept your flaws are part of your make-up and make you the person you are today with all of your gifts and strengths, you unlock freedom from self-doubt. You free yourself of the mental torture of doubting yourself, and questioning whether you're "really" valuable, or capable of achieving things you want to achieve.

When you open wide and don't shy away from the not-so pretty parts of yourself, the stronger and more powerful you feel. You also naturally grow stronger and more confident when encountering challenges, rather than feeling weakened, crippled, and defeated by them.

Your weaknesses are your kryptonite and if you're holding a safe space for them rather than hiding them, no one can use them against you. In that place, you're unbreakable. Confidence frees you from fear and anxiety. Remember, it's not about walking into a room with your nose in the air thinking you are better than everyone else. It's about walking into a room and not having to compare yourself to anyone in the first place.

When you are inwardly fluent,

you are outwardly influential. But likewise,

if you are inwardly lost, you are outwardly influenced.

From that humble place you know you can accept, handle, learn, gain, and benefit from any situation, circumstance, or outcome. With that mindset, you naturally replace fear and anxiety with greater confidence in yourself and your abilities. You're constantly looking for the lesson, the silver lining, the blessing.

When you are clear about who you are, who you truly are at the core and what's important to you and what you stand for, you free yourself from social anxiety. This is why I took you through those chapters on discovering your values, what's important to you, what you stand for, how you want to show up in the world, and what footprint you want to leave behind.

The more secure you feel in your self-worth, regardless of how others see you, the less concerned you are with what others might or might not think of you in social situations. You're not manipulated by status, fashion, money, or opinions. When you are inwardly fluent, you are outwardly influential.

But likewise, if you're inwardly lost, you're outwardly influenced. Owning all parts of yourself sets you free. You will find more peace of mind and less stress. Freedom from self-doubt, fear, and anxiety naturally translates into greater peace of mind and a more stress-free life with more energy and motivation to act.

The more confident you are that you can achieve things you want to achieve (like personal goals or dreams), the more motivated and energised you are to take the action to achieve them. The happier and more confident you are, the more relaxed, comfortable, and at ease you are. This naturally puts others at ease more around you. Also, with these qualities, others trust, respect, value, welcome, and cooperate with you more; the overall result is better, and you'll have more enjoyable social interactions.

People can feel when you're living in alignment with your truth, you radiate that energy and vibrate at a higher level. It's contagious and lifts up those around you! I bet you that right now you know someone who is at that place, somebody comes to mind, right?

You can feel their energy as soon as they walk into the room, their aura, their body language, their tone, their carefree laugh, their conversations reek of confidence. They are someone people naturally radiate towards at networking events, or pay money to see, hear, or speak to.

I'm sure they've had to put in the work and go within to get to that place through personal, professional, and spiritual development. They have spent the time (even money to attend conferences, complete courses, and educate themselves). They've been willing to sit in places of discomfort to forgive, accept, and truly see all parts of themselves, even parts they have been denying, suppressing, or hiding for years.

But once they let it shine, people feel it. They want more of it; they want to be around it. They also want a piece of it and will try to tear you down (more of this in the next chapter). Confidence, clarity, and acceptance of who you are also leads to better sleep and health; less fear and anxiety, less stress. It means the body doesn't turn on and start attacking itself, (which research has found can trigger lots of autoimmune diseases), more peace of mind, and ultimately, more happiness.

The flow-on effects of confidence are endless, for ourselves, our loved ones, our happiness, and our health. It all starts and ends with you. You, loving and owning all of you. No one can do that for you. If you go within, you will never go without. You can practice and build on your confidence by ensuring you're living in alignment.

By now, if you've rolled up your sleeves and done the work in previous chapters, you know who you are; you know what your values are and what is important to you. You know how you want to show up in the world. What you want to be known and remembered as, and how the ideal and best version of you would consciously respond to situations by referring to your mission statement.

If you catch yourself playing below the line and not living in accordance to your truth, redirect, realign. Be congruent in what you say and what you do. If you do things that do not align with that, that upon reflection aren't how you ideally would have liked to respond to the situation, apologise.

Universal Assignment:

Who is someone that pisses you off? What about them pisses you off? Where in life are you doing that? What parts of yourself are you not owning and loving?

Be humble.

People connect with authenticity and transparency, not perfection. That is unattainable and therefore unrelatable. Acknowledge and accept you're not perfect. No one is. Admit when you're wrong, ask how you can be better and do better, before asking for forgiveness.

By doing this, not only are you shining light on the not-so-pretty parts of yourself. Because you have taken the time and space to familiarise and get to know those parts, you will also be able to see and recognise those parts in others. This makes it easier to forgive and give love and be loved in return.

> Every person on your path is there to teach you something, are you willing to learn?

We are all the same, we all make mistakes, we are all capable of doing things we aren't proud of. People will just mirror back to you the unloved parts of yourself. Every person placed on your path is there to teach you something, are you willing to learn?

Realising one's potential is a personal endeavour that depends on where one's creative, intellectual, or social potential lies. Self-actualisation is not about making the most money or becoming the most famous person in the world.

Instead, self-actualisation is about reaching one's personal potential, whether that means becoming a painter, a mum, a politician, a philosopher, a teacher, or anything else. At the risk of sounding cliché, self-actualisation is truly about achieving your dreams!

This "confidence" I speak of also aligns with what research and Psychologist, Abraham Maslow (being the leading figure in the tradition of humanistic psychology and the modern Positive Psychology movement), describes as being found when you self-actualise.

You know the people who have transcended to maximise their

potential, and are doing the best they can do because they embody the below twelve characteristics which Maslow outlines in his book *Motivation and Personality*:

1) Self-actualised people embrace the unknown and the ambiguous. (They are not threatened or afraid of it; instead, they accept it, are comfortable with it, and are often attracted by it. They do not cling to the familiar.)

2) They accept themselves, together with all their flaws (She perceives herself as she is, and not as she would prefer herself to be. With a high level of self-acceptance, she lacks defensiveness, pose, or artificiality. Eventually, shortcomings come to be seen not as shortcomings at all, but as neutral personal characteristics.)

3) They prioritise and enjoy the journey, not just the destination.

4) While they are inherently unconventional, they do not seek to shock or disturb.

5) Growth motivates them, not the satisfaction of needs.

6) Self-actualised people have purpose.

7) They are not troubled by the small things. Instead, they focus on the bigger picture.

8) Self-actualised people are grateful. They do not take their blessings for granted, and by doing so, maintain a fresh sense of wonder towards the universe.

9) They share deep relationships with a few, but also feel identification and affection towards the entire human race.

10) Self-actualised people are humble.

11) Self-actualised people resist enculturation. They do not allow themselves to be passively moulded by culture. They deliberate and make their own decisions, selecting what they see as good, and rejecting what they see as bad. They neither accept all, like a sheep, nor reject all, like the average rebel. Self-actualised people: "make up their own minds, come to their own decisions, are self-starters, and are responsible for themselves and their own destinies. Too many people do not make up their own minds, but have their minds made up for them by salesmen, advertisers, parents, propagandists, TV, newspapers and so on." Because of their self-decision, self-actualised people have codes of ethics that are individualised and autonomous rather than being dictated by society.

12) Despite all this, self-actualised people are not perfect.

Building your confidence by getting to know and own all your parts takes time, experience, courage, maturity, and practice to build and perfect. But what if I told you you could fake it until you make it, and you could enjoy the journey? The next chapter is for you, girlfriend!

"In a society that profits from your self-doubt, liking yourself is a rebellious act."

CAROLINE CALDWEL

CHAPTER EIGHT

Enjoy the Journey

So you've got a journey ahead of you, Babe. We all do. And I feel we have gotten to know each other pretty well by this stage so you know I am not here to sugarcoat it for you, I respect you too much for that. I won't lie to you and say it will be easy, but don't wish for it to be easier, wish you were better!

Be excited for the person you'll become along the way and grow into. Every single challenge or obstacle you come across, know it was deliberately placed on your path to help you, to teach you something, to grow and stretch you. It is a universal lesson (or as we like to call, a "blesson") preparing you for the next level of awareness, consciousness, abundance, wealth, and leadership. Like all the universal assignments I have scattered throughout this book for you to help you grow and raise your vibration and awareness.

Without that lesson you won't have the skills, knowledge, experience, perspective, confidence, or self-worth to handle the amount of abundance that waits for you at the next level of transcendence. Without this bump in the road, you would self-sabotage the next level of success because you won't feel worthy of receiving it.

There is no shortcut to unlocking success in life, relationships, or business, you have got to stay in line and do the work. A tiger earns its stripes. You see this all the time with people who "win" their success and fortune in the lottery and all of a sudden receive an abundance of wealth, opportunities, and choices without the journey that would have moulded them. They're unprepared for that level of abundance and unequipped with the skills, mindset, lessons, and self-worth to effectively manage it, let alone build on it.

They say your net worth is a direct reflection of your self-worth. By jumping the cue and short-cutting the journey, failing to build their self-worth and skills, lottery winners are more likely to declare bankruptcy within three to five years than the average American.

> The Universe ONLY gives you what you can handle
>
> but in saying that, it won't give you anymore
>
> until you can learn to handle what you've got.

What's more, studies have shown winning the lottery does not necessarily make you happier or healthier. Evidence shows most people who make it to the top one percent of income earners usually rarely stay at the top for long. Economist Jay L. Zagorsky further explains studies found instead of getting people out of financial trouble, winning the lottery got people into more trouble, with nearly a third of lottery winners declaring bankruptcy not long after. Meaning they were worse off than before they became rich.

Other studies show lottery winners frequently become estranged from family and friends, and incur a greater incidence of depression, drug, and alcohol abuse, divorce, and suicide than the average person. The universe ONLY gives you what you can handle, but in saying that, it won't give you anymore until you can learn to handle what you've got.

Just know whatever challenge you are facing at the moment, that this is *on* the way, not *in* the way. This, too, shall pass, but in the meantime, ask yourself some better questions, like we spoke about earlier. This is where the growth versus fixed mindset comes into play.

Ask yourself: *What is the lesson here? How can I grow because of this? How can I help others because of this? How am I stronger, wiser, a better person because of this?* Learn to enjoy the journey as much as the arrival at the destination, because when you look back you will realise the small things were the big things. Every triumph along the way makes the achievement at the end so much more meaningful and bittersweet.

I am sure you have heard of that saying, "good things come to those

"Slow dance

Have you ever watched kids on a merry-go-round?
Or listened to the rain slapping on the ground?
Ever followed a butterfly's erratic flight?
Or gazed at the sun into the fading night?
You better slow down, don't dance too fast.
Time is short, the music won't last.
Do you run through each day, on the fly?
When you ask: How are you? Do you hear the reply?
When the day is done, do you lie in your bed
with the next hundred chores running through your head?
You'd better slow down, don't dance too fast.
Time is short, the music won't last.
Ever told your child we'll do it tomorrow?
And in your haste, not see his sorrow?
Ever lost touch, let a good friendship die,
cause you never had time to call and say hi?
You'd better slow down, don't dance so fast.
Time is short, the music. Won't last.
When you run so fast to get somewhere,
you miss half the fun of getting there.
When you worry and hurry through your day,
it is like an unopened gift thrown away.
Life is not a race, do take it slower.
Hear the music before the song is over."

ANON

who wait", but do they really? Let me distinguish the difference between slowing down, enjoying the journey, and not starting the journey at all, because there is a distinct difference. I am a massive advocate of mindfulness, being present, self-care, and self-love, but that is something I catch people using as an excuse for self-sabotage.

Living a Life Above Zero is about creating a life of health, wealth, and abundance. It's about creating a life you love in accordance to your values, opposed to settling for one; leading and loving a life that has you lit up, inspired, and living with purpose.

What I find is most of the people coming to me, whether I'm coaching them in business, in health and wellness, or life and relationships, want above-average lives. But they're not willing to put in the above-average action to make that happen.

We live in an era where life is fast-paced, and we want it NOW. We want people to promise and deliver quick fixes and results. A generation so spoiled with technology, machinery, apps, and fast foods, and we're like, "I want this, and I want it now. If it is not here today, or tomorrow, that is not good enough. I don't want it anymore."

Let's talk about relationships

A lot of us aren't willing to put in the work, energy, and time it takes to get there. So many of us want these long-term, meaningful, romantic relationships, relationships that give us that satisfaction of connection, belonging, security, safety, love, and loyalty.

What people don't realise is, to have that depth in relationships, it's about long-term commitment, it's about shared memories and shared triumphs. It's about understanding those relationships don't come without hard times. Those relationships don't come without lessons. When bumps and challenges come up in relationships, it's about sticking it out.

It's about asking; *how can I learn more about my partner, learn more about our communication style to get through this, so I have that long-term relationship that gives me the satisfaction and loyalty I truly want?* I am sure you know someone who bounces from relationship to relationship right?

Because they have a problem that continues to arise, they don't realise that *Hey, you'll have that problem in most relationships. It is not them. It is you.* Until you stop to look within and find the lesson, you will continue to be challenged with it and see it pop up in other relationships with other people because relationships are our best mirrors.

If you continue to keep tapping out at the first sign of struggle, discomfort, and growth, you will never enjoy all the magic that lies on the other side of it. If you're continuously being tempted by new, exciting relationships that are easy without the challenging and confronting conversations that go deeper than that, you're facing short-term satisfaction of lust versus called long-gratification of love.

> If you continue to keep tapping out at the first sign of struggle, you will never enjoy all the magic that lies on the other end of it.

Let's talk about health

Essentially, in psychology, what they call delayed gratification also happens in health. So many come to me and they want help with health. They're like, "Ok, so I want to lose this much weight. I want to be happy. I want to be positive. I want better skin. I want to have more energy and vitality." What they really want is to have those results in a week.

They're looking for quick fixes, quick fads, and if they don't get the results in a week or even a few months, they think, *No, that's not working. I don't want that anymore,* or *that is not worth me investing time and money into,* and they go from one fad to another, yoyo dieting and self-sabotaging their health and happiness.

Instead of sitting there and being like, *you know what? I'll commit to learn and implement small, sustainable healthy lifestyle changes, to eat well consistently and long-term. I will invest in whole foods that nourish and fuel my body.*

I will be patient and put the time aside to learn how to manage stress better and commit to consciously moving my body every day and doing

Universal Assignment:

What is the universe trying to teach you right now? What is the lesson you are failing to see and learn?

Note: The universe will keep giving you this lesson, in different forms, situations, and through different people until you learn it. If you're wondering why you can't catch a break, it is because you can't pick up the clues.

something I love and enjoy. That is the health and wellness I'm after. Instead, they do it for a few days or look for memberships or coaching they only have to commit to for a month and then they look in the mirror and are like, *ugh, I don't look any different. I so deserve that cake. I've tried so hard the last couple of days. This obviously isn't working.*

I know I've struggled with that, too, sometimes. I'm someone who loves that little treat but know it is just a quick fix, that short-term gratification of a sugar high and emotional eating. The long-term satisfaction of fuelling and nourishing my body without the energy crashes will serve me longer.

The same principles apply to loving the journey and loving the lessons. Let's say, even if you did a quick fix or a yoyo diet that works for you, without the skills, education, discipline, and habits, you will self-sabotage. You won't sustain it and will return to your pre-fad diet state.

Now let's talk Business

This trend of short-term satisfaction is so common in business, too (which, personally, is why I think so many businesses fail). So many women I mentor in business, they come in and they want to work for themselves. They want to have that time freedom. They want to have that money freedom.

They want to work when they want, with whom they want, whenever they want. But what they don't understand is they have that employee mentality. Most of us start off working for a boss. You might be fourteen when you get your first job, so I get why it's hard to not think like this when you have been conditioned to think in a certain way for so long.

You show up consistently to work on creating someone else's dream, and many of us still might be doing that now. Which is fine, entrepreneurship isn't for everyone, it doesn't align with lots of people's values and skillset. But if you're one of those people who have decided the entrepreneurial world is for you, you need to remember when you used to work for someone else.

At the start, they overpaid you. I bet you didn't really know what you were doing. You got in there, and they paid you to learn. Do you remember your first week at your last J.O.B? I remember the first week of my job in child protection. I was like, "I get paid a full-time wage for the first few weeks, right?"

I felt awkward and kind of guilty that I didn't know what I was doing. For the first few weeks (who am I kidding, it was more like the first few months); I was following people around like a lost puppy until I got the hang of things. Which I was still trying to get my head around four years later with the forever-changing policies, procedures, and red tape that come with working for the government.

In that employee-employer mentality, we're overpaid at the start, but you quickly become and remain underpaid. What people don't understand in business with this long-term gratification is, you will be underpaid at the start, but if you stick with it, you have the potential to become overpaid in the long run.

You will come in and you will put more work in than you did for your nine to five. Because if you slack off, the only person you're ripping off is yourself, not a millionaire at the top of that corporate ladder. Chances are, at the start, you will feel like you're not getting anywhere.

You probably won't see as many results early on, and definitely won't see the financial rewards there either. It's about understanding you aren't getting paid the big bucks as you learn, so the best advice I can give you in the business space is to fail forward fast.

A lot of entrepreneurs, when they start businesses, say, "I'm not making as much money as I thought I would after a year. It's not for me," or, "I'm not seeing the results, I am not cut out for this." That is because they are thinking like an employee not an entrepreneur.

It comes down to understanding the pain of discipline over the pain of regret. What you are experiencing is that short-term pain for long-term gain. What it is costing you now versus what it will give you later. Please refer to the change quadrant we did in chapter five if you need to see it all mapped out on paper. I know we are pretty good at convincing ourselves otherwise in our heads.

If you can stick it out, remind yourself of your "why." Be consistent, and see that long-term vision will far outweigh the short-term gratification of a stable and capped salary. And having someone dictate how you will live your life, where, and when, you will enjoy time with loved ones and the values that mean most to you.

It won't happen overnight, so instead of you making it into a hard slog and moaning and whinging the whole way, make a conscious decision to

"You can't give a million-dollar dream a minimum-wage work ethic."

ANON

enjoy the journey. The turtle really does win the race. You don't have to accomplish it all today, but you need to start, be gentle and patient with yourself.

There is no such thing as quick fixes in life, health, happiness, relationships, or business. It is a marathon, not a sprint. So many people, like I said, because of the age we're living in and the fact it is so fast-paced, are going for that quick fix. It breaks my heart, because so many want a Life Above Zero.

We all want this above-average life, but so few of us put in the above-average effort to get there. In saying this, you know how much I love my research.

I love sharing my love and light, but I know often it is easier for people to dismiss hard truths believing I am just a happy-go-lucky, young, privileged, white girl talking for the sake of it. Someone who doesn't know what she is talking about as that is not how it works. This is why I love sharing my messages with research to back it up in hopes you will stop trying to belittle or shrug it off when you have these studies staring at you plainly in the eye.

One of my favourite studies I referenced earlier is the "Marshmallow Study", done by Stanford University in 1960. It was that one I spoke of which demonstrated the power in delayed gratification. Passion mixed with perseverance really is the secret sauce for success.

Apply the same concept of having one marshmallow now and deciding to have the discipline and long-term vision to wait and be able to double the return of your investment and be rewarded with two marshmallows tomorrow.

When people are talking about wanting success in business, they want success in life, or success in health, and they want success in relationships. I try to explain to them you *can* really have your cake and eat it too, but it won't happen overnight. There's no such thing as a quick fix.

There will be pain. It's the pain of discipline. It's about understanding the sacrifices you make now will reward you in the long run. You can't expect to have an above-average life with time freedom, money freedom, the best relationships ever, and be the healthiest and happiest version of yourself if you're not willing to make short-term sacrifices and be disciplined about it.

So, eat healthy, more often. When you have a fight with your partner, don't just throw in the towel like, "Ah, he doesn't care/get it." Work it out.

> *"Choose your hard; choose the pain of discipline over the pain of regret."*
>
> LAUREN KERR

Explain you want a meaningful relationship. You want for you both to understand each other. Ask yourself how can I stick around and do this? How can I learn from this? How can we be better? How can we be stronger?

In business, understand most people who start a business have to come up with the money to fund massive outlays. There's a lot you've got to learn. If you've got employees, you've got to pay other people before you pay yourself for that business to grow.

Most people who start a business don't break even for the first one or two years. Guys, if you've got a business and you're breaking even and at the end of the week you've got money in your pocket, you're an entrepreneur! You're killing it! I am not sure if you have read Robert Kiyosaki's book, *Poor Dad Rich Dad*, you have that "rich dad" mindset Robert talks about. I believe this is the ultimate guide to helping any entrepreneur shift their mindset when traditional schooling has conditioned you to think and work in a certain way.

It is a different mindset. It's a different way of thinking. It's about understanding long-term gratification pays off; work smarter, not necessarily harder. Ask yourself better questions. If you still don't believe me, go talk to successful people (whoever you look up to and aspire to be more like) and see what sacrifices they made at the start.

Read books, research, go read the Marshmallow Study by Stanford University in 1960 in detail. It has been replicated many times. They followed participants for many years to measure the tangible long-term effects of delayed gratification in health, wellness, happiness, relationships, careers, and finances.

Now, on this journey, don't think you have to have your shit together to succeed. I promised you in the previous chapter to share some tips and tricks on how you could fake it until you make it, and I am a girl who sticks to her word. Don't think the people who are seriously bossing it in life right now know what they are doing.

They commit to consistently moving forward. If you're not growing, you're shrinking and dying. They understand the magic happens outside of their comfort zone. They know their "why" is bigger than their excuses, and the vision and voice inside of them is clearer and louder than the opinions of the people on the outside.

> If you're not growing, you're shrinking and dying.
>
> They understand the magic happens outside of their comfort zone.

That doesn't mean they don't get nervous, they don't get scared or they are immune to anxiety. Even the most successful people who get on stage regularly and publicly speak in front of thousands still get butterflies. EVERYONE GETS THEM!

If you don't, it means you're not pushing yourself hard enough and putting yourself in situations that will stretch yourself. No one is immune to cortisol and increased blood pressure. We may label it as anxiety and become fearful of it, but it is our body's fight and flight hormones. They've evolved over billions of years to prepare us for something that will happen that requires more than normal energy to execute.

Fear is just excitement without breath. Breathe into it and be excited you're about to step into growth rather than staying stagnate in mediocrity.

I am guessing by now you're smoking what I've been chopping, right? I love positive psychology! Growing up, my favourite movie was the 1960 film "Pollyanna." It's about a young orphan girl who believed a positive attitude and pragmatism could always be surmounted by life's most difficult problems.

Pollyanna teaches others how to play the "glad game", where no matter the situation, always look for the positive, the silver lining, the lesson, something to be glad about. I live by concepts like the law of attraction. "What you feel, you attract." You must learn new ways to think before you can learn new ways to be.

I am not a complete hippy; I swear. (Although that may be how I dress. I am a sucker for high-waisted flares or long, flowing skirts… guilty!) I strongly believe in how much power we hold simply in our mindsets. My existing belief in how powerful the mind can be was just reinforced by my studies in Psychology.

I live by corny quotes you find in the book, *The secret*, and one of my favourites is "Whether you think you can or can't, you are right." In saying

"What you do every day matters more than what you do once in a while."

GRETCHEN RUBIN

that, the more I study, the longer I live, and the wider I read, I find there is science and research that backs up my beliefs, so I don't feel like a complete flower child.

Here's a little psychology for you…

Here are some phenomena based on psychology research which reinforce the power of perspective, faith, and belief, having more influence than reality or actual ability:

Placebo effect

In any well-done study these days, there has to be a cohort or control group to who they administer no treatment or manipulation. This is to test whether there is a correlation or cause and effect between a stimulus and response the researcher or study is trying to test.

The Placebo effect (also called the placebo response), is a remarkable phenomenon in which a placebo, a fake treatment, an inactive substance like sugar, distilled water, or saline solution, can sometimes improve a patient's condition. Because the person has the expectation it will be helpful, if they believe in something enough, it can cause physiological response in the body.

This is one reason why I am such a massive advocate of holistic health and healing. We can heal ourselves biologically with our mind if you train that muscle to become strong enough.

Self-fulfilling prophecies

Positive or negative expectations about circumstances, events, or people may affect a person's behaviour toward them in a manner he or she (unknowingly) creates situations in which we fulfil those expectations.

For example, you may believe no one likes you at a party so, unconsciously, being insecure, you withdraw. You use closed off body language, cross your arms, avoid eye contact, and give off this "piss off" vibe. You pop yourself in the corner of the room where you don't have to put yourself in situations where people can reject you. But likewise, they feel like you don't want to be approached either, or you'd rather be left

"When we take action on the things that truly matter deep in our hearts, move in directions that align with our values and mission, clarify what we stand for in life and act accordingly, then our lives become rich, full, and meaningful, and we experience a powerful sense of vitality. This is not stress; this is not even some fleeting feeling of happiness – it is a mindset that appreciates and understands a life well lived. And although such a life will undoubtedly give us many pleasurable feelings, it will also give us uncomfortable ones, such as defeat, fear, and frustration… This is only to be expected. If we live a passionate life, a life lit up, we will feel the full range of human emotions… so work hard but enjoy the journey and the person you become along the way!"

ANON

alone than mingle with new people.

More often than not, that is exactly what other people do because they, themselves, are worried you don't like them or think you're better than them and don't want to be there. But really, now you get to tell yourself you were right, nobody spoke to you because nobody liked you. Ironically, you brought that about yourself and fulfilled that prophecy because of the way you acted.

Pygmalion effect

Pygmalion effect is another form of self-fulfilling prophecy, which entails if you think something will happen you may unconsciously make it happen through your actions or inaction. In the workplace/educational system it is the phenomenon whereby the greater expectation placed upon people, the better they perform.

A teacher who, for example, expects the students to be low achieving and rowdy, will likely treat them in a way that will elicit the very response he or she expects. A famous study demonstrated this phenomenon done in 1970. Jane Elliot, who was a third grade teacher did this experiment on her students. There is no way this would pass the ethical board now.

She divided the class by who had blue eyes on one side and who had brown eyes on the other side. On the first day, she told the blue-eyed children they were superior. She explained all the positive qualities of blue-eyed people and all the negative qualities of brown-eyed people.

She even made the brown-eyed children wear collars so they would be more easily identified. She repeated the same process the next day with the same children, only their roles were reversed. In those two days, the children's abilities had shown through their statuses.

The brown-eyed children completed an exercise, when they believed they were inferior, in five and a half minutes. On the second day, they completed it in two and a half minutes. The blue-eyed children's time went from three minutes on the superior day, to four minutes and eighteen seconds on the inferior.

Stereotype Threat

This is another Psychological Phenomena that demonstrates the power of belief in others affecting their performance rather than pure ability itself is Stereotype Threat. A growing body of research has shown individuals who are members of stereotyped groups suffer from a performance deficit in the context in which their group is generally considered weak. This occurs when a negative stereotype about their group becomes salient (Croziet & Claire, 1998; Steele & Aronson, 1995).

For example, many women may wish to gain entrance into the field of technology but must first demonstrate competence in math and science. However, because of negative stereotypes about women in these domains (Steel, Spencer, & Aronson, 2002), these women may be apprehensive about confirming the stereotype women do not perform as well as men on these tasks. As a result, their performance may suffer.

According to the Stereotype Threat Model (Steele & Aronson, 1995), members of a stereotyped group (e.g. African American), who perform a difficult task in an area in which their group is considered weak (e.g. academic performance). They often report feeling anxious at the prospect of confirming a negative stereotype about their group.

Stereotype is widespread in this stereotyped group (African American) and similar social groups have shown comparable declines in performance when negative stereotypes about their group's abilities were made salient. We have depicted this in numerous studies and was what I wrote my thesis about while getting my psychology degree.

Some studies identified this phenomenon with women falling victim to stereotype threat. When I read and learned about this, it made me feel so much better! I honestly never used to think I was a bad driver. When it was just me in the car, I would make hardly any mistakes. If my dad, my partner, brother, or any male friends got in the car and they made me aware of the stereotype "women are bad drivers", I would somehow do something silly. Which I had never done before, yet would confirm the stereotype.

Like, seriously! A simple awareness or joking mention of the belief "ahh, shit, I don't want to get in the car with you, Lauren, you're such a bad driver," would trigger my performance deficit.

Now you understand how these psychological effects work, are you recognising where these have played out in your life previously? You were

*"Great minds discuss ideas;
average minds discuss events;
small minds discuss people."*
ELEANOR ROOSEVELT

probably thinking, *what the hell, why did I do that or where did I pull that from?* Well, now you know why. It is just your brain playing tricks on you.

These self-fulfilling phenomena have been found in numerous studies and really reinforce again the power in surrounding yourself with people who lift you up and believe in you. It's also depicting how important it is for children to have someone who believes in them.

Your perception and belief in yourself is more influential than your actual ability. It's hard to have an unshakable belief of yourself and your mission if the people around you are focused on bringing you down and believe something different.

So, do you believe me now that your mindset is your super power? The cool thing about this is, until you get to that point where you are inwardly fluent and are so confident in who you are and what you stand for, *you can fake it until you make it.*

Virtually, every social interaction involves reciprocal evaluations and the stakes are often higher in one direction than the other, with one party often having more power to impact the future of the other, such as controlling access to resources.

For example, in a job interview, the interviewer has power over the job candidate's future and consequently, the importance of the interviewer's evaluations of the candidate has greater implications than the evaluations the candidate has of the interviewer.

> You're perception and belief in yourself is more influential than your actual ability.

Or, on a date, let's be honest here, the woman wears the pants in today's dating world. The woman has control over whether this date will go anywhere after the first coffee. When was the last time you were nervous or being judged? When was the last time you were doubting how valuable you were or lacked belief in yourself?

Maybe you're thinking of a job interview, a first date, preparing to deliver a speech in front of the class, or pitch a sale or idea at an important meeting, or even taking on a leadership role and having to present at an event. Most of us shrink in our chairs, hunch over our phones, notes, or speech cards, adopting postures that cause us to feel even more powerless.

But what if we did the opposite? What if you were to stretch out and occupy more space, rather than slouching and taking up less? In both human and non-human primates, expansive, open postures reflect power, whereas the opposite (closed and contractive) reflect low-power, and not only do these postures reflect power, they PRODUCE it. Prove it?

In a study by Carney, Cuddy, and Yap (2010), a brief power pose induction was sufficient in biological testing to produce elevations in testosterone, decreases in cortisol, increased self-reported feelings of power, and a greater self-reported tolerance for risk.

Another study by Amy Cuddy, Caroline Wilmuth, and Dana Carney from the University of California at Berkeley, 2012 demonstrated holding a high-power pose increases both your implicit and explicit feelings of power and dominance. (The benefit of power posing before a high-stake social evaluation). Also, increasing risk-taking behaviour, action orientation, confidence, performance, pain tolerance, and testosterone (being the dominance hormone), whilst consequently also reducing stress, anxiety, and cortisol.

This study tested whether changing one's non-verbal behaviour prior to a high stakes social evaluation (such as a job interview) would improve performance in the evaluated task.

They manipulated participants to either hold a high-power pose (e.g. standing up straight with the hands on the hips). Or a low-power pose (e.g. touching the neck while sitting) for seven minutes before a job interview.

As predicted, high-power posers performed better and were more likely to be chosen for hire, and this relationship was mediated only by presentation quality, not the speech's quality. The high-power posers in contrast to the low appeared to better maintain their composure, project more confidence, and present more captivating and enthusiastic speeches, leading to higher overall performance evaluations.

It's suggested by non-verbally manipulating power, the high-power poses took advantage of the psychological and physiological perks typically associated with high-power, despite being in the low-power position in relation to the evaluators.

So, how can you fake it until you make it? It is true, you don't have to be confident, but you can trick your body into believing you are, which makes others believe you are! What is the difference? No one has to know you are shitting your pants, but you!

So, the next time you

go on a date

walk into a party

go for a job interview

have to deliver a presentation

feel powerless due to hierarchical status within organisations

presenting/reporting to a manager

competing for a promotion

Or you're in any other social situation where you feel you are being judged or assessed, FAKE IT! Pretend you are Beyoncé and get it done!

Take five minutes for yourself. Get in the zone. Stand confidently with your hands on your hips or lay back in your chair with your legs up on the desk and your hands behind your head. Take up as much space as possible, it's your space, you deserve to be here.

Own it, you are powerful, believe in yourself, believe in the power of the mind, breathe it in, embody it. Now go get them, Queen B! Continuously look for opportunities to do this little experiment yourself and have fun. Giggle! Learn to laugh at yourself and not take life so seriously. Enjoy the journey! Always be looking for the lessons, because there is no such thing as failure, only feedback.

If you occupy your time and energy with low-priority bullshit, you will attract petty problems. Stand on the shoulders of giants, surround yourself with the movers and shakers. If you are using your time and resources on big projects that will make a big impact, you won't have time to be sucked into the everyday petty dramas most people waste their time whinging and moaning about, whether it's gossip, the weather, or the news, which dramatizes and instils fear, and fuels prejudices.

> If you don't choose your challenges, the universe will assume you're bored, restless, and have too much time on your hands and will choose them for you.

Remember, great minds discuss ideas; average minds discuss events; small minds discuss people. If you don't choose your challenges, the universe will assume you're bored, restless, and have too much time on your hands and will choose them for you.

Seek out the next mountain you want to climb. Challenge your perception of anxiety, get addicted to growth, love the butterflies, become an adrenalin junky, and chase that natural high that comes with mastering a skill and testing yourself. When is your next hit?

Learn to enjoy the journey and the people you meet along the way. If you don't seek challenges, they will seek you. I promise, life is happening for you, not to you.

Universal Assignment:

Schedule your next challenge before the universe assigns you one. What is the next mountain you will climb? How will you stretch and grow yourself?

CHAPTER NINE

Playing Small Doesn't Serve the World

When you are aware and own of all parts of you, you know what you see and need in others. You realise there is so much more that connects us than separates us. This is why I am such a big advocate and lover of personal development, because the more you can understand about yourself, the more you can understand others. We are all more alike than you think.

In saying that, we are all very unique individuals; we live in a society that celebrates that individuality. No two humans have ever had or will ever have the same genetic make-up. But how unique are we really? Did you know our DNA isn't 100% unique, it's not 50% unique, not even 1% unique? Geneticist Dr. Craig Venter found our DNA is only 0.06% unique.

The differences in who we are lie in such a minute point of difference. We are, in fact, 99.94% the same person as Beyoncé! Feel empowered now, gf? Business strategists have explored this fact and applied it to the psychology behind branding and consumer behaviour.

They have found the reason consumers choose one product or brand over another, like Nike vs Adidas, BMW vs Mercedes, McDonalds vs Burger King, Woolworths vs Coles, Apple vs Android. It is because of the loyalty that lies in the .06%. When 99.94% of the specifications of comparative products are the same, it's the .06% that creates consumer allegiance with the company.

What is that? Fady Hanna does a great Ted Talk on this explaining it all comes down to the companies' ability to make the consumer feel understood. The ultimate measure is if the company can make the consumer feel and say, "they just get me." Consumers align themselves with companies who share the same values. Consumers buy products that feel like the products are made specifically for them by someone who is exactly the same as them.

This is why you may drive pass three cafes on your way to work that make better coffee than your local. They may even offer better customer service, but you will still go to your local because "they just get you" there, you fit in. They know your name, they know your friends, they probably even went to the same event on the weekend as you. These are your people!

It's ironic that, ultimately, just understanding this simple fact is the key to unlocking the success and ease of which you navigate life, relationships, and business. All three come down to our ability to feel understood, connected, and supported; love really is the only way. Corny, huh?

This is a similar process to how we select our friends. I don't know about you, but I don't have friend ceremonies, auditions, or application forms, but all my friends are very individual, unique, and I was attracted to them. But what makes them different was, in fact, the 0.06% that resonated with me and my personality. There is an alignment, and that alignment is what we call friendship.

In the same way we "just click" with brands, their 0.06% aligns with our values, we feel a connection to their values, because their point of difference and our point of difference is aligned. We feel heard, understood, supported, and essentially, loved.

Social psychology research has even found that .06% can be found in the attractiveness of a person. I know I would often hear the boys at university curious as to why the hot girls always have hot friends. It's not like they say, "all take a vote" (contradicting to what you may say have seen in the "Mean Girl" movie) and agree "you're pretty, you can sit with us."

There is psychology and research behind it. We naturally radiate towards people like us. Like attracts like. It makes us feel like we have that connection; we are understood, we are the same, and so we feel comfortable. Unconsciously, we radiate towards people on their attractiveness scale, and if two parties feel like they are around the same level on that scale, like attracts like. A connection and allegiance is established, and we can build a friendship.

Likewise, people lower on the attractiveness scales rarely create a strong bond with someone higher up if they are insecure in themselves. Because that discrepancy doesn't make them feel comfortable or understood, they compare and feel inferior because their point of difference is not aligned.

Like I said earlier, there is way more that connects us than separates us (99.94%, in fact), but if you haven't reached that level of maturity or self-actualisation yet to see that. Most people rely purely on the .06% of difference to measure and assume their level of connection.

Once you get this, like *really* get this, you can apply it to your life, relationships, and business and win that war on approval. So many people I see and hear from in my job, whether it be in parenting, friendship circles, romantic relationships, family networks, workplace, career or business, are constantly seeking approval.

In pursuing this, they self-sabotage and stop working on their own goals, their mission, their dreams, and prioritising their values. They believe if they don't get that support they are wrong or not worthy. Support is bullshit. I know that may be a hard pill to swallow but stay with me and let me break this down for you.

When people support you, whether that be in your decisions regarding parenting, health, business, or politics, the reason isn't because they support "you" as a person. It is because whatever you're doing or saying is aligned with their values and what they believe is important.

Likewise, when someone doesn't support you, it's understanding that it is not because they don't support "you" as a person. Your values are not aligning with theirs and what they believe is important in the world. You know how earlier in the book I was talking about heuristics? Well, the world is full of information, yet our brains can only process a certain amount.

If you tried to analyse every single aspect of every situation or decision, you would never get anything done! To cope with the tremendous amount of information we encounter and to speed up the decision-making process, the brain relies on these mental strategies and cognitive biases to simplify things. Then we don't have to spend endless amounts of time analysing every detail.

Fortunately, heuristics allow you to make such decisions with

*"I can't give you a sure-fire formula for success,
but I can give you a formula for failure:
try to please everybody all the time."*

HERBERT BAYARD SWOPE

relative ease without a great deal of agonising. However, there are types of cognitive biases that can distort your thinking. One of which is "Confirmation Bias" which is the favouring of information that conforms to your existing beliefs and discounting evidence that does not conform.

This is a heuristic that comes into play when talking about support. There are other cognitive biases which I will tell you about later, too, so you can call yourself on it when you catch your brain taking shortcuts and not being 100% truthful to you. We all, as humans, have our own rights, own opinions, and freedom to choose what our highest values are.

In chapter three, we spoke about values, and that is exactly what life is about, having awareness of what is important to you and living in alignment with that. When someone has similar values as us, we support them. We passionately rally behind them like "yasssss, you go Glen Coco, you go." We get fired up because "they get us." Their point of difference is the same as our point of difference.

We feel that connection and alignment. We believe this is a sign we are correct and right, but there is no right or wrong in life. There is no "one reality", only your perception of what is happening or what has happened through our own cultured lens, which we view the world through, which is biased by our own values.

If I look at a cup and see it half full and you look at a cup and see it half empty, who is right? If I am colour-blind and you ask me to look at a shirt and tell you what colour I see, you see purple and I see blue. Am I lying to you or just seeing the world through my eyes?

When you have someone who doesn't support you, please know it has nothing to do with you. It has everything to do with their .06%; it is their values and whatever you're saying or pursuing just doesn't align with their .06%, but don't forget we have more that connects us than separates us.

Sometimes we need to take a step back and be grateful and tolerant of difference. Remember this when we are being judged, criticised, or throwing ourselves our own pity party. Instead of being so offended why someone or even a group or population of people doesn't agree or support us, snap yourself out of it and look at it from a bird's-eye view, the bigger picture.

It is what makes the world so colourful, diverse, and full of lessons. We all have so much to learn from each other, enjoy, and celebrate. I see this all the time, especially in Australia with our tall Poppy Syndrome. Australians generally don't like others to do too well, or (to use another popular Australian term) to "big-note" themselves.

We have this tendency in Australian society to cut down people who are considered to be too successful or prominent ("cutting the tall poppies down to size"). Poppies are tall flowers, but they don't grow taller than the rest of the flowers, so there's a mentality where people are really happy for you to do well; you just can't do better than everyone else or they will cut you down to size.

I see this even more so in the entrepreneurial space, when we see others having success or doing something crazy that is controversial, straying from the "norm" and unlike anything they speak about or do in their own little clique. Therefore, they struggle to gain the support and encouragement they need to back themselves and build their confidence and belief in what they are doing.

I have even seen others go as far as creating hate pages to bring others down, which is so sad. But when you look at the bigger picture you can understand why a whole bunch of people come together to hate on a person or a group of people. This is how prejudices work. And they totally dis whoever for whatever reasons.

Successful people are the people who get this. They understand how the war of approval works and they thrive when they hear something like this is happening and being directed at them because they know that is a sign they are doing something right. They are standing for something they are passionate about and are having an impact or leaving a significant imprint in the world.

If you stand for nothing you will fall for everything. If you're helping a thousand people, there will be at least ten people who will claim they don't like you. You cannot help someone without pissing off someone else, because we all have different values.

Would you rather be hated for doing something than loved for doing nothing? If you're wanting to have more impact, help more people, and create more influence, be aware you will also have more criticism and rejection. You cannot have one without the other. Everything in life comes in duality.

Would you rather be hated for doing something or loved for doing nothing?

It is sad there are people out there who have the time and are willing to use harmful words and actions in spite in the attempt to bring others down. But now I hope you can understand why, because you are not that different from them. Think about how you feel when others support you (whatever opinion that might be.) You feel loved and a sense of belonging when you have a community that supports you and believes in what you believe in.

When you share a post or picture and they all like and comment saying they agree with you, sharing that passion and commonality, don't you feel understood? It doesn't matter what post you shared. It could have been uplifting, positive, negative, or even derogatory. But if you gain support in it, you feel like you're not alone in your beliefs. Essentially, you feel loved, right?

It is sad but hate pages/prejudices are the same thing, serving the same purpose. People want to feel loved; it is ironic they use hate to try find it. But we are all longing for that sense of community, that support and connection with people who are like minded and share the same values and opinions as us.

Those people might say some nasty, terrible things, but they are just like the rest of us, just trying to feel loved and supported. It is that 99.4% we all are, so send them love and light. I feel sorry for these people who need to use such hurtful words to find that connection. And I wish they knew the ramifications of that because what you think; you become.

Dis-ease, feelings of envy and jealousy cause exactly that – disease. A great book, if you want to educate yourself and explore this further, is, *When the body Says No; the Cost of Hidden Stress*, by Gabor Mate. The author talks about the science and research that have found the correlation between negative talk to self and others showing up negatively in your body, whether that manifests as an inflammation, cancer, or sickness.

If only those people knew what they were sending out in the universe and that there are nicer ways to find that connection without causing harm to themselves and others. I know there are so many people who struggle

"Our deepest fear is not that we are inadequate. Our deepest fear is that we are powerful beyond measure. It is our light, not our darkness, that most frightens us. We ask ourselves, who am I to be brilliant, gorgeous, talented, fabulous? Who are you not to be? You are a child of God. Your playing small does not serve the world. There is nothing enlightened about shrinking so that other people won't feel insecure around you. We are all meant to shine, as children do. We were born to make manifest the glory of God that is within us. It's not just in some of us; it's in everyone. And as we let our own light shine, we unconsciously give other people permission to do the same. As we are liberated from our own fear, our presence automatically liberates others."

MARIANNE WILLIAMSON

to get this which is why I have devoted a whole chapter on it. They freak out and think *how can I get this page/post down? Why don't they love me, support me, like me? How can I change their minds? I will stop what I am doing; I will give up on my passions, beliefs and values because other people don't get me/agree with me/see what I see.*

If you feel you're being pushed or not getting the support where you currently are, it is because you're outgrowing the people around you and it makes them feel uncomfortable. Trust the process and know in a year's time from now, I promise, you will be grateful. This lack of support will push you to seek out new situations, new relationships and support networks that will nurture and inspire you. They will support you to be the best version of yourself rather than dimming your light, holding you down and back from pursuing your dreams.

Take a breath, take a step back, and give yourself permission to look at what is happening in the bigger picture. Whatever is happening right now for you, as long as you're aligning yourself with your values and your mission and using that to benefit the many, I promise you're doing the right things.

Self-sabotage is a word that is often overused and misunderstood; essentially, what it means is there is a conflict of values. The two values in conflict the most are relationships (with others and self) and money.

For example, if you have a very high value on relationships and the people around you have a high disregard for money, they may call money evil, greedy, or believe the people with lots of it have scammed or cheated others. Once again, a typical example of the tall poppy syndrome. This is an experience well known by far too many entrepreneurs. These people have their own baggage and their own dirty money story they're carrying around. They may be unconscious of it; most people aren't aware of their money story and have inherited it from their own parents. They lack the understanding they can change it, as often it is this bullshit, limiting belief which blocks them from experiencing abundance themselves.

If you hold those relationships or value of friendships in a higher regard of your value of growth, business, and impact, and they witness your behaviour around the pursuit and desire of creating a business or wealth, those people will attack, condemn and reject.

Unconsciously, you will modify your behaviour to fit back in with the rest of the poppies in the field. Most people will allow themselves to be drawn back in because it's predictable, it's comfortable, it's safe. They feel all warm and fuzzy inside and are held back in the comfort zones with untapped potential, unlived dreams, because it makes their "clique" feel better about themselves.

And that's ok, that isn't weak, it is human. One of the number one drivers behind human psychology and behaviour is certainty and safety. Self-sabotage is primal behaviour, deep-rooted in 8,000 billion years of evolution in your reptilian brain, governed by social order and social hierarchy.

You have an unconsciousness mechanism in your psychology that uses self-sabotage to prevent rejection from your herd/clique. Back in the day, it served a purpose. It would ensure you weren't left vulnerable to be attacked by an intruder or be left out alone in the savage weather conditions. Or eaten by a sabre-tooth tiger because you would have a tribe sticking together and looking out for each other.

Today, the quickest and fastest way to eliminate self-sabotage from your environment is to have a good look at your tribe, your community, the people you are spending most of your time with. Hang around the right people. When you surround yourself with the right people, people with the same values, passions, and missions as you, they lift you up; they inspire you.

When they see you doing things that are sabotaging your efforts to reach your goals and not doing the things you declared were important to you, and living your truth, they will call you on it! They will help you realign rather than distracting and detracting you to pick the easier route. The one with less resistance and more acceptance, the noise, the opinions of people that don't matter, the distractions, the new, shinier objects.

Your herd will make you or break you. That saying "you become the people you surround yourself with" isn't a cliché, it's science. You need to seriously start examining the relationships in your life right now. I am not suggesting you cut off all your loved ones and cut out the people in your life who don't share the same values and look at the world the same way you do. That is what makes life beautiful and challenges us to be innovative and check in with ourselves to ensure we are, in fact, living in accordance to our values.

Universal Assignment:

Who are the people you spend most of your time with?

Are they making you or breaking your dreams/goals?

Where do you see yourself self-sabotaging in your life right now?

> Today, the quickest and fastest way to eliminate self-sabotage from your environment is to have a good look at the people you are spending most of your time with.

I am suggesting, however; you review how much time you spend with them. The level of self-sabotage you're experiencing right now is a direct reflection of the time you're spending with people who see your progress as unacceptable. If you want more, prioritise your values.

I know from my experience in business, when I started off I truly only had a vision. I knew what I wanted to create, and I also knew why it was important to do so. Not just for me and my loved ones, but for how I wanted to show up in the world, the footprint and legacy I wanted to leave behind.

Most of my loved ones (and wider society), they didn't see what I saw; they didn't understand it. They didn't understand why I would leave a job I was good at, studied for years to get into, that offered me as a young woman all the security I would need. I had a good salary, annual, sick and maternity leave. I left it to pursue a business that used an untraditional business model and wasn't predominately considered the "norm" in society, with lots of people having misconceptions around the network marketing industry and profession.

It was hard for them to support something they didn't understand. For years, I would receive backhanded compliments or snide remarks that would belittle the success I was having. It wasn't until I understood and really grasped this idea of the "war of approval" myself that I could accept them and understand where they were coming from.

> The level of self-sabotage you're experiencing right now is a direct reflection of the time you're spending with people who see your progress as unacceptable.

Universal Assignment:

Who are the five people's opinions that matter to you? These are the people who you care what they think of you. Next time someone gives an opinion, cross check it is one that matters and ensure it is an educated one before taking it on board.

It wasn't they didn't support me; it's just their values weren't aligning with mine. They loved me and they weren't consciously trying to hurt my feelings or dim my shine; they were worried about me doing something foreign to them. They were coming from a place of love and seeing the world through their past experiences, their knowledge, and their values.

A great tip I used in the early stages of my business when I did not have the support I was longing for, was thinking of the five people in my life whose opinions mattered to me. At that point it was my mum, dad, partner, business mentor, and best friend.

When I heard or read something that would shake me and my confidence I would consult my five people and ask for their feedback and opinion. Their opinions are really the only ones that counted. And on that note, just because they gave their opinion, doesn't mean it changed mine.

I would always take it on board before making a decision of my own, incorporating my own values, education, and goals. I know they want what is best for me and their advice won't be self-serving or manipulative, but they don't always know what is best for me.

I know what field they are experts in, and I aspire to be more like them, but I also know what I am an expert in. If I am more educated on that subject, I will know. I am sure you are learning by now; I read far and wide. I don't do something because someone told me to or because everyone else is doing it, without being confident it is the right thing for me to do in accordance with my values. And also, in the attempt to help as many people as I can in the process.

So know, although the opinions of your loved ones are coming from a place of love, they aren't always educated, so love them, thank them, and keep doing your thang, Sister!

I would also ensure I took advice from people who I looked up to, people who had what I wanted, and had achieved what I was trying to create. Or was impacting the world the way I wanted to be remembered and known for. So often, it is the people who have no money, who are surrounded by shitty relationships and are living week to week and falling sick often, who are more than happy to offer you their opinion.

You wouldn't want your hair done by a hairdresser who had a shitty haircut, would you? The same applies in life, relationships, and business. A lion does not lose sleep over the opinion of sheep. Like I mentioned

"What divides us pales in comparison to what unites us."

TED KENNEDY

earlier, at the time it was a hard pill to swallow, not having the support and appraisal from the people who meant the most.

However, looking back now, I am so grateful for that. Because of them I persevered. I didn't want to just tell them my vision; I wanted to show them. I wanted them to witness the impact and thousands of lives I helped by staying true to my mission and vision.

I will be forever grateful for the lack of support because it provoked me to go find people who would give it to me. From there, I manifested business mentors who introduced me to amazing, influential people in the world doing amazing things, alongside creating "Babes in Business", my very own clique, #theBIBclique. A generation of thousands of passionate, hard-working, ambitious, heart-driven women around the world who share the same passions and love to empower others to live their own Life Above Zero. A life of health, wealth, and abundance.

It really is your voids that lead to your biggest values. I would love to share a quick story about one of the beautiful women I mentor in the "Babes in Business" clique. I feel most of us learn through storytelling, so for this story I will change her name to April.

April had a massive "why" she was on her health and wellness journey after holistically healing herself from the symptoms that came with a poly cystic ovaries diagnosis. However, she gave too much weight to the opinions of others and allowed it to dim her light. She stopped getting out of her comfort zone and sharing her journey with others about what had worked for her in the fear of what a few small-minded, uneducated people thought who would constantly cut her down.

Because of this, she played small. She didn't maximise her potential. She didn't allow herself to flourish in the attempt to protect the people around her from feeling uncomfortable. But it wasn't until she caught up with a dear friend who, little to her knowledge, was going through the same painful journey, that she realised the truth. Her friend had been told conflicting advice and pressured to do things to her body that didn't align with her values. This was because she had not heard or met anyone who shared her view of the world and value of holistic health.

It was in that exact moment April realised that, in making it all about herself and what other people thought of her, she neglected her mission and the people out there who needed her. She realised playing small didn't serve the world, and it definitely didn't help her friend who was going through this painful experience all alone.

Did you know?

In a given day you consume over 1kg in solid material, 2.5 kg water, and interchange 1kg air? 7% of your air exchanges out every single day, so 7% of what was you yesterday, is not here anymore. And the stuff you are now, tomorrow, 7% of that will be gone.

You may not have a sense of what roughly 7% of your body is, so let me paint a picture for you; it is essentially the mass of your arm. Every day, one of those limbs is leaving, and another one is coming in. Over the course of two weeks, you exchange an equivalent to the entire body mass of your body, so you think you are you, but really, from two weeks ago, you aren't.

Comparing yourself to the person you were a year ago, you're definitely not the same person. You're always in a state of inter-becoming. Air reaches the other side of the planet in just four to five days with winds that blow up to 150 km/h. The air you're breathing in now was literally on the other side of the planet only a week ago.

It also means the air you are exhaling right now could become a flower in France or be inhaled in a baby's first breathe in Mexico. This is not theoretically what is happening, this is literally what happens. Part of you today was these plants only a couple of days ago. And part of you tomorrow will be them; both locally around you in the next couple of minutes, and globally, in the next couple of days.

This is how much we are interconnected with our planet and each other. This is why we need to protect nature, our environment, our animals, and each other, because we find a little piece of ourselves in all of that. I am you and you are me. Moving forward, I hope you protect your dreams with the same drive, dedication, honour, and commitment you have for the desire to belong to something bigger than yourself.

We all have gifts and a reason why we are here. Don't waste those talents you have today in trying to fit in when you were born to stand out (because you won't have them forever). Find solitude in knowing there is way more that connects us than ever will separate us, but you playing small does not serve the world. Grow you and serve the many!

CHAPTER TEN

Feel the Fear and Do it Anyway

Let's talk about the naughty four-letter "F" word. "Fear." Everyone has a different relationship with fear, so I wanted to create the space to talk about it because it is one of the biggest manipulations in the world. Fear (whether it is real or perceived) has the same effect on you and your nervous system.

It triggers the same emotions and hormones to be released in our body such as cortisol, which is the stress hormone that provokes the feeling of anxiety. I am not sure if you are someone who is into psychology or if you have ever seen a life coach, a clinical psychologist, or sport psychologist/coach. But you will often see and hear these professionals talk about techniques and strategies such as visualisation and mental rehearsal. Like some of the strategies I was talking about earlier regarding vision boards and letters to your future self.

That is because your psyche and nervous system cannot tell the difference between what is "real" and what is "imagined."

It creates the same psychological response to stimuli such as things that make you feel fearful. I would love to show you how powerful our imagination is and why I am so passionate about helping others to understand how much power they hold just in their minds. And to show them how they can harness that if only they took the time to understand how to control it with techniques such as goal setting, manifestations, affirmations, and forgiveness. Meditations and visualisations aren't wishy washy. They are science!

If I haven't convinced you yet and you're still sitting on the fence, I want you to do this quick little activity with me. (Especially if this is all new to you and you haven't read about or looked into the laws of attraction and quantum psychics and you're thinking I am woo-woo).

Close your eyes and imagine you're walking to your fridge. You open your fridge and you see two big, ripe, juicy, yellow lemons. When you pick one up and it squishes a little under the pressure of your grasp. You can tell it is ripe and full of the zesty sour juice, being softer than the one next to it.

You place it on a cutting board and cut it straight down the middle. The juices drip down your finger and are so acidic it stings a small cut you have on your thumb. You pick up one half of the lemon, bring it to your mouth and start squeezing it like a stress ball. All the cold juices dribble down your tongue along with a few seeds.

Did you feel your cheeks tighten? Did you squish your face up and feel a pinch in your jaw as if you were about to torture yourself with a lemon? Look down at your hand. Are you holding a lemon? That is what I am talking about! You created that whole physiological and psychological experience in your head.

That is how strong the correlation is between a psychological experience and our physiological response! It doesn't matter if the experience is real or imagined, our psyche and nervous system cannot decipher the difference and still responds the same, regardless.

So, what experiences are you having? Remember what I was talking about earlier when I explained there is no one reality? We only have our perception of reality which is based by the values we see the world though, our very own cultured lens.

We can apply this same theory to fear. Once you understand it, you will understand why it can manipulate your perception and the way you respond both psychologically and physiologically to events.

For an example, let's say you robbed a bank with a fake gun. Even though you couldn't have really harmed anyone with that fake gun, you would still be charged with armed robbery because your intent was to inflict fear, and fear makes people think irrationally.

Fear can manipulate people to abandon their values

==and logical ways of thinking and==

==do things they probably would not usually do.==

In this case, for example, the victim is manipulated to hand over money or belongings, even though they know it's not something that they would like to do or should do under normal circumstances. Fear can manipulate people to abandon their values and logical ways of thinking and do things they probably would not usually do.

Fear is the tactic terrorists use. Some people have different values. They see the world differently and have biased prejudices based on what they have experienced or been told. Terrorists use fear to manipulate people and cloud their judgement, to make people feel scared. Instead of coming from a place of love and remembering there is way more that connects us than separates us, they come from a place of fear. They find the smallest things that make us different to judge others in a way to protect themselves and keep their loved ones safe.

It doesn't matter if the threat is real or perceived, fear manipulates the masses to discriminate and abandon their values and what they know is right and rational. Fear is also a tactic the governments use to make us do things we probably wouldn't normally do or don't want to do, like pay taxes. Most of us would rather keep that money for ourselves and our families.

Fear is what the government uses to manipulate us into not just walking into a shop, picking up everything we want, and walking out without paying for it. (As much as I would love, absolutely *love* to have free rein in the Tiger Lilly or Spell store). We are fearful if we did that we would be arrested and be charged for shop lifting. Then we are even more fearful of what wider society would think of us if we got caught.

Fear is what your parents used when you were sixteen to manipulate you from not sneaking out on the weekend. They wanted to stop you going to that underage party and getting your friend's older brother to buy you a bottle of Passion Pop in case you got caught and would be grounded. I know it didn't stop all of us. But there were boundaries, and we use the fear of consequences to implement them.

When I was living over in Hawaii on the Island of Oahu studying a university semester of sex and gender psychology, there was a tsunami warning. I can look back on it now and laugh, but at the time it was pretty traumatising.

It was Halloween in October in 2012 and, ironically; I was dressed for high seas as a pirate! Halloween is obviously a big hype in the USA, so my other friends who were also international exchange students, the majority from Germany and Sweden, and I were excited to be amongst it all.

We had drunk all day and were celebrating at a street festival in downtown Honolulu with delicious food, music, and the streets crowded with people dressed in other crazy costumes. Suddenly, my group started getting calls, one-by-one, from their families overseas asking them if they were ok because a Tsunami was about to hit.

Apparently, it was on international news after a powerful earthquake with a magnitude of 7.7 hit Canada's Pacific coastal province of British Columbia earlier that day. The U.S. Geological Survey said the quake was centred 123 miles (198 km) south-southwest of Prince Rupert at a depth of 6.2 miles (10 km).

The Earthquakes Canada agency said the quake in the Haida Gwaii region was followed by numerous aftershocks as large as 4.6 and that a tsunami had been recorded by a deep-ocean pressure sensor. Within minutes, the music stopped at all the various stages with the performers warning the crowds, "This is not a drill. A level five tsunami is coming, and you all need to get to higher ground."

Almost simultaneously, warning sirens could be heard blaring out across the island, prompting an immediate rush of panic. Keep in mind, fear clouds judgment (and being severely intoxicated does not help, let me add). I rang my poor best friend and parents crying saying goodbye thinking I would die because I was too drunk to swim.

I kept thinking of the movie "The Impossible" that had only come out earlier that year showing the terror of the Indian Ocean tsunami that hit Thailand in 2004. This did not help the drunk dramatizing I was creating in my head. I remember imagining a wave of that magnitude hitting Oahu and just being like, "I am way too drunk to even know which way is down or up to swim."

My poor parents, halfway across the world, could do nothing to protect or calm their drunken and terrified nineteen-year-old daughter. I

"I don't want to look back in five years' time and think, 'we could have been magnificent, but I was afraid.' In five years, I want to tell of how fear tried to cheat me out of the best thing in life, and I didn't let it."

ANON

remember Dad saying, "Just do what they are telling you and get to higher ground." I remember everyone running, cramming, and rushing to get into cars and crazy traffic jams.

I even remember some people fleeing and instead of rationally helping others, they were pushing other people out of the way and pulling them out of rides from taxis so they could get in. Which I would like to think, logically, under normal circumstances, they wouldn't act like that and would have manners. Fear manipulates us to do things and act in ways that we probably wouldn't usually do.

100,000 to 150,000 people who live in Hawaii's coastal zones had been urged to move to higher ground. Residents were being evacuated and tall, high-rise hotels opened their doors with crowds being ushered onto the top floors for safety. They encouraged people stuck in traffic to consider getting out of their cars and walking to higher ground.

I remember one of my beautiful German girlfriends taking me under her wing. She got me to the top floor of a hotel, for me to only be so drunk I passed out waiting for the wave to hit. Like I said, hilarious now. Reflecting, I must have concluded and accepted I was too drunk to save myself so decided a nap was a better way to spend my last hour alive.

But even if I HAD stayed awake, there wouldn't have been much to see, fortunately! By the time the wave hit Oahu, it was a small barrel. There were hooligans out in the surf who rode it! It was a running joke. The following week for my birthday we were celebrating with the gang in Hawaii that I was alive, and they even bought me a t-shirt that read, "I survived the tsunami."

It was a surreal experience for me, though, to think how quickly life could have been changed and to witness how fear manipulates the way you think, behave, and respond. The numerous car accidents happening that night in the surge of panic, with people hurting more people, caused more harm than the tsunami did.

Rather than logically thinking and knowing the best way to look after ourselves and each other was to stay calm, the masses (including me) rushed, pushed, and panicked. This is a real-life example of how our psyche and nervous system cannot decipher the difference between fear, regardless of whether it is real or imagined, it responds the same.

As a child, did you ever stop breathing and feel your heart racing out of your chest because you convinced yourself the boogie man was under your

"What a terrible waste of life it is to always take the easy path, to never know what it is to risk everything for what you love."

BEAU TAPLIN

bed and you were too scared to run to your parents' room in fear it would grab your feet? My point, exactly! We all have different fears; rational or not. Mine, still to this day, are needles and birds. Even when I learned how to treat phobias in my degree of exposure therapy, I couldn't shake them.

What a lot of us don't talk about is the fear that we inflict on ourselves. We fear what others may think, things we want to do, things we want to be, or try.

I bet you have something on your bucket list that remains unticked because you're scared. Maybe it's sky diving, snorkelling, shark cage diving, getting a tattoo, or quitting your stable job. Perhaps taking the leap of faith to build your own business and doing something you are passionate about, buying your first property and taking on a lot of debt, etc.

Are there things you have always wanted to do but you've been too scared to? I know for me, personally, making a career change was scary. But you know what's scarier? Regret. Don't let fear stop you from making your dreams your reality. Those who dare to fail miserably can achieve greatly.

Tease it out and try to work out what that fear is for you. Is it fear of failure? Is it fear you will give it your all and it won't be enough? Or is it fear of regret or judgement? Are you fearful of what others will think of you? Are you fearful you'll succeed?

That is one we don't often hear and many people aren't aware of, but what if you're great at it? What if you enjoy it? What if you get everything you ever wanted, and it's not enough or you don't feel like you think you should or would have when you get it or achieve it?

And what if you become successful at it? Is that something that maybe has been unconsciously scaring you? Are you fearful of succeeding? What if you are great at it and then there is pressure for you to continue to perform? What if you stand out so much you make the people around you feel uncomfortable and you become a target for people to criticise and cut back down to fit in with the rest of the poppies?

These fears stop us from thinking logically. It hijacks our prefrontal cortex and instead of thinking rationally; we abandon our values and everything we know, our mission, how we want to show up in the world. It can rob us from experiencing magical moments and prevent us from saying yes to the most amazing opportunities that come our way and walking through new doors that present themselves to us.

> *"If you want to increase your success rate, double your failure rate."*
>
> THOMAS WATSON

I see this so often; people complain they are unhappy in a relationship and the conversation comes up where they could walk away but fear of being alone stops them. They are unhappy in a job and a new opportunity comes along, but fear of failure stops them.

People want to get healthier and happier and a girlfriend invites them to sign up for a half marathon in three months, but fear of judgment gets in the way and they say no. Then, the same people moan about life twelve months later when nothing has changed. They look up to God (or whatever they perceive the divine to be. Like I said, for me, it's the universe and its laws) asking for a sign or a break, without realising they were given so many opportunities over the last twelve months to create a different reality. But because of fear, they didn't see them, let alone take them.

"A fellow was stuck on his rooftop in a flood. He was praying for God to help. Soon, a man in a rowboat came by and the fellow shouted to the man on the roof, "Jump in, I can save you!" The stranded fellow shouted back, "No, it's ok, I'm praying to God, and he is going to save me." So the rowboat went on. Then, a motorboat came by. The fellow in the motorboat shouted, "Jump in, I can save you!" To this, the stranded man said, "No thanks, I'm praying to God, and he is going to save me." I have faith. So the motorboat went on. Then, a helicopter came by and the pilot shouted down, "Grab this rope and I will lift you to safety!" To this, the stranded man again replied, "No thanks, I am praying to God, and he is going to save me. I have faith." So the helicopter reluctantly flew away. Soon, the water rose above the rooftop and the man drowned. He went to Heaven. He finally got his chance to discuss this whole situation with God, at which point he exclaimed, "I had faith in you, but you didn't save me, you let me drown. I don't understand why!" To this, God replied, "I sent you a rowboat and motorboat and a helicopter, what more did you expect?"

If you don't believe me, reflect. Reflection and reverse engineering are the best way to predict and plan how you'll best manoeuvre the path forward. Think about the best things that have ever happened to you in your life, whether it was a decision, a person, or an experience.

Maybe it was having the courage to approach your lover for the first time and ask them on a date or even asking them to marry you. Maybe it was packing up your life and moving overseas. Or maybe it was buying your family home or falling pregnant with your first child.

Maybe it was starting your own business or a trip where you travelled

"Always go with the choice that scares you the most. Because that is the one that is going to help you grow."

CAROLINE MYSS

around the world solo. It may be one of those pivotal moments you identified earlier in chapter one. Whatever comes up for you, I bet before you acted, before you decided, before the event, you were nervous, your blood pressure rose, your heartbeat quickened, your hands sweated, you got butterflies in the pit of your stomach; you were fearful, or you were unsure what would happen next. But imagine if you had let that fear cheat you out of the best things of your life?

> But imagine if you had let that fear cheat you out of the best things in life.
>
> What would you have missed out on?

What would you have missed out on? Where would you be now if you hadn't felt the fear and done it anyway?

Next time you feel fear come up for you, don't let it cheat you out of something amazing, you've done it once, you can do it again! Great things never come from comfort zones!

The walls of your comfort zone are lovingly decorated with your lifelong collection of favourite excuses. They don't say the magic happens out of our comfort zone for nothing. You can't be comfortable and grow at the same time, so you have to pick one or the other. Remain stuck in your comfort zone doing what you've always done, being the same person you've always been, having what you have always had. Or do you jump out of your comfort zone and do something that will scare you shitless? Feel the fear and do it anyway.

When you feel fear come up, I would love for you to take a step back and acknowledge it is a manipulation. Remind yourself your body doesn't know the difference between perceived and real threat, so give yourself the space to check in and ensure the fear is real. Are you thinking logically, could you honestly be harmed or hurt right now? Could your loved ones?

Universal Assignment:

What have you been putting off because you're fearful? What are you fearful of?

==Nobody gets there without failing,==

==failure is success in progress.==

Or is your mind playing tricks on you and trying to rob you from an amazing opportunity? What could you gain from it? What could you learn from it? Quickly do the change matrix tool in your head. Or on paper if you're someone who needs to visually make sense of all the chaotic feels and self-talk being thrown around in your head and flipped around in your stomach.

Whatever you perceive success to be for you, go read books, listen to podcasts, talk to mentors, watch documentaries, do your own research online. Nobody gets there without failing, failure is success in progress.

Take a breath, embrace the excitement, trust the process, and know magic is about to happen. Anyone who jumps out of an airplane to go skydiving will explain to you, they are shitting their pants, and thinking a million things a second. One of which is probably yelling at themselves, questioning why they put themselves in this position in the first place, willingly deciding to jump out of a perfectly good aeroplane 14,000 feet above safe ground! (If you have, you'll know exactly what I am talking about!)

Yet, once they do it, they turn around and say it was the most amazing thing ever. They remain on that natural high for hours! You can see it in their face. They are glowing; they are wide awake, all starry-eyed and lit up, enthusiastic, and ecstatic about how beautiful life is. Instead of relying on caffeine, alcohol, or drugs for that induced adrenalin, learn to love the body's natural ecstasies.

I know as kids growing up on the border of New South Wales and Victoria in Albury on the Murray River, we were constantly jumping off bridges, waterfalls, and trees into the river. You would sit there for what would seem hours, just staring down at the water below you, contemplating. The longer you left it, the more time you gave yourself to psyche yourself out and make imaginary scenarios in your head which would just make the anxiety snowball.

But then you would just close your eyes, feel the fear, and do it anyway. Once you did it once, you would race straight back up just to do it again. We are all just junkies looking for our next hit. Learn to love and get enthusiastic

Universal Assignment:

What will you do today that scares you?

about life! There are opportunities every day to say yes to things that scare you, things that stretch you. It doesn't have to be something as crazy as jumping off bridges, and looking back as an adult I truly do not recommend that being something you try at home either, kids.

I encourage you and support you to say yes to more things that challenge you (and also keep you alive, may I add). Feel the fear and do it anyway. Are you playing it safe? If you died tomorrow, would you be happy with how you have spent the days gifted to you or have you left things on your bucket list because you're letting fear get in the driver's seat?

I remember I played a game one year where I decided to be like Jim Carey in the movie "Yes Man." Every opportunity that presented itself to me I would close my eyes, and just say "yes" and work the rest out later. So many magical opportunities came my way that year, including a second scholarship, volunteering on a mental health helpline, travelling the USA with my best friend, and moving to Hawaii.

I double-dare you to do something every day that scares you! It doesn't have to be something big. It may be starting a conversation with someone you don't know when you're out. Or it may be doing a sales pitch, speaking up in class, talking at a conference, volunteering to host an event, being vulnerable and telling your partner how you really feel, or trying a new recipe or workout. Put some spice back in your life, girlfriend!

> Inaction breeds doubt and fear
>
> action breeds confidence and courage.

When we are babies learning to walk, we stumble, we fall repeatedly. We resort back to crawling until we get the courage to get a piece of furniture to help pull ourselves back up and try again. Our parents, siblings, and people around us, they continue to love on us and encourage us.

It's not like they go "Oops, you failed, give up, obviously you're not meant to walk, walking just isn't for you." They trust they we will get there in our own time, and when we are meant to. Use this same analogy, apply the same patience, unconditional love and kindness to yourself.

Whatever goals you have, they will be scary. You'll probably fall, but that is all part of the journey. Your journey. We all have our own and you need

*"Success is not final, and failure is not fatal;
it is the courage to continue that counts."*
WINSTON CHURCHILL

to trust the universe's divine timing and know everything will happen exactly when it's meant to, but you still need to do your part; you need to show up and take consistent action.

Inaction breeds doubt and fear, action breeds confidence and courage. If you want to conquer fear, do not sit at home and think about it. Get busy. Stay in your own lane, understand everything is on the way, not in the way.

Get in tune and listen to your body. It will tell you what you need to do. Your body will contract when you're scared. You'll notice you cross your arms and legs; you bow your head and hunch your shoulders; you occupy less space in an attempt to disappear.

You will even notice your heart glazes over, like you've closed your heart off and a shield pops up to protect yourself from getting hurt emotionally, too. When you can catch yourself unconsciously doing this, this is a sign you need to consciously decide to open wide. Say yes to more!

Open yourself up to new opportunities, friendships, relationships. You don't know what door may open from that one conversation. Tough times don't last. Tough people do. The temptation to quit will be greatest right before you succeed, SO, inhale courage and exhale fear. And repeat.

"Fear and doubt kill more dreams than failure ever will! Failure is nothing more than a chance to revise your strategy."

ANON

CHAPTER ELEVEN

It's Ok to Not be Ok

I love to read widely to strengthen my practice and keep it up to date with the latest research. I am a firm believer in walking my talk, and I encourage my clients to always be learning and growing.

I understand everything comes in duality yet with the pressures and unrealistic expectations imposed upon us in the Western world by social media, people's perception of life is skewed. They're honestly believing they have to be happy all the time and achieving all the time. And if they aren't, they are falling short of normal standards and something is wrong with them or they aren't living in alignment with their truth or values.

Living a Life Above Zero isn't about being happy all the time; what is happiness to you anyway? Even if you are living in alignment with your values, there will be days, weeks, or even months where you hit a wall, where your faith and belief wavers, where you feel challenged and uncomfortable.

Living a Life Above Zero isn't about "succeeding" all the time either, like we spoke about previously. What is your definition of success anyway, through your cultured glasses? I loved it when I stumbled across Russ Harris's book, *The Happiness Trap,* in my degree. It helped explain (better than I ever could) the psychology research, statistics, and theory behind what I was personally witnessing happen today in society and in my own world of relationships and experiences.

I am passionate about educating and helping people not only understand their emotions but to self-regulate them. In some of my workshops I get down on the floor and play with colourful water to teach parents and children how to talk about their feelings. We all have them,

"My friends on the mainland think just because I live in Hawaii, I live in paradise, like a permanent vacation. We're all just out here sipping Mai Tais, shaking our hips, catching waves. Are they insane? Do they think we are immune to life? How can they possibly think our families are less screwed up, our cancer's less fatal, our heartache less painful?"

THE DESCENDANTS

folks, so why is it most of us struggle so much to express them?

Let me tell you a secret; what if I was to tell you almost everything you believed about finding happiness turned out to be inaccurate, misleading, or false? There is a growing body of scientific research that suggests we are all caught in a powerful psychological trap, a vicious cycle in which the more we try to find happiness, the more we suffer.

Friends posting on Instagram what their partner did for them, magazines feeding us what we have to look like to be desirable. TV advertisements manipulating us to believe we need to own materialistic objects to be happy. Government policies forcing us to conform to a lifestyle and belief we need to "work" five days a week, 260 days a year to deserve a couple of weeks' break. Society selling us the concept of having a career, your own home, and settling down with kids of your own is the epitome of happiness. Why is it then we have an increasing amount of middle-aged, middle-class women suffering from depression and anxiety?

They followed the recipe book for a fulfilled and happy life to a T, then found themselves full of despair and confusion when they don't feel as ecstatic as they were told they would be.

But… I am supposed to be happy, right?

Wrong. In the Western world, we now have a higher standard of living than humans have ever known before. We have better medical treatment, better housing conditions, better sanitation, more money, more welfare services, and more access to education, justice, travel, entertainment, and career opportunities.

Today's middle class live better than the royalty did not so long ago. And yet, humans today don't seem very happy.

Oh yeah, says who? Research says. The statistics speak for themselves; in any given year, almost 30% of the adult population will suffer from a recognised psychological disorder.

The World Health Organisation estimates depression is currently the fourth biggest, costliest, and most debilitating disease in the world and by the year 2020, it will be the second biggest. In any given week, one tenth of the adult population is suffering from clinical depression, and one in five will suffer from it at some point in their lifetime.

Even more startling is the fact almost one in two people will go through a stage in life when they seriously consider suicide and will struggle with it for two weeks or more. Scarier still, one in ten people will at some point attempt to kill themselves.

I'll give you a moment for those numbers to resonate with you. Think of your friends, your family, your co-workers, the random masses of people walking around your local shopping centre. Almost half of them will at some point be so overwhelmed by misery they seriously contemplate suicide. One in ten will attempt it. It becomes obvious that lasting, ever-flowing happiness is not normal!

But why can't I always be happy?

Let me take you on a brief psychology lesson exploring evolutionary theory. Today, our modern human minds have evolved with amazing abilities to analyse, plan, create, and communicate.

This evolutionary process has taken a long time, not like the agonising week-long wait for the next episode of The Bachelor to come out. (Not like any of us watch that garbage reality TV, right? *Cough, cough*). More like a hundred thousand years (no exaggeration).

Why your brain plays tricks on you

First on the planet were these badass homo sapiens. They were equipped with minds to help them survive in a world full of danger. They weren't lazing around telling jokes with "bae" or counting how many 'likes' their last Instagram post got. Their only concern was meeting their four essential needs to survive and reproduce: food, water, shelter, and sex.

However, none of these things mattered if you were dead. So the number one priority: look out for anything that might harm you and avoid it. The smarter mind could avoid more bullies, which meant they could live longer, which meant they had more time to have jiggy-jiggy and make babies.

As the story goes, with each generation the mind became increasingly more effective in predicting and avoiding danger. And now, after one hundred thousand years of evolution, the modern mind is constantly on the lookout; is it dangerous? Harmful or helpful?

However, these days we aren't on the lookout for sabre-toothed tigers. Instead, it's losing our job, being rejected, getting a speeding ticket, getting cancer, embarrassing ourselves in public, or a million other things. As a result, we spend a lot of our time worrying about things that more often than not, never happen.

Another essential for the survival of any early human is to belong to a group. If your crew or squad booted you out, it wouldn't be long until the wolves found you. So, how does the mind protect you from rejection of the group? By comparing yourself with others, both friends and foes, to assess if your membership is at threat; am I fitting in? Am I doing the right thing? Am I as good as the others?

Sound familiar? Our modern-day minds are continuously warning us of rejection and comparing us to the rest of society. No wonder we spend so much energy worrying if other people will like us. No wonder we are always looking at ways to improve ourselves or putting ourselves down because we don't "measure up."

One hundred thousand years ago, we only had a few members of our immediate tribe to compare ourselves to. Today, we only need to glance at a newspaper, a magazine, or swipe down on our Facebook or Instagram newsfeeds to instantly find a whole host of people who are skinnier, richer, sexier, more powerful, more famous, or more successful than we are. The crazy filters and photo shop does not help the already unrealistic expectations we have on ourselves, either.

When we compare ourselves against these glamorous media creations, we feel inferior or disappointed with our lives. To make matters worse, our minds are now so sophisticated they can conjure up a fantasy image of the person we would ideally like to be. And then we compare ourselves to that! What chance have we got? We will always end up feeling not good enough.

Now, for any Stone Age person with ambition, the general rule for success is to get more and get better. The better the weapons, the more food you can kill. The larger your foods stores, the greater your chances for survival in times of scarcity. The better your shelter, the safer you are from wild weather and animals. The more children you have, the greater chance some will survive into adulthood.

It's no surprise our evolved mind also carried this strategy forward. Today, we are still led to believe "more and better"; more money, a better job, more status, a better body, more love, a better partner, more likes. And if we succeed, if we get more money, or a better car, or a bigger house, or buy a bigger set of boobs, then we are satisfied, for a while. But sooner or later (usually sooner), we end up wanting more.

Thus, evolution has shaped our brains so we are hardwired to suffer psychologically; to compare, evaluate, criticise ourselves and others, to focus on what we are lacking, to rapidly become dissatisfied with what we have, and to imagine several frightening scenarios, most of which will never happen. No wonder we find it hard to always be happy.

What is happiness? We all want it. We all crave it. We all strive for it. Even the Dalai Lama has said, "The very purpose of life is to seek happiness." But what exactly is it? The word happiness has two different meanings. The common meaning of the word is "feeling good."

In other words, feeling a sense of pleasure, gladness or gratification. We all enjoy these feelings, so it's no surprise we chase them. However, like any human emotion, feelings of happiness don't last. No matter how hard we try to hold on to them, they slip away every time.

A life spent in pursuit of happiness is, in the long-term, deeply unsatisfying. In fact, the harder we chase after pleasurable feelings, the more we are likely to suffer from anxiety and depression. The other, far less common meaning of happiness is "living a rich, full, and meaningful life."

When we take action on the things that truly matter deep in our hearts, move in directions we consider valuable and worthy, we clarify what we stand for in life and act accordingly. Then our lives become rich, full, and meaningful, and we experience a powerful sense of vitality. This is not some fleeting feeling. It is a mindset that appreciates and understands a life well lived.

Although such a life will undoubtedly give us many pleasurable feelings, it will also give us uncomfortable ones, such as fear, sadness, and anger. This is only to be expected. If we live a full life, we will feel the full range of human emotions. Happiness being among them.

"It is not happiness that brings gratitude, but gratitude that brings happiness."

ANON

==If we live a full life,==

==we will feel the full range of human emotions==

==happiness being among them.==

Have you heard of the pursuit of happiness? In psychology it's known as the Hedonic Treadmill. It entails we want or long for something, claiming our happiness depends on it and when we get it, our happiness adapts, and we require bigger, better things to attain the same fulfilment.

Essentially, the more you have, the more you want! This is why they say it is not happiness that brings gratitude, but gratitude that brings happiness. We need to learn how to be happy with what we have and who we are, otherwise, happiness will always be out of reach.

This is something you may not have heard of before. It's called sadness, and yes, it is normal.

I still don't get it. Is it possible to be happy?

We all enjoy feeling good, and we should make the most of the pleasant feelings when they appear. But if we try to have them all the time, we are doomed to fail. The reality is, life involves pain.

There is no getting away from it. As human beings, we are all faced with the fact that eventually we will grow frail, get sick, and die. Eventually, we all will lose valued relationships through rejection, separation, or death. Eventually, we will all come to face with crises, disappointment, and failure.

This means that in one form or another, we will all experience painful thoughts and feelings.

So, you mean to be truly happy I don't have to be happy?

More or less, yes, by truly understanding the grass isn't greener on the other side, it is where you water it.

The good news is, although we can't avoid such pain, we can learn to handle it much better, to make room for it, reduce its impact, and create a life worth living despite it.

The sad thing is, for so long, society has told us something different. From a young age we are taught we should be able to control our feelings.

When you were young, I am sure you heard many expressions like, "don't cry", "stop feeling sorry for yourself", "there's nothing to be afraid of", "stop being a sook", etc. With phrases such as these, the adults around us are sending the message again and again that we ought to control our feelings. But what was going on behind their closed doors?

They may have been drinking too much, having an affair, throwing themselves into work, or suffering in silence whilst slowly developing stomach ulcers. Whatever method they used to cope, I bet they probably didn't share those experiences with you. This is something you may not have heard of before. It's called sadness, and yes, it is normal.

On those rare occasions when you witnessed your parents' loss of control, I am betting they never explained to you, "Okay, these tears are because I am feeling sadness. It's a normal feeling, and you can learn to handle it effectively."

That's not too surprising, they couldn't show you how to handle your emotions because they didn't know how to handle theirs. The idea you should be able to control your feelings was undoubtedly reinforced in your school years. Do you recall kids who cried at school being teased for being "cry-babies", or "sissies", especially if they were boys?

Then, as you grew older, you probably heard phrases (or even used them yourself) such as "get over it", "snap out of it", "shit happens", "move on", "chill out" and so on. These phrases imply you should be able to turn your feelings on and off at will, like flicking a switch.

But everyone else looks happy.

And why is this myth so compelling? Because people around us seem, on the surface, to be happy. They seem to be in control of their thoughts and feelings, they always post happy photos on their Instagram and Facebook, but "seem" is the key word here.

The fact is, most people are not open or honest about the struggle they go through with their own thoughts and feelings. Social media are people's highlight reel (or for most people out there now, their business strategy to promote their latest campaign). Do not compare your *whole* life to their best parts.

Everything in life comes in duality, you can't have yin without yang, men without women, a rainbow without the rain, happiness without sadness. Like a coin, you have heads or tails. One is no more "right" or "common" than the other. It is just as normal to feel happy as it is to feel sad.

> One is no more "right" or "common" than the other. It's just as normal to feel happy as it is to feel sad.

When you feel sad, don't be so quick to suppress it, shrug it off, or make yourself feel guilty for not feeling ecstatic that day. Feel it, be aware of it, and even ask what it is telling you. Our feelings serve a purpose, and they are a good indicator when we are feeling rejected, loved, guilty, jealous, envious, grateful, or safe. It really is ok to not be ok; it is normal. Feel the emotion instead of trying to deny its presence, and tell yourself, this too shall pass.

Let's talk about the feeling of loneliness, too, while we are here talking about our feelings. Just like hunger is a warning sign that our blood sugar is low, and we need to eat, thirst warns us we need to drink to avoid dehydration, and pain alerts us to potential tissue damage. Loneliness tells us we need social connection, something as critical as our wellbeing as food and water.

Denying you feel lonely makes no more sense than denying you feel hunger, yet we deny our loneliness. If you doubt the idea starvation and loneliness are equally life-threatening, let me share the results of a meta-analysis of studies on loneliness. Researchers Julianne Holt-Lunstad, Timothy B Smith, and J Bradley Layton found living with air pollution increases your odds of dying early by 5%, living with obesity 20%, excessive drinking 30%, and living with loneliness? It increases our odds of dying early by 45%.

There is nothing to be ashamed of by admitting you're lonely. Historically, admitting this came with the negative connotation or stereotype you were a "loner" and had no friends or poor social skills. Today, despite being more connected than ever online, so many of us are feeling disconnected offline as I shared in the statistics, and you're not alone.

Did you know a 1990 study found the average person had 3.8 significant friends they would share important life info with, trusted friends and advisors? Today, even with social media platforms like Facebook suggesting friends, reminding us of significant events and birthdays, showing us what interests we share. The average person has 1.8 trusted close friends. Our support networks have halved despite being more connected than ever!

Like I explained earlier, we humans are social beings, we need connection for our survival. Make time, make an effort to catch up and connect with friends and family. Ask how colleagues, neighbours, and strangers really are and listen to what their body language says, not just their reply.

Soon you learn we are all more connected than you think, and you could be the one person who saved their life that day just by stopping by and caring. Because of how we were raised, depending on how well your parents understood and self-regulated their own emotions and how much education you got around feelings, this will influence how aware you are of your feelings. Also, what tools you have in your tool box when learning to manage them, and your ability to read how others are feeling. Which is ironic that most of us are taught so much in school, but we neglect to understand ourselves.

This skill is referred to as "emotional intelligence." When emotional intelligence was first discovered, it served as the missing link in the peculiar finding that people with the highest levels of intelligence (IQ) outperform those with average IQ just 20% of the time. Yet people with average IQ outperform those with high IQs 70% of the time.

Scientists realised there must be another variable that explained success above and beyond one's IQ, and years of research and countless studies have found emotional intelligence (EQ) is the critical factor.

Emotional intelligence is so crucial to success research has found it accounts for 58% of performance in all types of jobs, and the cool thing is like the trait "grit", you can improve it!

You can pay to do the emotional intelligence appraisal test online which will give your score and sixty-six strategies on how you can improve your four dimensions of EQ being; self-awareness, self-management, social awareness, and relationship management.

It is something worth you investing in and improving with research; finding the link between EQ and earning is so direct that every point increase in EQ adds $1,300 to an annual salary. This is another reason why I truly believe the biggest investment you can ever make is in yourself, whether that is your health, your happiness, or your education!

When I did workshops with children and their parents, I would explain our feelings by breaking them up in our ABCs to make it as simple as possible. "A" stands for affect. This refers to our emotions and the affect they have on us or how we would describe they make us feel. We have identified the five core emotions as happy, sad, angry, afraid, and ashamed. Each have variations in intensity which you can see on the next page graph.

"B" stands for behaviour. This refers to what our feelings look like, and it is important to remember they look different for everyone. Often, because of gender stereotypes, men show emotions differently to women because of what we condition them to believe is acceptable in society. It doesn't mean they don't have the same underlying feelings.

For example, I don't know what frustration looks like to you, but for me, when I am frustrated, I cry. People who don't know me assume I must be sad. I know what my emotions looks like. When I am sad I don't cry; I withdraw and don't talk at all. Which, if you know me, is not like me, because usually if I am happy you could never get me to shut up in a small social gathering with friends and family.

Another example I have is this weird habit of laughing when I am scared. When I watch a horror movie, I giggle the whole way through it. It is not because I think it is funny; it is because I am shitting my pants! I remember when I first moved to the Gold Coast, I was living with a girlfriend. One night, while we were waiting for the electricity to be turned on after we had moved in, a squatter broke into our unit.

Intensity of Feelings	HIGH	MEDIUM	LOW
HAPPY	Elated Excited Overjoyed Thrilled Excuberant Ecstatic Fired up Passionate	Cheerful Gratified Good Releaved Satisfied Glowing	Glad Contented Pleasant Tender Pleased Mellow
SAD	Depressed Agonized Alone Hurt Dejected Hopeless Sorrowful Miserable	Heartbroken Somber Lost Distressed Let down Melancholy	Unhappy Moody Blue Upset Disappointed Dissatisfied
ANGRY	Furious Enraged Outraged Boiling Irate Seething Loathsome Betrayed	Upset Mad Defended Frustrated Agitated Disgusted	Perturbed Annoyed Uptight Resistant Irritated Touchy
AFRAID	Terrified Horrified Scared stiff Petrified Fearful Panicky Frantic Shocked	Apprehensive Frightened Threatened Insecure Uneasy Intimidated	Cautious Nervous Worried Timid Unsure
ASHAMED	Sorrowful Remorseful Defamed Worthless Disgraced Dishonored Mortified Admonished	Apologetic Unworthy Sneaky Guilty Embarrased Secretive	Bashful Ridiculous Regretful Uncomfortable Pitied Silly

ADAPTED FROM AND REPRODUCED BY PERMISSION FROM JULIA WEST

I remember us hiding in a corner of a room in the pitch darkness and hearing them open the balcony door but not being able to see anything. I was so freaking scared I broke out hysterically laughing. My girlfriend thought I was in on the whole ordeal and thought it was funny and didn't believe I had no idea who was walking into our apartment!

It is crazy how feelings can look different for different people. There is no right or wrong. A fun little activity to do is go through these emotions on the table above to reflect on what they look like for you. I bet you can describe what they look like for your loved ones who you spend a lot of time with, like your partner, children, parents. Sometimes even better than they do themselves.

Self-awareness is one of the four dimensions that come into play when talking about emotional intelligence. This is a cool activity you can do to help you become more aware of your own emotions and what they look like for others so you can learn to better manage them.

"C" stands for cognition. This is the thought process that usually happens after something triggers the emotion. We try making sense of what they mean or what they are trying to tell us in understanding why we are feeling a certain way. Sometimes we aren't aware of how we feel about something until we have a physiological response (so our body literally tells us).

The daily challenge of dealing effectively with emotions is critical to human condition because our brains are hardwired to give our emotions the upper hand.

For example, maybe you found out your friends caught up on the weekend and you weren't invited. You thought you were ok and tried to shrug it off, but you got home and something your house mate or partner said triggered you and you started crying.

Upon reflection, you know it wasn't anything they had said, but it was just the straw that broke the camel's back and you were really upset and offended your friends left you out. Maybe you go on a date or to a party and thought you were feeling really confident about it but as you get there, you feel your hands sweating and your heart racing. You didn't realise you were nervous until your body told you.

One I know too well is, I think I am energised and fired up, then suddenly, I get run down and have some really sexy cold sores pop up on my bottom lip. My body is telling me I am stressed. The daily challenge of dealing effectively with emotions is critical to human condition because our brains are hardwired to give our emotions the upper hand.

Everything you see, smell, hear, and taste travels through your body in the form of electric signals. These signals pass from cell to cell until they reach their ultimate destination, your brain. They enter your brain at the base near the spinal-cord but must travel through to the frontal lobe (or behind your forehead) before reaching a place for rational, logical thinking to take place.

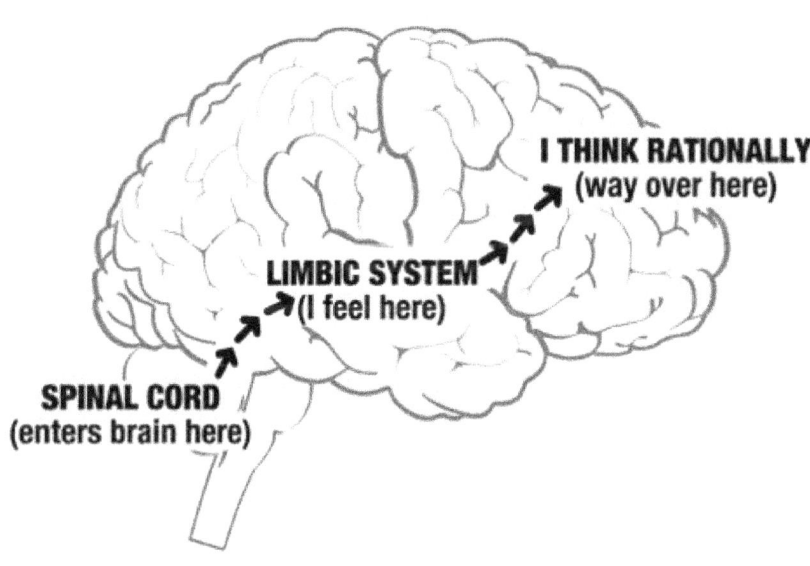

The trouble is, as you can see from the image above, they pass through your limbic system along the way, the place where emotions are produced. This journey ensures you experience things emotionally before your reason can kick into gear. The rational area of your brain (the front of your brain) can't stop the emotion felt by the limbic system, but the two areas influence each other and maintain constant communication. The communication between your emotional and rational brain is the physical source of emotional intelligence.

When I am explaining feelings to kids, I get a demonstration out using a jug and some coloured water. You can understand something as complex as emotions by breaking them down using a simple analogy like a cup!

Let's say, every morning you start with an empty cup. You sleep in passed your alarm (so you then pour some water in your cup). Then you grab a coffee on the way to work and your normal barista isn't there that day and the coffee they make you is shit house (so you pour a little more water in your cup). You get stuck in traffic and you're already running late (so you pour some water in your cup). You get to work, and your boss rolls their eyes at you as you walk in late and gives you the stink eye all day (pour some more water in your cup). Then you get home late and the kids are asking a million things from you and your partner hasn't helped prep dinner yet and your cup overflows and YOU SNAP!

Sound familiar? Obviously, we all have different days, different triggers, different sized cups and patience which influences how quickly our cups fill up. But this, in a nutshell, is how you regulate your emotions, by checking in throughout the day and seeing how full your cup is.

I would love for you to look at that table above and reflect on the pleasant emotions listed under happy and think about some things that create that emotion for you. I like to call it a "glad list." Think about the things you can do to empty your cup – for you!

Maybe it is a form of self-care; make a "Menu of Happiness" and literally have twenty things listed you can do (that don't cost a lot of money) nearly on any given day. This is what we were talking about earlier in chapter three about having that awareness of what makes you happy.

If you don't know, how can you expect a parent, a child, or a job to do that for you? If you're stuck, here are some things on my glad list:

LAUREN'S MENU OF HAPPINESS;
- Ten-minute meditation
- I take three deep breaths and think of three things I am grateful for
- Yummy candles or essential oils
- A bath

- Journaling
- Goal setting
- Yoga class
- Run
- Dance class
- Cuddles with my partner
- Call my mum
- A wine with my best friend
- A green tea
- Listening to music
- A yummy nutritious meal
- Nap in the sunshine
- Reading a book
- Getting a massage

Now, imagine I had that beaker with coloured water, and I had that same challenging day. After I slept passed my alarm, maybe I took three deep breaths which would allow me to pour some water out of my cup. Maybe on my lunch break I did a ten-minute meditation, so I get to pour some water out of my cup. And maybe when I got home I hugged my partner before responding to the million things that needed tending to, which allowed me to pour a little more water out of my cup.

After the kids are in bed, I treat myself to a chapter of a book with a green tea or even a bath. This is the same day, but I checked in and knew my cup was filling up quickly, so I took control and ownership of my emotions. This stopped my cup from overflowing and prevented the explosion.

This is what it means to self-regulate, *but* only *you* can do that. Some tips when making your glad list: make sure the things you put on there don't make you just feel good in the short term, but worse off, in the long-term. For example, cookie dough used to be my go-to after a bad day in child protection (soo good) but it would leave me feeling even more tired, sluggish, and depressed after the initial sugar hit wore off. Remember, the intention is to fill your cup up, not pour from it! Really, question, *is this constructive? Will this fulfil me long-term?*

Being aware if you are an introvert or an extrovert also helps you in creating a glad list that will work best for you. Another reason why I am not

Universal Assignment:

Make your own glad list or happiness menu.

surprised when people learn I am an introvert is because so many people are not aware of what the true meaning is of these words.

Unlike what most are led to believe, "introversion" and "extroversion" is not a theory about how outgoing or shy we are, in psychology and research. It relates to where we get our energy from, how we recharge our brains and batteries, or how I like to say – how we fill up our cup!

Introverts (or those of us with introverted tendencies) recharge by spending time alone. For example, for me that's walking, one-on-one coffee or wine dates with my girlfriends, watching a movie with my partner, going for a long walk, sitting at the beach *alone*, meditating, and journaling. We lose energy from being around people for long periods of time, particularly large crowds. Extroverts gain energy from other people. Extroverts find it saps their energy when they spend too much time alone. They recharge by being social.

So many clients I coach in wellness feel guilty when they go through a breakup, a death, or just a few bad days in a row (it doesn't have to be extreme). They feel bad because their friends are trying to get them to go social gatherings and get out there. They don't want to go to big social gatherings as it feels more like a chore for them they have to drag themselves to, rather than something that gets them excited and lit up.

Maybe they're saying, "I don't wanna do that," and you feel like they're deflecting or they're suppressing emotions because they're avoiding people. But, really, it's educating and being understanding they might be an introvert. There's a difference between suppressing emotion and avoiding people.

If you understand your personality type,

you can make smart decisions on how to regulate

your emotions in a way that is healthy for you.

"When I was five years old, my mother always told me that happiness was the key to life. When I went to school, they asked me what I wanted to be when I grew up. I wrote down 'happy'. They told me I didn't understand the assignment, and I told them they didn't understand life."

JOHN LENNON

If you're an introvert, you're practicing healthy self-regulation. If going to a party is taking all your energy, the best way for you to self-regulate and get your energy back (if you're an introvert) is to have time by yourself. Especially when you're in a space right now where you don't have energy to give.

Going out would just be putting a Band-Aid on it. Temporarily distracting themselves with noise, suppressing their feelings with alcohol, drugs, or even casual sex, rather than sitting in their own company and making peace with their emotions.

For extroverts, the best thing for them when they're feeling lonely or upset is to go to a party! That's what gives them energy, to socialise, to be around people, to bounce off other energies just to see that there's love and there's light out there outside of their head.

If you understand your personality type, you can then make smart decisions on how to regulate your emotions in a way that is healthy *for you*. (And not feel guilty if going to your friend's party isn't the best thing for you do to right now). If you're an introvert, you can understand why and how I use my "Business jacket" I spoke about earlier when I embrace the suck and work with large groups of people. Consider this if you're already in or embarking on stepping into the business world, which is all about *marketing* yourself as an extrovert to get your mission and message across.

Understanding others and yourself is the key to spreading kindness and compassion, and the world needs more of that.

Talking about feelings with kids

I know it is hard to talk about feelings for most people and even harder for kids. Have you ever tried to ask kids how their day was? Or how school was? How are you? I am sure what you usually hear is, "Good, Fine, Ok." It makes it so much easier when you are using the same terminology!

If you have kids, get a water beaker and explain this to them, talk about feelings and how full their cup is. We learn so much better with visuals! Make it a family affair and one night, all sit down to create your own "Glad lists." This way, as a parent or even a partner, if you can feel or see your partner or child has come home from work or school frustrated and overwhelmed, chime in with, "Hey buddy, I can see your cup is nearly full. How about we go kick the soccer ball for twenty minutes before we sit down to do a little homework

"People get lost when they think of happiness as a destination. We're always thinking that someday, you know, when you get a car, get that job, go on that holiday, or meet that person who will fix everything… we will be happy. But happiness is a condition, not a destination. It is like being tired or hungry. It comes and it goes, and that's ok. And if people thought of it that way, we would find happiness a lot more often."

ANON

before dinner?"

Replace soccer with something on their glad list they have come up with that also works for you. You will get better results this way rather than adding something to their already overflowing cup, which will just cause them to explode and pour water in yours!

There are great resources you can find online with scaling questions and visuals children can use to colour in to explain how they are feeling. This also helps them to become more self-aware of their emotions and how to manage them. Too many people are feeling guilty for not being happy.

The secret to happiness is not always being happy but understanding the concept of happiness by practicing mindfulness, allow your perspective to be challenged. Everyone's pain deserves to be validated. We all have permission to be upset.

It is Ok to not be Ok. We are all human; it is part of our evolved design, and it is not weak to speak about it, as I highlighted the statistics earlier. You are definitely not alone and there are services that can help if sadness is hanging around for prolonged periods.

Life is only as good as your mindset, so here are some quick life hacks.

Mindset Hacks

1) Do not be manipulated by status, fashion or money. Don't allow society to dictate to you what should make you happy. With this book, you should know your values by now. Live in alignment with them.

2) Practice self-awareness and mindfulness. Are you aware of what makes you happy? Be motivated by your values, live your life in accordance to what is important to you. And be aware when you feel yourself being pulled away from your truth and redirect with gratitude for the lessons.

3) Acknowledge when you're not feeling Ok. Accept it. Allow it. Try to change the way you think about it. Did you learn something? Did you grow? Did it make you happy at the time? Did it allow you the opportunity to reassess your values? Did it give you the opportunity to have a good old-fashioned cry, devour a tub of cookie dough ice-cream, and let it all out? Or even have a cuddle with your bestie or mum and really connect on a deeper level than you had ever before?

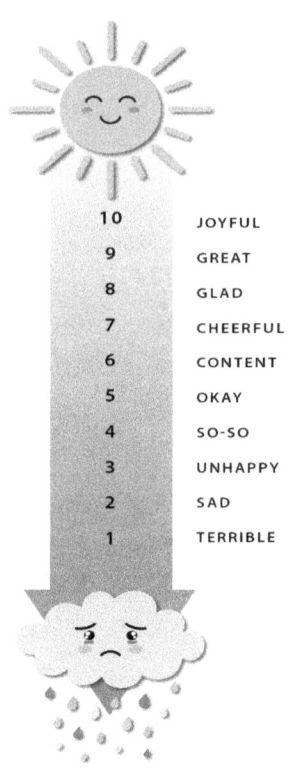

4) Remember, everyone demonstrates emotions differently, so dig deeper using your ABCs. You know what behaviour you're seeing but what do you think the cognition behind it is? Why are they behaving like that (or if you are self-reflecting, *why did you behave like that? How are you really feeling?*) What is the emotion triggered that affected you/them?

5) Monitor how full your cup is. Have some healthy and easy go-to's to help you empty your own cup, like a Glad list. If you are a parent, prompt self-regulating strategies for your children and model healthy self-regulating strategies yourself. It is important to understand emotion regulation starts with you and what children learn early on in life, which affects how they respond to everything that happens to them later in life.

CHAPTER TWELVE

Manifest and Show Up

Do you feel like you're stuck in quicksand trying to keep your head up? Stop fighting it, stop resisting change. Acknowledge it. Accept it. Remain calm and breathe. Just like you cannot define gravity, what you resist persists.

Instead of being a fish swimming against the current, there are Universal Laws you can use to your advantage and find flow instead of force, community over competition, presence over pressure, and compassion over judgment. Alignment is the new hustle because when you are aligned with your deepest values and truth, "the force" is always within you.

Picture yourself being caught in a rip out at sea. The worst thing you can do is to fight against it. You will just tire yourself out and be left feeling defeated and helpless. Instead of swimming against the current, swim with it. Go with the flow in life, trust the pull. Life is fluid. Embrace it. Nothing stays the same forever but nothing is ever lost.

You cannot lose something without gaining something else, so trust the process, be open to change and learning, look for the lessons. Maybe the universe's plan is to show you the next beautiful beach?

As you learn and understand the universal laws, you will notice them and the role they play in life, health, relationships, and business. The evident theories are underlying most of the things I have spoken to you about already in psychology, faith/religion, research, gratitude, forgiveness, mindfulness, self-love, and self-talk. It's about being a good person and doing the best you can with what you can, as long as you can.

When we ignore the natural Laws of the Universe, often you will experience struggle, resistance, unfulfilled destiny, pain, and lack of direction.

It has always been in the nature of humanity to believe mostly in the things we can see, feel, taste, hear, or touch while doubting anything else beyond the perception of our immediate senses.

However, whether you believe it, these Universal Laws influence our everyday lives and you cannot change that. You can liken these Universal Laws to a very deep root of a tree buried underground which the ordinary eyes cannot see, yet the root exerts so much influence on the tree because without the root, a tree cannot stand.

The Law of Divine Oneness.

Everything is connected to everything else. What we think, say, do, and believe will have a corresponding effect on others and the world around us. This is what I was talking about earlier when I was explaining the science behind finding more that connects us than what separates us.

Everything consists of and exists as energy. Your subatomic particles aren't fixed. In fact, particles may flow into and out of you now from: this page, the sky, the floor, your best friend, and your worst enemy. There is no separation. How would you behave if you really knew you were not separate from life, your friends, colleagues, the Earth, animals, and every being that has ever existed?

I am guessing, probably differently. What you do to others you do to yourself, and likewise, how you treat yourself sets a standard of how others will treat you. If you don't love, respect, and believe in yourself, you're teaching others they don't have to either.

All of humanity and God (whatever you perceive God to be) are one. We are always connected to the force of the universe because the energy of the universe is everywhere at once, and permeates through all things, living or material.

The universe's energy is infinite and always available to us, each soul is a part of that same energy. Whether you follow and believe in religion or science, there is a divine energy that vibrates in every single thing. That is the divinity.

Everything that exists seen and unseen are connected to each other, inseparable from each other to a field of divine oneness. Divine all knowing, the matrix, pure consciousness, or universal mind energy, sometimes also known as Life Force or God. Everything is one.

Increasing your awareness of this law will increase your awareness of God and awareness of being connected to everything. It is important for us as a human race to realise and understand this law.

As we do, we will realise what we think of each other should only be for acceptance and love. As we think of the good in others, so they will think of the good in you. It is essential the thoughts, feelings, and actions be for good, for we "reap what we sow."

You are not a tiny, insignificant drop in a vast ocean. Your goal is to learn to see the ocean within the drop. Those who see themselves as perpetually "small" are sending vibrational energies that are also "small." Instead, you are a part of an energy source that is so vast, so immeasurable, the mind cannot comprehend it. This lies at the core of you and every being.

Law of Vibration

This law states energy makes up all things. I am sure you've heard the phrase "vibes" as in "I didn't like that place; it had a weird vibe." We can intuitively sense the energies around objects, places, and other people. Science reveals everything in the manifest universe is ultimately composed of packets of energy; quantised units vibrating at specific frequencies.

Quantum physicists has shown that, although matter may appear to be solid, it is ultimately, mostly empty space interspersed with energy. When you look at it through a high-powered microscope, it is broken down into its smallest components: molecules, atoms, neutrons, electrons, and quanta (the smallest particles measurable).

So, in essence, everything is comprised of energy and empty space. Everything that appears solid is the frequency of the vibration of the energy that makes it up. An interesting fact about this is the denser the object, the higher the speed of vibration. The lower the density of an object is, the lower the speed of vibration.

Anything that exists in our universe, whether seen or unseen, broken down into and analysed in its purest and most basic form, consists of pure energy or light which resonates and exists as a vibratory frequency or pattern. When you hear people say, "like attracts like," they are referring to how a vibrational energy can resonate with or is attracted to the same or a similar vibrational energy.

If you are not happy with your current vibration, make a conscious choice to focus your energy more on positive emotions and less on negative emotions to raise your vibration higher beyond the one you do not want in your life.

If you do not want more bad news coming to you, do not be the one to spread it around to others. By giving others that which you desire, you indirectly increase that which comes back to you. This is why I am so passionate about understating how to control your thoughts because our thoughts are where it all begins.

> As your conscious mind dwells habitually on thoughts of a certain quality, these become firmly imbedded within the subconscious mind.

As your conscious mind dwells habitually on thoughts of a certain quality, these become firmly imbedded within the subconscious mind. They then become your dominant vibration. This dominant vibration sets up a resonance with other similar vibrations and consequently draws them into your life.

Your feeling at the present moment dictates your vibration. People say feelings are words used to define conscious awareness of vibration. So, your feeling at the moment is your vibration you are in which sets up things of like nature. Positive feelings = positive circumstance, negative feelings = negative circumstances.

Law of Action

Like I promised at the start of this book, I am all about positive vibes, but also, with some tough love, the universal laws are the same. They are not woo-woo. We base them on science, and this law entails you must act for us to manifest things on Earth.

You cannot sit on your butt and expect things to fall into your lap without effort. *Does this mean you have to struggle? Absolutely not!* If you are "struggling" to reach your goals it means you are not aligned with them properly, or they are not the right goals for you.

Don't use this law as a cop out to give up on your dreams because it hasn't been easy, either. Working towards your goals (when it is something you are passionate about) should be challenging, but also seem to follow a meaningful flow. Remember, there is a difference between "hard work" and "working hard."

> Working towards your goals should be challenging but also seem to follow a meaningful flow.

The Law of action states you must do the things and perform the actions necessary to achieve what you are setting out to do. Unless you take actions in harmony with your emotions, thoughts, and dreams and proceed consistently towards what you want to accomplish, there will be absolutely no foreseeable results.

It is here, with the law of action, that most people falter when pursuing success. It could be their fears or laziness that get in the way. Manifest those crazy dreams girlfriend, but don't forget you need to also show up!

Only by taking actions which correspond with your free will and desires will the universe know what to bring into your life. If you wish to learn, then take the action steps to learn. Read books, study, enrol in courses, attend networking events. Only then will the universe know what it is you are striving for.

When you take action, from the smallest thing like writing a to-do list in the morning to scheduling dates and meetings in your calendar, you set into motion corresponding effects that change your immediate future. If you follow up day after day, it can become a habit or way of living and the results will be exponential.

But if you fail, to take that first action, you might as well forget the rest of the laws. This is also why I am a passionate advocate for mastering the art of saying "no." Say no often, say it clearly, and say it unapologetically. Many of us over-commit and say yes to projects and commitments we think we have to do. Which just adds to our already overwhelming to-do lists, making us busy instead of productive.

If it is not something that aligns with your values, if it is not something that will get you closer to your goals, don't say yes purely because you feel obliged. Otherwise, the universe will think those initial goals you set aren't that important to you because you haven't prioritised them.

All the universal laws explain you cannot gain something without losing something else. Let's say you get to make that appearance to your colleague's BBQ on Sunday (that you didn't really want to go to but felt you had to). Now it means you have less time to spend quality time with your family, which is a high value for you, or less time writing that book that was a goal of yours around full-time work. Or less time to food prep and get organised for the new week as health was a high value of yours. Guard your time.

Money we can get back, time we cannot. Every action has a consequence, so be deliberate with the action you do make. Keep in mind when choosing to do nothing, it is an action too, which also brings with it its own cascade of events and consequences.

Law of Correspondence

This Universal Law states the principles or laws of physics that explain the physical world energy. Light, vibration, and motion have their corresponding principles in the universe. "As above, so below," "As within, so without," or "Whatever is above is like that which is below," and "Whatever is below is like that which is above."

Your outer life reflects of your inner life. There is a direct correspondence between the way you think and feel on the inside and the way you act and experience on the outside.

If you want to change external circumstances in your life, you need to accept responsibilty for your own life and change your inner world first.

Your relationships, health, wealth, and position are mirror images of your inner world. Simply stated, you are destined to experience what you think about and your world reflects this to you every day. If you want to change external circumstances in your life, you need to accept responsibility for your own life and change your inner world first.

Those who seek inner peace and clarity find their daily lives and routines flow more easily and harmoniously. They are better able to cope with life's little upheavals and carry on. Which is why I am a massive advocate for self-regulation and meditation to help you get those thoughts and emotions in check!

Those who get stuck in anger, resentment, and other self-sabotaging emotions and beliefs find they draw more chaos into their lives. And most don't even realise they are doing it!

Law of Cause and Effect

Nothing happens by chance or outside the Universal Laws. Every Action has a reaction or consequence. "We reap what we sow." Many spiritual traditions have taught this universal wisdom in various ways. The most well-known is "karma." Ralph Waldo Emerson said the Law of Cause and Effect is the "law of laws." We see the most important lesson involving human conduct and interaction in the Cosmic Law of Cause and Effect. "For every action there is an equal and opposite reaction."

Every human thought, word, and deed is a cause that sets off a wave of energy throughout the universe, which creates the effect whether desirable or undesirable. Likewise, inaction is also an action which carries with it a cascade of consequences.

With every thought of intention, action, or even emotion that transmits from you, a person sets into motion an unseen chain of effects. These vibrate from the mental plane thought the entire cellular structure of body out into the environment and finally, into the Cosmos. This is how physical manifestation works. This is why good thoughts, words, emotions, and deeds are essential to do good in the world.

*"If there is light in the soul,
there is beauty in the person.
If there is beauty in the person,
there will be harmony in the house.
If there is harmony in the house,
there will be order in the nation.
If there is order in the nation,
there will be peace in the world."*

BUDDHA

Law of Compensation

This Law of Compensation is the extended arm of the Law of Cause and Effect. We apply this to abundance and blessings that flow into our lives in the form of friendships, gifts, money, inheritances, and other forms of blessings. These various forms of compensation are the visible effects of our direct and indirect actions carried out throughout our lives.

You get back what you give to others. There is a saying, "misery loves company." It means when you are miserable, you attract other people who are also miserable, and it becomes a vicious circle that feeds on itself.

Fortunately, the opposite is true!

If you want to receive more of something in your life, be what you want to see! Give freely to others what you hope to receive. Does this mean if you need more money you should throw away the money you have? No, but you should be generous and share abundance according to your current capacity to do so.

Provide for those who are in need by giving of yourself. Be generous and share abundance in its many forms with others and abundance and prosperity will return to you. This is a secret I have noticed talking to lots of successful entrepreneurs and people I look up to have also figured out!

So many people wait to receive before they give. They wait until they have money before they donate. They wait until they catch a break before they slow down and practice gratitude. And they wait until they are being treated the way they believe they deserve to be treated before they fully give 100% of themselves to a partner, friendship, or job.

But successful people do the opposite. They give before they receive. They understand universal laws; they understand what comes around goes around. You have no control over how it comes back to you but trust that it does.

If you are feeling poor, go donate. If you're feeling lost, go volunteer. If you're wanting a better relationship, step up and treat the other person how you want to be treated first; go plan a romantic weekend getaway! If you want a thriving business, go add value and give back to the existing customers you already have. In a world that is all about 'take, take, take,' what have you given today?

Law of Attraction

This law demonstrates how we create the things, events, and people that come into our lives; our thoughts, feelings, words, and actions produce energies which attract like energies. Negative energies attract negative energies and positive energies attract positive energies. It doesn't matter whether you want the negative. What you place your attention on is what you attract into your life.

> Gratitude is the easiest way to shift your focus and energy almost simultaneously.

If you dislike the negative, you just need to raise your vibration higher and away from it in order to fully apply this Law of Attraction to work for you. For example, when anyone starts out thinking negatively, it lowers their vibration.

As the focus on the problem rather than the solution becomes intense, the size and number of the problem will magnify as that's where the person's focus is. This is why it is important to focus on manifesting positive energy through the use of the various laws of the universe.

It goes beyond merely "wishing" or "hoping" or "visualising" as so many others teach. If you want to attract positive energy, line up with it and apply yourself. Gratitude is the easiest way to shift your focus and energy almost simultaneously.

Life is full of difficulties, adventures, challenges, and more importantly, lessons, so we can grow and become the person we need to be, to attain the life we want to live. It takes the same amount of work and energy to put yourself down and to the paint world grey as it does to lift yourself up and paint the world in vibrant colours, experiences, and lessons!

When you feel yourself vibrating at a low frequency, use gratitude as a tool to help make the conscious shift and be alleviated to shake those bad jujus and attract more of the good stuff!

The Law of Perpetual Transmutation of Energy

The energy of the Universe is always moving and transmuting into and out of form. This law of nature further tells us energy is always in a state of motion. It will take one form and move to another form, but it's always in motion and never standing still.

This law relates to the universe and our consciousness through the realisation everything seen, and unseen is constantly changing. We can harness this energy and transform it into whatever form we desire. We should then realise the energy with us can be focused toward good and then the things around us and within us will change for the better.

The energy is flowing into our consciousness constantly. We transform this energy into whatever we choose through our focus of attention at the moment. The formless energy is open to be shaped by our minds.

Through learning this law, we see that change is all there is. We must see we are either growing or dying. Everything is always changing. Do not resist the change. If a person does, then they will be going against the law. Resisting change is resisting growing, and those people go backwards and prevent learning and continual improvement.

Use this law for your benefit in the way of shaping the formless flowing to and through you at all times into good "causes." Continue to improve all aspects of your life and grow with the changing times. We all have within us the power to change the conditions of our lives.

> If you don't like the path you are on,
>
> change it, or more importantly,
>
> "allow" it to be changed.

Higher vibrations consume and transform lower ones. Thus, each of us can change the energies in our lives by understanding the Universal Laws and applying the principles in such a way as to effect change. If you don't like the path you are on, change it, or more importantly,

"Happy people don't have the best of everything, they just make the best of everything."

ANON

"allow" it to be changed.

At the start of the book I talked about feeling the universe's "pull" to move to the Gold Coast by myself to start a new chapter when I had just turned eighteen. There was something in me that wanted more, that was ready to evolve and grow.

Instead of fighting it and doing what was "easier" and following my high school boyfriend to Canberra or all my high school friends who moved to Melbourne, which was only three hours away from home, I tuned into my intuition. I trusted the universe, went with the flow, and "allowed" the change to happen rather than trying to make sense of it or rationalise it.

Rather than force your will on people or circumstances, rearrange the way you think and empower yourself. I call this the "learning to go with the flow" law. When we resist change or assert a false sense of control over the external world, it always leads to struggle.

We must learn to embrace change, work with energies and "allow" circumstances and opportunities to manifest according to divine providence. The ego's need for a false sense of control can block the flow of positive energy that will bring you the ideal circumstances you are searching for.

It is fear-based thinking and can undermine your progress in all the other areas if you don't recognise it. Once I learned to truly understand this law, I stopped struggling and suffering. I learned to trust that closed doors were never truly meant for me, and the universe knows what is best for me better than I do.

It created me, didn't it? It takes control and ensures my heart continues to beat and my central nervous system continues to send messages reminding me to breathe, even while I clock off every night to sleep for eight hours. So why doubt its skills in the driver's seat now?

Law of Relativity

Each person will receive a series of problems (tests of initiation, or as I love to call them as I have assigned to you in this book, "universal assignments or lessons"). The challenge is to remain connected to our hearts when proceeding to solve the problems to strengthen our inner light, our truth, faith, or certainty.

*"Every adversity, every failure,
and every heartache carry with it the
seed of an equivalent or greater benefit."*

NAPOLEON HILL

This law also teaches us to compare our problems to other's problems into its proper perspective. No matter how bad we perceive our situation to be, there is always someone in a worse position. It is all relative. Nobody is ever given a problem they cannot handle, as we were born with everything already needed to handle them.

Do not spend your time looking for happiness from the outside as it already lies within you. What is in me is also in you. It is what it is. Nothing is good, bad, big, or small until it has been experienced through our cultured lenses and we compare it to something else and assign it a meaning. This law also tells us that sometimes "shit happens." Energy is always manifesting. Period.

> Nothing is good, bad, big, or small until it has been experienced through our cultured lenses and we compare it to something else and assign it a meaning.

This law teaches that every soul will face some challenges; it's what you do with those challenges that define you and determine what you become. You can "fold" under the pressure or rise above and allow your trials to strengthen you. Learn to use your life's challenges as stepping stones rather than stumbling blocks.

One strategy that works when you feel a bit overwhelmed is to know, regardless of what you are suffering at the moment, someone has it worse. Keep things in perspective. That broken arm might hurt, but somewhere, someone else may have broken both arms and their leg! "This too shall pass." In times of sorrow or adversity, learn to glean the wisdom and the blessings.

The spiritual and metaphysical aspects of this law of relativity tells us everything in our physical world is made real by its relationship or comparison to something. Light only exists because we compare it to dark. Good can only exist because we compare it to bad. Hot can only exist because we compare it to cold.

Happiness can only exist because we compare it to sadness. Support can only exist because we compare it to criticism. I have explained when

"In form, you are and will always be inferior to some, superior to others. In essence, you are neither inferior nor superior to anyone. True self-esteem and true humility arise out of that realisation. In the eyes of the ego, self-esteem and humility are contradictory. In truth,
they are one and the same."

ECHHART TOLLE

understanding emotions in health or lack of support in business, you cannot have one measure of the spectrum without a mutual appreciation for the opposite. One does not exist or have meaning without the other.

In fact, everything in our life "just is" until we compare it to something. Nothing in life has any meaning, except for the meaning we give it. It is all in how you look at your situation and what thoughts and perspective you think about the situation. This is what I talk about when I refer to our "cultured glasses or lens. " Every one of us wear and see the world differently because of past experiences and values. From a spiritual point of view, we can remove barriers of labelling and accept everything "as is."

Law of Polarity

Everything is on a continuum and has an opposite. We can suppress and transform undesirable thoughts by concentrating on the opposite pole. It is the law of mental vibrations. We can see you cannot have a left without a right, an up without a down, failure without success, a good without a bad and so on. It is a world of duality.

However, these opposites have no absolutes. There is not one point where you can say one starts and the other begins, it is a scale range. There are two poles or opposites, the difference between the two extremes of one thing is called polarity. There are degrees of difference between the extremes or poles no but no absolutes. In fact, these opposites are different manifestations of the same thing!

Example: there is not one point where you can say that cold stops and heat begins, it's all on the same pole.

An understanding of the principle will enable you to change your own polarity, and that of others. Thoughts and ideas that are not working for your highest good can be removed by consciously directing your attention to their opposite.

Feeling sad? Watch a funny movie. If you feel angry, rather than dwell on that emotion, focus on what you can do to manifest its opposite like our glad list. In this way, you find solutions that are inspired and empowering. Anger is often demonised and as a result, we push it down until it explodes into something destructive.

Instead, now you have the awareness of how the laws work. If

"Everything is dual; everything has poles; everything has its pair of opposites; like and unlike are the same; opposites are identical in nature, but different in degree; extremes meet; all truths are but half-truths; all paradoxes may be reconciled."

THE KYBALION

something angers you, don't complain or lash out or wallow in your frustration. DO something proactive to work yourself up the opposite end of the pole. Imagine if you had $86,400 in your account and someone stole $10 from you. Would you be upset and throw the remaining $86,390 away in hopes of getting back at the person who took your $10?

Or move on and live? Right, you move on and live. See, we all have 86,400 seconds each day. Don't let someone's negative ten seconds ruin the remaining 86,390. Don't sweat the small stuff. Life is so much bigger than that and man, is it beautiful! Use this analogy to help you get back the other end of that Pole, girlfriend!

Law of Rhythm

Everything vibrates and moves to certain rhythms. These rhythms establish seasons, cycles, stages of development, and patterns. Each cycle reflects the regularity of God's Universe. Be patient with yourself and trust the process. There a season to plant seeds and there is a season to sew, no one blooms all year around!

The Law of Rhythm states the energy in the universe is like a pendulum. Whenever something swings to the right, it must then swing to the left. Everything in existence is involved in a dance, swaying, flowing, swinging back and forth. Everything is either growing or dying.

The more the pendulum swings one way, the universal law dictates it will swing that extreme the other way. The best way to make stable decisions is to centre your energy. Do you notice in relationships, if someone is longing for a relationship where they are with their partner all the time? That's only because they have been at one extreme too long and feeling neglected with little or no time together.

Or, if you are starving, when you do finally get food you aren't polite or mindful of each mouthful you take. Instead of being centred and tuning into your body's cues, you binge! When you feel life pull you one way, don't feed it, don't invest your energy into it. Breathe! It is what it is and let it go. This too shall pass.

We can even see this law in the cycles of economies. There is a high period then a low period. Think of the seasons, all of which form a full year. Each season has its own purpose and function but is a vital part of

"Everything flows, out and in; everything has its tides; all things rise and fall; the pendulum-swing manifests in everything; the measure of the swing to the right is the measure of the swing to the left; rhythm compensates."

THE KYBALION

the full circle. If you track women's menstrual cycles or the moon's cycle, both are guided by a constant flow of evolving emotions, cleansing, and regeneration.

Trust the universe's rhythm. It governs our economy, health, relationships, and spirituality. What seems to be random is very orderly. Let's say you're at peak potential with your health and fitness. If you realise you're at the peak, then you can expect your health and fitness will drop a little sometime soon in the future.

However, instead of viewing this "drop in health" as something being wrong with you, you now view it as a sign to rest your body. Then, by law, you must grow to a better and higher state of potential.

Masters know how to rise above negative parts of a cycle by never getting too excited or allowing negative things to penetrate their consciousness. The key to success in mastering this law is in balance. Never allow your emotions to swing too far to the left or right.

Learn to harmonise with the higher vibrational energies you seek to attract. Raise your vibration through the understanding and practice of the other universal laws and harmonise with those higher energies. Meditation is a means many use to connect their energy to their source and as a result, they maintain "higher frequencies." That sense of connection throughout the day to the universe's natural pull, ebbs and flows.

Law of Gender

The Law of Gender states everything has its masculine (yang) and feminine (yin) principles, and these are the basis for all creation in the Universe. All things require space, time, and nurturing to grow. This law tells us when we plant a seed (masculine) it requires time to grow and manifest (feminine).

This is the law that requires both patience and persistence and tells us not to give up before we reach the goal. As spiritual beings, we must ensure there is a balance between the masculine and feminine energies within us in order for us to become true co-creators with God (whatever you perceive GOD to be) as we require both for life to exist.

We all have cycles where we are predominantly running on masculine energy; strong, fast-paced, powerful, resistant, unemotional, rushed, unbreakable, headstrong, resilient. However, like the law of rhythm suggests, there are also periods where all of us need to get in touch with our Feminine Energy; soft, slow, vulnerable, emotional, gentle, nurturing, love, self-love, and awareness.

Both energies, yin and yang, are needed to look after ourselves in health to prevent burn out, to connect and relate to others to nurture our relationships which, together, helps businesses thrive.

Chapter Thirteen

How You Do Something is How You Do Everything

How are you feeling? I am so grateful for you and proud of you for honouring yourself to have gotten this far in the book. We have covered so much in such a short space. It is crazy how this stuff isn't taught in schools, yet the one thing I can promise you in this lifetime is you have to spend every single day of the rest of your life with yourself.

Understanding yourself, knowing yourself, and loving yourself, wholly. Honestly, it is the best investment you can make. This will return ten-fold in your relationships, happiness, health, wealth, career, business, and life. I have really tried my best to educate and pass on the research and science to you sprinkled with love, light, and laughter from my own stories. This way you understand how we as humans are all hard wired, yet we also have all these beautiful things that make every one of us different; our experiences, our lenses, our values, and our lessons.

One on my biggest lessons I learned in my life (quite early on) is funnily enough, also one I see come up a lot with my clients. It's probably one of the most powerful lessons I've ever learned in my life, and it applies to every aspect of it.

It is something my mum taught me in primary school. To this day, I apply it to my friendships, my relationship with my partner, my work, and society. It helps me become grounded. It helps me stay focused. It helps me stay humble, and it also helps me live each day authentically.

So, the biggest lesson I've ever learned is not to place your expectations on other people. That might sound really simple, but it has literally taken me years to learn, and yet, I am still working on mastering it. When I was in primary school, so between the ages of eight and twelve years old, I was always that friend who was trying to catch up with all my friends and organise fun stuff. (I'm not sure how many of you guys can relate).

I was always like, "What are you doing this weekend?" or checking in to see if they were ok. I felt like I was always making the effort, and I would get this yucky feeling. Give me some love if you have also felt this, or even if you have got kids of your own and realise your child is that one who's always trying to make all that effort. My inner mean girl/the dark passenger would sit on my shoulder taunting me saying things like *Oh, they don't want to hang out with me. How come they don't make the effort?* Or, *How come they don't reach out to come see me?*

It is because they don't like you, Lauren. It was something that was coming up a lot for me growing up and my mum tried to create the space to teach me not to place my expectations onto other people and discipline my disappointments.

Just because I wanted to be a "good friend" didn't mean I could then place that expectation on others to treat me the same way. Understanding that even more meant coming to the realisation it wasn't about them "not being a good friend" at all. It was more about my expectation I placed on myself that I needed to be "a good friend" and my definition of that. The way I measured that through my cultured lenses, was to make that effort, or by reaching out or checking in and being concerned with their feelings and how they're going.

But that doesn't mean those expectations I placed on myself and that meaning I gave to the word "good friend" was universal or it was then fair to place them on somebody else. That is where I would then get that yucky feeling of insecurity, doubt, and rejection because I would start measuring myself. I'd start comparing and making assumptions like *Oh, they don't value this friendship as much as I do. They don't want to hang out with me,* or, *They don't enjoy our time together as much as I do.*

That frustration is just misplaced expectations. As I was getting older, it was funny because this lesson kept coming up for me in my relationships, whether it was at school, in sports, with colleagues, and with my high school boyfriend. As I got older, the value I used to measure friendship with was "loyalty."

I am one of those friends, if you need something, I will be there. If I say I'll do something, I will do it. If I make a promise to you, I will do everything in my power to uphold it. I am a woman of my word, and I would be a loyal friend. If somebody did something or said something about my friend or partner, I would be one of those people that would stand up for them because loyalty is something really important to me and how I measured my relationships.

When the roles were reversed and I would hear something would happen or something was said about me, I would get this icky feeling. Oh Lordy, young girls can be sooo bitchy in school. I'd be so hurt to find some people wouldn't do the same for me as I would do for them. Then my mum would have to remind me, "Remember, they are your expectations you placed on yourself, they didn't ask that of you. You don't do those things just so you can expect that back from other people."

It is funny because it is such a simple lesson in theory, but as you learn this and understand it and apply it, you see it come up and play out in so many areas of your life. Even now, fifteen years on, I am still learning in business, in friendships, in marriage, as a parent, as a person in society. Life is about what you give, not what you get.

It's about learning the universal laws and principles and understanding you don't give to receive. Life is not about tit for tat. You don't be a good friend because you're expecting them to do that back for you. You don't be a good parent because you expect your child then owes it to you to be a good child.

> The real reason you show up and give your time, energy, respect, and love is self-serving.

You don't be a good member of society and expect others to then show up and advocate for the same projects and causes you do. You give because you want to give, because you want to be a good person who upholds to the values and expectations you place on yourself.

The reason you go above and beyond for those people and those causes is because they are things that are important to you. The real reason you show up and give your time, energy, respect, and love is self-serving. It is to make sure you're living in alignment with your values so you can look yourself in the mirror and be proud of who you are, what you stand for, and your efforts.

It is because you want to believe *you are* that kind of person. You want to be that kind of friend/partner/citizen/employer/boss. That is something that's important to you and you don't want to look back with regret wondering *what if I had…*

This lesson continues to come up for me as a reminder to put myself back in check. Even recently, there has been a person in my life who I go above and beyond for. I care for them. I want to do everything in my power to be there for them, yet when I've needed them, they haven't been there.

An opportunity can come up for me to be there for them, and it is really easy for us to catch ourselves saying to ourselves, *No. They wouldn't do that for me. They wouldn't be there for me,* or, *They've never done that for me.* But it's about realising it is not about them, it is about you. Who do you want to be? How do you want to show up in the world?

For an example, let's say you're a mum and wife and you've gone away for a trip for work. Your partner has had a really testing week at his work this week whilst also trying to juggle the kids while you've been away. You can sense it in his voice on the phone he's tired and stressed. Meanwhile, you're sarcastically thinking in your head, *welcome to my world buddy. This is my reality every day juggling work, the house, and the kids.*

You want to do something nice for him, so you buy him a gift at the airport knowing he never does that for you, but that's not the point. You want to show him you love him and appreciate him. You do this because you want to do something nice for him because that is the person you want to be.

Just because he doesn't do those things for you doesn't mean he isn't a nice person, love, or appreciate you. He just shows his appreciation and affection in other ways and measures it differently. There is a great book called *The 5 love languages* that is a whole book devoted to help you understand this theory more in relationships. I won't go into detail in it here, but that is another great one to pop on your list if this is something you find you struggle to understand and accept in your own relationships.

You do what you do not because it's what others would do for you, it's because what you want to do for yourself. I remembered the person I wanted to be, and that loyalty is something really high on my values list and being a good friend and person in general.

I think about what I would want to happen to me. It doesn't mean they would do that for me or be that person for me, but what kind of person do I want to be? How do I want to show up in the world? What kind of friend do I want to be to my friends?

> I owe that loyalty and alignment to myself, not to spite.

I owe that loyalty and alignment to myself, not to spite. When something is coming up for you, check in and see if these are expectations placed on you by others or by yourself. When you have expectations, admittedly, that is when you give yourself the opportunity to be let down or disappointed. If they are self-imposed, it's also an opportunity to make yourself proud of how you showed up.

Remember not to place your expectations on other people whether it is in romantic relationships, in your friendship circles, in the workplace, or just in wider society. Especially when you find you are getting frustrated because someone is not doing things to your standard or they're not returning you the favour or treating you how you treated them.

You live up to your expectations. You live up to your values. And you do that because that's what you need to do to be proud of yourself and to wake up with intention and integrity and be in alignment with your values. My biggest lesson, it's something I apply every single day, is to give my best anyway; to try not to place my expectations on other people (because I am not perfect and still catch myself doing that).

Remember, everybody thinks differently. Everyone regulates emotions differently. Everyone shows emotions differently. Everybody has different values, so make sure you're living in alignment with yours.

Working in child protection, I've definitely had struggles with my world view, my expectations of myself and those I placed on others, and my understanding of humanity. Each day (as most people do) I learn from experience and self-reflection.

There are big discrepancies between what I know, what I have personally experienced, and what I see and hear. It is usually your voids that lead to your values. For example, those who suffer injustice often work in helping serve justice, whether as a police officer or lawyer. Those who were bullied at school or struggled to find a place where they belonged often work in the educational system to help children know they are enough.

Similarly, a lot of people have the perception to be a Life Coach you must have gone through something pretty traumatic to motivate others on how to overcome triumph and achieve success. Sorry, but no sob story here. I won't lie to you. That was one of my strengths as a Child Safety Officer and as a Life Coach. I am transparent.

Like I explained earlier, I come from a normal upbringing for a young, white girl, living in a nuclear family unit in the western world (and for that, I am already more privileged than most). However, I can vouch that all my successes I have achieved on my own, nothing was handed to me.

I know the value of hard work and independence. Well, at least that is what I used to say to myself.

I have done a lot, seen a lot, and know a lot for my age. I used to take pride in the fact I did it on my own. However, since working in Child Protection, I realised something different.

My Story

My Mum and Dad taught me good things come to those who wait and if you wanted something you had to earn it. Even before my first job I had to do chores, babysit and help my mum clean offices to receive pocket money. This amount was small, so I started my first job at fourteen (with a letter of consent from my parents that I could work under the legal age of fourteen and nine months). I bought my first car, studied hard, and got my High School Certificate.

I was the first person in my family to be accepted into a university, let alone even apply. I gained a scholarship for university. I moved fourteen hours away from everyone and everything I had ever known at eighteen. I worked four jobs. I wasn't eligible for government assistance, so I paid my own bills.

I studied hard, gaining myself another scholarship, which enabled me to study overseas and travel. I finished my degree and got into Honours, which lead me to a Graduate position working in the Queensland Government's Child Protection Services.

As I try to shorten my life story in a paragraph in my attempt to explain; I am not a stranger to hard work. But working with families in Child Protection, I came to realise I didn't do it by myself. Yes, I looked those scary dreams in the eye and went in for battle. However, I was never alone.

I have always had the support of a loving mum, dad, and two younger brothers. A nuclear family unit within itself is a gift. So many today come from broken families and homes, being brought up by a single parent, being traumatised by sour separations and divorce. They're carrying around guilt that maybe it was them or maybe they weren't worthy of love, which is why they never knew one or both of their parents. Then they carry that heavy story on their back throughout their journey of life which affects the tint of the glasses they see the world through.

> In this world there are alot of things that are out of our control, but our actions aren't one of them.

From a young age, my parents encouraged me to be whoever I wanted to be. I could go wherever I wanted to go, I could achieve whatever I could dream. To their dismay, I don't think they anticipated I would have been chasing those dreams so fast. In this world there are a lot of things that are out of our control, but our actions aren't one of them.

Don't get me wrong, my childhood wasn't sheltered, and like most, I somehow survived unscathed. Like most kids I battled the schoolyard demons. Having buckteeth in primary school didn't make it easy to avoid the bullies. I think it's from those experiences I learned young that people's actions and words weren't a reflection of who I was.

It didn't make a difference how pure my intentions were or how nice I was; they would act like that regardless. I had no control over it. It reflected their reality. All I could do was to have control over my actions. This is a lesson I teach in my practice today. For a few years it seemed I was in a scene from the movie "Mean Girls." Despite being fearful of catching the school bus with these bullies and having some nasty girls in my year at school, I put my head down and studied hard at school. After 3pm, I would invest myself in a different area and a different group of friends. I am so grateful to have had some beautiful friends who remain my soul sisters to this day and walked me down the aisle on my wedding day.

This lead me to true friendships and what became my outlet for years – dancing. From here, I kept building on my perspective of the world, becoming more accepting, positive, and at peace with my place in it. I had the self-confidence instilled from family.

I had a sense of autonomy and mastery having had the space and opportunities by my parents to grow and test myself. I knew my self-worth because a loved one never treated me badly. Let me note, I wasn't dating yet; those heartbreaks were yet to come!

You are not your past.

I am not saying you need to come from a loving childhood to achieve success. I am not saying for your future to be bright you can't have scars from the past. And I definitely do not believe your past defines you, otherwise I would not be working in the area I am.

I am saying, understanding the effect of having a loving childhood or having support or the lack of from family can help comprehend the differences. This is why some are having trouble achieving the same goals as others later in life or living to different social standards or holding different values.

For one, a goal may be to expand on their investment portfolio. To another, it might just be to look in the mirror and not hate the person they see. It might be to last a whole week sober, to understand why they self-sabotage every relationship they enter, or to understand why their parents struggle to show them love. Behaviours are reflections of beliefs.

> *I am not saying you need to come from a loving childhood to achieve success. I am not saying for your future to be bright you can't have scars from the past.*

People's pasts and upbringings affect the thoughts, beliefs, and values they have. The unhelpful ones in particular, self-limiting beliefs, are the ones that cause the most disruptive behaviours and resistance. But the good news is, that's all they are; beliefs. They are not your reality. They can be challenged and changed.

If you could believe in Santa for fifteen years, you can learn to believe in yourself, girlfriend! For outsiders, you need to understand behaviours are reflections of people's beliefs. If someone is not respecting their bodies, their health, or is allowing others to treat them badly, they need someone to remind them of their self-worth. Encourage them to believe in themselves.

If this is you, I hope this book is helping you to understand why you think the way you do. Why you behave the way you do, why you feel the way you do, and even better, how you can think, feel, and act differently! Two of the biggest contributors and predictors of success in life, relationships, business, and sports research has found is Emotional Intelligence and Grit (passion matched by perseverance).

As I have explained earlier, neither are dictated nor predetermined by circumstances such as heritage, race, gender, age, or socio-economic status. We can strengthen both with strategies provided in this book and resources referred to, to continue to build those muscles and increase your score of those traits!

Only YOU have control over that. How daunting and refreshing all at the same time! Want something different? Teach yourself to think something different! You may not have had control over some situations and circumstances that moulded you into the person you are today, but you have control over who you grow into and how you show up.

> You may not have control over some situations
>
> that moulded you into the person you are today,
>
> but you have control over who you grow into.

People are not their behaviours

Accept people. Assist them in changing their beliefs to change their behaviour. I'm often asked how I worked in child protection and that was my secret; I wholeheartedly accept every one of my clients. I didn't judge them; I heard their story, and they were more than enough.

I was often told I was naïve by people working outside of the system because we would see the best in people. I didn't believe a dad who would abuse his children was a bad person. I believed he was a troubled person fighting his own demons, not that that condemns his actions.

I wouldn't believe a mum who would constantly return to a domestic violent relationship and put her children at risk was a bad person. Don't get me wrong, I would get frustrated. It would keep me up worrying all night I'd wake up and it be one of those cases I hear on the news where another mother had been killed by her spouse. But I also knew she had low self-worth and limited support, skills, and resources to think she could do life alone.

> I strongly believe that there is no such thing as an unresourceful person, just an unresourceful mind.

I strongly believe there is no such thing as an unresourceful person, just an unresourceful mind. People do the best they can with the knowledge and resources they have available at that given time. Cut people slack. We, as humans, can be so self-righteous and quick to judge others thinking our own shit doesn't stink.

But I understand why, like I explained earlier. Our brain has developed shortcuts called heuristics, which help the brain to not have to analyse every single piece of information we expose it to. There are some cognitive biases that come into play which, when you come aware of and can understand, can help you have a more objective view of the world and the people in it.

There is the Self-Serving Bias:
This is the tendency to blame external forces when bad things happen and give yourself credit when good things happen. For example, when you have one of the biggest months ever in your business with customers you conclude it is because you were on your A-game. You showed up every day with the right attitude and created an awesome promo. While when you have one of your worst months you say it is because of the time of the year or your team not working hard enough.

Attentional Bias:
This is the tendency to pay attention to some things while simultaneously ignoring others. For example, when deciding whether you think Sally is a good friend you may pay attention to the fact she rarely calls you or reaches out to organise to catch up. But you ignore the fact she has never forgotten your birthday. And when your mum had a heart attack, she dropped everything in her life to be there for you and helped with the kids' school pick-ups and drop-offs and cooking.

Actor-Observer Bias:
This is the tendency to attribute your own actions to external causes while attributing other people's behaviours to internal causes. For example, you forgave yourself when you snapped at your colleague and spoke abruptly attributing it to the fact you had a bad day and "we are all human." But when your boss snaps at you, instead of giving them the grace of understanding they may have had a bad day and going through their own dramas, you attribute it was because they are a self-absorbed and thoughtless person.

People may think I am naïve because I can see the best in people. I give everyone the benefit of the doubt and forgive quickly. BUT I think it's because I understand these cognitive biases and how quickly our brain tries to put ourselves on a pedestal and everyone else in a pit.

What is in you is in me, and vice versa. Yes, some people do sad, spiteful, and hurtful things. But truth be told, we are all capable of doing those things and I bet some of us secretly have.

You can't expect a bird that has been caged for its whole life to one day, when the gate is left open, fly free and survive. But I assure you, slowly, and with support and encouragement and the desire, it might.

We all need a little support and a little understanding.

CHAPTER FOURTEEN

Living with Intention; Choose to Thrive, Not Just Survive

Now, it wouldn't be a book about unlocking the code to success in life, relationships, and business without a chapter on health. As you know by now, I am all about creating magical moments, living life on your terms, making an impact, and doing something constructive with our short time here. Have fun in pursuing your goals and mastering how to harness the power we hold in our mindset.

Which is also why I am a massive believer in investing in your body, in your health, and your future, because, guess what? That is where you will spend most of your time. How can you help and support your kids or make an impact in wider society or the world if you're not here?

Some of the best days of your life are yet to happen and your body is the only way you'll get there to enjoy them, so you need to look after it! When people think of health, I know for some; they think of boring, green kale smoothies, boring food like chicken, broccoli and rice for lunch and dinner and having a gym membership, right? Wrong!

Well, for me, anyway. Health is about nourishing the mind, body, and soul with self-love, conscious movement, and wholefoods. A massive love of mine is supporting people to make small but sustainable healthy lifestyle choices for a happy heart, head, and body. So much comes into play when we are talking about holistic health.

My health and wellness journey so far. (Because we never truly arrive.)

I guess my awareness of health and wellness didn't really start for me until when I was eighteen. I had just moved to the Gold Coast all starry-eyed; I was really excited.

It was the first time I had ever moved away from home. I was always an active girl. I loved dancing. I always loved running. I loved my netball. I never ever thought about my skin, my diet, or having to consciously "work out." I was a very lucky teenager.

I didn't have any of those struggles. I just lived an active lifestyle, and so when I moved to the Gold Coast, I was fortunate to be welcomed by some gorgeous girls I met through dancing, who are now some of my best friends. I got sucked into the dancing world up here, and I had so much fun. I loved it!

It probably wasn't until about six months in, I had my very first real heartbreak. That was when things with the high school boyfriend got sour and I realised my happily ever after didn't exist, well, not with him, anyway. The universe secretly had just flown my prince charming over from the UK but was deliberate to not place him on my path for another two years until I was loving myself again and able to receive love in return.

I'm sure all of us girls, or boys, you have had it or will have one of these at some point in your life. Life isn't all sunshine and rainbows. I had my very first heartbreak. The faith destroying one that turns your life up on its head and makes you doubt everything you have believed about the world, including your own existence. Suddenly, all these things started happening to my body that I had never had an issue with before. (On top of the sexy cold sores in and around my mouth and all over my face induced by the stress).

I've always been a naturally slim girl, but suddenly, I just started to pile on weight. It was over a period of about four or five months I put on about ten kilos. Anybody who's seen my journey can vouch for this. You can see my photos. My face got bloated, the only bonus was my boobs seem to magically grow to a double D overnight. Winning!

But in all seriousness, I just got bigger all over. It was so odd because nothing had changed in my diet or exercise. In the dancing world, I was surrounded by all these other beautiful women who were a few years older than me and really into their health.

They were going to the gym, counting calories, and weighing their food. I had never been introduced to that world before, but suddenly, I thought, *Oh my God. I have to do these things. I've blown out. What is this?* I forced myself to go to the gym. I hated the gym. I've never been somebody who loves the gym.

Then, I started being really conscious of what I was eating. I was restricting myself. I was calling these things "diets", and I've never been one for diets. I've never been more conscious, ever, of what I was putting into my mouth and I started exercising excessively.

Like I said, I've always been somebody who's really active and I did it because I loved it. I loved running because I loved clearing my mind, getting in the "flow", focusing on my breath, and getting out in the sunshine. I danced because I loved losing myself in the music (and secretly, I was good at it!). But suddenly, I went to the gym or running more to punish myself.

It wasn't coming from a place of love; it was coming from a place of fear. I started running to punish myself. I was like, *Oh my God. I ate this massive bowl of pasta last night. I'll have to run for fifteen KM tomorrow.*

It became an obsession; it consumed me. It consumed my life. And it consumed how I thought. It got to a point where I was even avoiding going to social outings because I was scared I wouldn't have the self-control not to indulge. I love cheese, biscuits, and cocktails. *Espresso Martinis are life!*

It got to a point where the waves of guilt that followed would far outweigh the enjoyment of a dinner or drinks with the girls. It was odd because it was the healthiest I have ever eaten. It was the most I've ever exercised, yet it was the biggest I had ever been, but, more importantly, *it was the unhappiest I have ever felt.*

I was like, *what is going on?* I thought, *this doesn't make any sense to me.* And then, it triggered a series of events. First, it was my weight, but then it was my skin. I've never had issues with skin. I was really lucky. I went through all my teenage years never having issues with my skin, and suddenly, it flared up!

I had all these random lumps all over my face, everywhere. It was acne, and I spent so much time and energy going to so many different skin specialists. Not to mention the thousands of dollars I spent as a poor uni-student trying to find a solution! I tried ProActiv. If anyone's used ProActiv before, you look at your towel! Give me some love, whoever shared this skin journey, because man, is it painful!

You look at your towel and it is bleached. If that's what it can do to a towel, I cannot imagine the damage it is doing to our delicate skin on our face. I tried dozens of things before resorting to Roaccutane. So, if anybody who doesn't know what Roaccutane is, it's a prescription drug I got from the doctors.

It's so strong it's illegal for them to give it to you if you aren't on some kind of form of contraception because if you fall pregnant, your babies are at risk of coming into the world deformed. That's how strong that drug is. Every month, or every six weeks, you would have to get a blood test to make sure it wasn't causing you kidney failure. That's how extreme the drugs were that doctors were giving me to try to fix my skin.

I felt like I was going around in a circle. I was upset. I was full of resentment and hurt and just all these heavy, heavy feelings of this heartbreak that I went through at this time of my life. My weight blew up. I couldn't get control of my skin, and I felt like I was just spending thousands of dollars on all these products, drugs, and treatments recommended by different health professionals telling me, "You need to try this. No, now you need to try this." But one professional would give me one drug that would help with one symptom of something but would then cause something else. That meant spending more money on a different drug to help with the next symptoms caused by that side effect. It was just bandaging one thing over another.

For an example, I was never fat. I may have been larger than my seventeen-year-old self, but I was never someone you could honestly look at and think I was overweight. The new weight just wasn't what I had always known, or others had known to be my figure.

When my skin broke out and they put me on Roaccutane, I also had to go on contraception, so the Doctor put me on the pill. The pill caused me to put on even more weight despite the fact I was eating minimally and exercising excessively. On top of the heartbreak and some serious self-loathing and negative self-talk, I was getting told that, in the dancing world, if I wanted any more gigs, I had to lose weight. This was my main source of income when I was studying.

Having this at eighteen, having something I was personally working through while being broken was soul crushing. I no longer had the support of my high school sweetheart, and my support network of close friends and family were over fourteen hours away. And then having something that used to be so fun to me being told I had to lose weight, especially when I wasn't overweight. I was lucky to weigh 65 kg!

I went to the doctors and they gave me prescription drug, Duromine. Anyone who doesn't know what Duromine is, it's a like legalised ecstasy. It's a drug doctors sometimes give to obese people to suppress their appetite.

Who does that? Although I admit I wasn't in the mental head space to treat myself with love, I asked for the drugs. But who gives them to a lost, unstable, eighteen-year-old girl who is in a healthy weight range?

That just played into my mind games. And then, like I said, my skin went to shit. I tried everything. I was then put on a different contraception pill as the pill aggravated my skin even more (I'm sorry to the guys reading this. I promised I wouldn't sugarcoat anything in this book). Then, I was like, okay, so they gave me Roaccutane for my skin, which meant I needed to be on the pill. This made me put more weight on, so they popped me on Duromine to lose the weight, which gave me anxiety.

Roaccutane made my face go so dry. My lips were cracking and bleeding. I was in so much pain (physically and psychologically). Anyone who has had bad skin, I know it sounds dramatised now, but unless you were in that position, it totally kills your self-esteem!

I remember not wanting to go out anywhere. I'd never leave the house without foundation on. It would hurt to dance with sweat and make-up for gigs. I would start saying no to social events because I thought in certain lights you could see all the marks on my skin, even though I tried to hide it under make-up.

I remember, I have this distinct memory (and I'm sure I have friends who can vouch for it), where my skin was so dry. That's what this drug does to your skin. It dries out your oil glands. I was now nineteen and my girlfriends and I went on this beautiful yacht out on the ocean.

Everyone was giving me a new Band-Aid thing

that would fix one problem

but yet create another one.

It was a beautiful day, we should have been carefree, happy. But I remember being in so much pain because of the salt in my skin, bleeding lips and being so self-conscious of all these girls around me who were so happy and carefree. I couldn't have my cake of make-up in the water and in the sun. I was in so much pain and just crying, thinking, *these are supposed to be the best days of my life. How come I'm so unhappy? How come this hurts so much?*

There's just got to be more to life than punishing my body, hating my body, and ultimately hating myself being full of anxiety and self- loathing. I just thought, there has to be. *Why? Why am I getting all this different advice?* Everyone was giving me a new Band-Aid thing that would fix one problem but yet create another one.

And then, what they don't tell you is that if you've got HPV virus (human papillomavirus) the contraceptive pill can aggravate the virus which puts you at high risk for cervical cancer. I found out later in life this is a story known far too well by many women as most women carry the virus. However, it lies dormant.

In 2002, the International Agency for Research on Cancer published a review that found a strong presence of cervical pre-cancers and cancers among HPV-positive women who used the pill consistently for five years or longer. Research since then has backed it up.

So, to top it all off, they ended up finding cervical cancer C3 cells on my cervix, and I ended up going through two years of procedures trying to get that all cleared. That was what prevented me from passing the medical to get into the Army, which, at that point in my life, was my aspiration to work as a psychologist.

I remember thinking, *what am I failing to learn here?* It was the most health conscious I've ever been, yet the unhealthiest and unhappiest I've ever been. From here, I decided to work on me and ironically, packed my bags and moved to Hawaii, where I knew no one, to rebuild myself and redefine myself.

I took myself off all pharmaceuticals and just got back to basics. Which is where I finally met the happiness and healthiest version of me, who had so much love to give and was worthy of that love in return. On a more positive note, when I look back on this chapter of my life, one amazing memory sticks out I will never forget and will always be truly grateful for. It's one of those moments I will remember with a smile when I am eighty, rocking in my rocking chair and reflecting on life.

When I was emotionally and mentally exhausted and officially hit rock bottom, I lost interest, passion, and drive for everything that once lit me up – *fun, dancing, running, food, friends, or learning.* My best friend I'd made on the Gold Coast through dancing and her mum (who became and still are my adopted family up here who I love so dearly) were really worried about me. They'd phoned my mum and helped organise her flying up to surprise me without me knowing.

Mum stayed with me for a week. She helped me get out of bed in the morning and reminded me to eat. Even though it hurt to as by this time the stress had resulted in cold sores all over my lips, chin, and in my mouth. She didn't tell me to feel better. She gave me permission to cry, swear, and be angry at the world and feel what I was feeling.

I remember she turned all the lights off in my apartment. She brought Cher's album up from Albury and she tuned up Cher's song "Strong Enough" full ball! (I am such an oldie at heart. Totally born in the wrong era when it comes to music.)

Before I knew it, we were dancing around in the dark and screaming at the top of our lungs with so much emotion of anger and hurt that had been building up inside of me. *"'Cause I'm strong enough to live without you, strong enough and I quit crying. Long enough, now I'm strong enough, to know you gotta go! There's no more to say, so save your breath and then walk away. No matter what I hear you say, I'm strong enough to know you gotta go!"*

We had it on repeat until light started to creep in, weight started to lift. A smile started to creep across my face with an immense feeling of gratitude for this beautiful woman I was so blessed to have as my mum. Someone who would do some crazy shit and risk looking like a complete nut case just to make me feel better. I will forever be grateful for this moment. I honestly believe it saved me.

Reflecting on this chapter of my life, I learned there isn't much in this world that a shoulder to cry on, a good boogie, and sing-along to Cher can't fix! But in all seriousness, I didn't really understand what was going on until years later when I teamed up with my own team of health and wellness gurus collaborating in our own online holistic health program!

We each have our own expertise and resources to nourish the mind, body, and soul. We've come together sharing the same love for advocating and educating others about holistic and preventative health and explaining what's really going on. This way, we can empower others to make informed decisions for themselves and for their loved ones with no Band-Aid effects or quick fixes, just self-love, conscious movement, and wholefoods.

One of the biggest things I have learned from our gorgeous team of health professionals is, even more so, the power the mindset has. For example, I now know everything I was experiencing, all those symptoms were stress related. There's no pharmaceutical drug that can fix any of that.

It had to come from within. I was filled with so much resentment, so much anger, so much pain, and I was just suppressing it. I had so much negative self-talk that was feeding my body and causing it to attack itself, and I was looking for all these quick fixes to fix it.

Autoimmune diseases; this is just a perfect example of what research has found. Stress is one of the biggest causes of autoimmune diseases, which causes your body to attack itself. Stress is one of the biggest contributors to all lifestyle diseases!

I witnessed my mum nearly die from a heart attack a few years ago. The cardiac specialist explained it was brought on by stress after watching her mum in her last hours before she passed away from Alzheimer's and dementia disease. Still to this day, it's one of the most traumatising days of my life. Images of her being airlifted to the hospital and my dad and brothers crying at the emergency room as they watched mum helplessly still haunt me yet remind me of the fragility of life.

We're primitive, we're animals. We've evolved from animals. So, when you're stressed, your body gets in a fight-or-flight response mode. Whatever stress it is, a heartbreak, financial stresses, relationship stresses, work stresses, or you're stressed from the daily hustle of just being on the go, go, go, go, go, your body is full of adrenaline. It's getting ready to fight and ticks over into the red zone.

Because of that, it's also getting ready to conserve. This dates back from the Stone Ages when we weren't sure when the winter would come, when we would eat again, or when we're getting threatened, our body stores fat. Our body holds onto our fat in fear it doesn't know when it is getting food next.

It doesn't matter what you're eating; it doesn't matter how much you're exercising, but if you're in that red zone and you're full of adrenaline and you're in that fight of flight mode, your body is storing your fat.

Now, when I look back, I'm like, *how come none of those health professionals told me I needed to work on my stress? Maybe to try some meditation to get out of that red zone to decrease my anxiety and cortisol levels. How come none of them told me I needed to work on my self-love?*

How come none of them told me it really started within? That I can take this drug and I take that drug, but it will only Band-Aid that and it will cause this effect? Nobody told me about that.

Friendly Reminder: It's perfectly ok if the only exercise you get today is flipping the pages of a book or stirring your tea or smiling with friends. Wellbeing means your WHOLE body. Make sure your soul is getting as much exercise as your glutes!

Now, I appreciate my journey (including the heartbreak) because now I can understand it. I can share and teach other people that, whatever your health and wellness goals, your physical health all comes hand-in-hand with your psychological, and the first place you need to start is on you.

It is funny I don't exercise as much now. I don't eat as well as I did then, but this is the healthiest and happiest I have ever been, looked, or felt, and a massive part of that shift has been understanding and honouring health being holistic.

Fill every weekend with reasons to celebrate with yummy, nutritious food, great drinks, and even better company. And with good reason. We should celebrate health, happiness, and lessons. For me personally, I am a sucker for a cheese platter and a Tia Maria with Coke! But now you can understand that it hasn't always been like that and I have done a lot of inner work to get to this place and relationship with myself.

Historically, being a girl in the western culture, we have been valued for our cosmetic make-up (and again, this is backed by evolutionary psychology as women are hardwired to use appearance to attract a mating partner). I know! I know! We have come a long way. Women and men have both fought for women's rights, now being more widely accepted and valued for our minds, our nature and our being.

However, this is even complicated again by the massive presence of social media. I have read a lot of arguments from both sides advocating for and against the pressure of social media on women's self-esteem, and they both have very good points. Social media can manipulate and taunt your ego but *only if you allow it to.*

We all know better, *on our best days*. It takes a strong-willed, confident, wise, and content woman to consciously resist the influence and temptation to compare themselves to the photo-shopped and filtered images of the ideal woman. They seem to be plastered everywhere these days; TV, movies, magazine, Facebook, Instagram, billboards, etc.

But who are these confident, invincible women? Sure, we are all her on our best days. We know and acknowledge that photo was probably her 50th attempt of sucking in, poking her ass out, and playing with the filter effects! But, we all have days where we feel inadequate; where we feel we fall short and we buy into the comparison game (even if you are that girl others are comparing themselves to), and that is ok. It has a lot to do with the evolution of our psyche, which I explained in that chapter earlier about being how we measure up to others in our tribe in fear of rejection.

I have been there.

Food is your friend

Not only am I a girl in the 21st century who has Instagram and Facebook to turn to for regular reminders of all the amazingly beautiful women out there to celebrate. But I am also a dancer who, out of all places, lives on the Gold Coast. I have been in the industry where I have been told I was too big.

I have been told before if I wanted more work, I would need to lose weight. I have been surrounded by the culture of girls experimenting with laxatives, prescription drugs, and discussions of the easiest ways to bring your food back up.

I have been surrounded by the lifestyle of weighing food portions and strict routines of eating, gym, sleep, repeat. I am a big advocate for a healthy lifestyle, but not when it consumes you.

It is a poisonous mindset.

I felt the more I focused on weight, the harder it was to lose it. In hindsight, I wish I knew about the effect women's hormones and contraception can have on weight. Punishing myself for something outside of my control did not help. I hated the gym but did it because I thought that is what I needed to do.

==I am a big advocate for a healthy lifestyle but not when it consumes you.==

I ate a bland, boring diet. I would get jealous of girls eating whatever they wanted because I knew I couldn't do that without experiencing a heavy weight of guilt. I deliberately committed to volunteering, three jobs and uni, so it wasn't even possible for me to attend these social events and be tempted by unhealthy choices.

It was a poisonous mindset that dominated every second of every day and dictated every decision I made. I was lucky; I realised early and made the changes I deserved. The fact I could recall a time of my life that I didn't think like that was enough motivation for me to do something about my mindset and self-talk.

Part of me felt my thinking habits were instinctual, normal. Like every girl thought like that, but slowly, I came to the realisation I was very wrong. There is so much more to life than continuously monitoring my intake and experiencing waves of guilt.

Food is your friend!

Now, I am not opening myself up for fire. I understand these symptoms I described earlier probably was the early onset of an eating disorder. Those who suffer such painful and sad diseases can't be magically cured by reading this book. They need the long-term support of a mental health practitioner.

I am not naïve, and I also understand this is not an issue that affects solely women. I acknowledge I am no diet or nutrition expert. However, I know about psychology, challenging, and changing perspective to experience gratitude, mindfulness and a healthy relationship with food and exercise.

Food *should* be your friend! Eating something yummy literally makes you happy by releasing endorphins and creating serotonin. Our culture, like so many others, is built around sharing food, drinks, and laughter with friends and family. We need food to fuel our body. It's imperative you build a healthy relationship with food, not only for your happiness, but your survival!

Some tips on building a healthy relationship with food and exercise so you can live and enjoy your Life Above Zero.

EAT TO FUEL YOUR MIND, BODY AND SOUL:

First, a conscious effort to incorporate healthy nutritional meals in your diet and limit junk food is great. However, how many of you have started diets? Finished diets? Then gone back to your previous way of eating? I am guessing most of you.

This can be fixed by changing your mindset. Don't limit yourself to a "diet." Don't deny yourselves food that literally makes you happy! Skip the diet, just eat healthy! Eat cookie dough when your heart wants it, and kale salad when your body needs it. A balanced, healthy diet means everything in moderation. Trust me, your mind, body, and soul will thank you.

> Eat cookie dough when your heart wants it,
>
> and kale salad when your body needs it.

BE MINDFUL:

When you are eating, make sure you enjoy each mouthful, savour the taste. Sure, when you are having your favourite ice-cream, you go right ahead and demolish it! You go, Glen Coco, you go! We aren't superheroes, everyone has their kryptonite. But, try to get in a habit of paying attention to your body.

Sit down at a table to eat, rather than eating on the go or while watching TV. Be aware of how your body is feeling. Are you full? Have a glass of water, leave it for ten minutes and give your brain time for your body's messages to register before you go for seconds. Those left overs could be your free lunch tomorrow. Let your body guide you.

BE GRATEFUL FOR WHAT YOU HAVE BEFORE YOU LOSE IT:

Like the relationship you had with your parents before they passed away, or a past friendship or lover lost, don't wait until it's too late before you realise what you have. Do you recall a time where you had even a cold or

"You are the food you eat, the books you read, the films you watch, the music you listen to, the people you meet, the dreams you have, the conversations you engage in. You are what you take from these. You are the sound of the ocean, the breath of fresh air, the brightest light, and the darkest corner, you are a collective of every experience you have had in your life. You are every single second of every single day. So drown yourself in a sea of knowledge and existence.
Let the words run through your veins
and colours in your mind."

ANON

flu and you told yourself you would do anything to be healthy again?

Well, use that same mindset with your body. You only have one, take care of it. Don't exercise to lose weight, don't exercise to get that bikini body, exercise to clear your head. Exercise to release endorphins, exercise to prevent cardiovascular disease, exercise to prevent diabetes, exercise to delay the onset of Alzheimer's.

Exercise is not punishment. It is a gift. There is someone somewhere who lives their life in a wheelchair and would give anything to go for a run. Don't take your ability for granted.

If you don't like it, don't do it! There is no use forcing yourself to go for a run if you hate every minute of it. Likewise, there is no point in dragging yourself to the gym if you don't enjoy yourself! It is so much easier to lead a healthy and active lifestyle when you are honest to yourself and play to your strengths. What do you like?

You hate exercise and find it easier to feed your competitive side, get involved in a team sport. You enjoy the energy and support of a gym, pump some weights. You enjoy the peace and solitude that comes with a morning walk, well put your runners on and enjoy "your time." Remember why you are doing it.

No one is forcing you to exercise. You're doing it because some part of it aligns with your values. You are doing this because you want to; you are doing this for you!

BE KIND TO YOURSELF, YOU ARE HUMAN:

As I spoke earlier regarding the mindset of "diets", you are setting yourself up to be punished. You are setting some distinct rules on what you can and can't do, and no one likes being told what to do! Rules are made to be broken, and as humans, it is in our nature to do exactly that. Otherwise there wouldn't be prisons, divorce, school detentions, or time-outs in the naughty corner!

After you have demolished that whole tub of cookie-dough ice-cream, don't beat yourself up and send yourself off on a guilt trip. I am sure the belly ache will be punishment enough. Instead, acknowledge that was naughty, oh, but so worth it, and maybe wait until the next weekend before you go do it again. That way it still has the novelty of being a treat.

PICK YOUR FRIENDS WISELY:

Choose your friendship, leisure, sporting, and work groups carefully. You have control over what circle you stay in, so make sure you are choosing contexts that support and encourage you to be the best version of you.

I am not sure if it is just a stereotype on the Gold Coast or if it is the impression the rest of Australia also has on the people that live here, but I often used to hear "The Gold Coast is so pretentious. People here are so fake."

Yes, I admit I understand how some people may have that perception, but that results from the environment they are in and the people they are choosing to mingle with. I love dancing, but because of the context that surrounded me for a while, I lost my passion for it.

> If you don't want to spend every weekend following your friend's unhealthy drinking habits, look for friends in different circles.

I consciously left that environment as I very well knew you become a product of your environment, and the values surrounding me no longer reflected ones I stood for. Yes, the Gold Coast has the best nightlife, but it also has the most beautiful beaches and rainforests.

If you don't want to spend every weekend following your friend's unhealthy drinking habits, look for friends in different circles. Put on your runners, and go for a hike, go stand-up paddle boarding.

Fill your friendship circles with healthy influences, people who pick you up, motivate you, remind you of your worth, and support your mind, body, and soul.

LEAD BY EXAMPLE:

Women, we are our biggest critics. It is very rare that you hear a man putting a woman down for her weight, eating, or exercise habits. We are the ones (the majority of the time) making a snide remark. "Have you seen her in real life? She is fat." "She's skinny-fat, she's not toned." "She would have the perfect body if she had an ass." "She is not even that pretty," etc. And the list goes on.

Have you heard the quote "girls compete with each other, women empower one another?" Once again, I don't agree with insulting a woman's maturity, but it is true to a certain extent. With experience, wisdom, and self-love, women realise competing with someone is just playing into your insecurities. You are beautiful. Every woman is beautiful, and this is *because* our bodies look different, our minds think different, and our souls yearn for different things.

To help other women and to do your part in changing women's mindsets, every once in a while, upload a photo of yourself or your girlfriends without a filter or any edits. Lead by example. Show other women it is ok to be you, the real authentic you (freckles, stretchmarks, and all)!

When you hear another woman critiquing/commenting on another's body, I don't advise you attack her or even instigate a heated debate. What about just commenting on something you love about her, rather than joining in on the slamming? Demonstrate to other women what supporting women looks like, so they can learn to do the same.

Lead by example, and hopefully with enough leaders leading the self-love movement and consciously resisting the urge to feed the ego. Instead, choosing to feed their mind, body, and soul, others will be encouraged and taught to do the same.

Simplifying Health

I remember after returning from a trip from Cuba a few years ago just after the embargo was lifted, feeling refreshed and enlightened. It was an awakening realising how fast-paced and complex our lives are compared to time-warped Cuba!

When did we get in such a hurry? When we went to Cuba, most did not have internet or TV, most did not have computers, laptops etc. It's crazy to think maybe Australia was like this sixty years ago. Without those distractions, our hosts would prepare fresh food with love, and eat the feast together as a family. Then they all sit on their porch, not locked inside with their eyes glued to a screen with little to no communication with their loved ones or guests.

If you go down any streets in Cuba, especially in Viñales, everyone has a

"Women really can have it all; they can have wealth, they can have health, and they can have abundance, but in the pursuit of achieving these things – it doesn't mean having more than the woman next to you. One woman's success is not another woman's failure."

CARA ALWILL LEYBA

rocking chair on their front porch. As you walk down the street, you will see lots of your neighbours sitting in their rocking chair, waving at the people driving. Or they'd walk by with the kids outside playing on the street or with their next-door neighbour, instead of playing video games.

That was so refreshing to see, and not having internet meant my partner and I were definitely out of our comfort zone! We don't speak Spanish well, so we had to trust humanity, and literally ask complete strangers for advice every day. We had to trust they're telling us the truth and not manipulating us for their own gain.

When do we do that anymore? Why do we second guess everything? In the Western world, we make things so complex. But in terms of our health and happiness, it really is simple; we need to get right back to the basics. We need to stop complicating things.

It's sad, but nearly everyone I personally know and the clients I work with are overwhelmed, overworked, overfed, yet undernourished. We are bombarded with so many options and so much information, we throw our hands up in the air and give up.

Let me simplify it for you. If you're feeling grumpy, unfulfilled, lethargic, stagnant, in a slump, do at least one, if not all the following things:

1) **Drink more water!**

2) **Put love back into your food.** Eat more Wholefoods! We're overfed, and we're under nourished. We're eating all these foods made of chemicals we can't pronounce and go on these fad diets looking for these quick fixes. We count calories and starve ourselves instead of just simplifying it and eating foods closer to the sun. If your food hasn't been touched by the sun, it doesn't have energy in it. It doesn't have nutrients in it! It has come packaged and made by guys in white cloaks. If you eat food made by guys in white cloaks, you'll end up being treated by guys in white cloaks! When you buy food, if you have to buy something that is not fresh, say, maybe you're buying some wraps, look on the back and check if they made it with five ingredients or less. When you're thinking about getting back to the basics, ask yourself: *did this food touch the sun?* Turn it over, look at the ingredients list. Can you identify the food that's on the ingredients label? *Is it real food?* A great question I love to ask myself, and I get my clients to ask themselves, is: Will *this food fuel me, or flaw me?*

3) Move your body every day! The ugly truth for the vast majority of us is we are so "busy." I try to avoid the glorification of the word "busy" and have erased the word "busy" from my vocab and instead choose the word "full" when describing my life. It changes my attitude from stressed to abundant. A lot of us are getting up early, working nine to five, coming home. We're wired with stress but tired, we're grumpy, we're not investing in our relationships with our family or friends. Often, we're not even making the time to move. Movement doesn't have to mean going to the gym and slogging your body for an hour, but instead, just include movement in your lifestyle, don't complicate it! Get out and go for a walk in the morning with your friends or after work go for a walk with your partner. Go across the road and kick the football or the soccer with kids. Go on a family bike ride. Walk to work, ride to work, take the stairs, play tennis. Go out and dance all night with your girlfriends.

Don't over complicate it. It's about getting right back to basics. It's just about conscious movement. We've got these technologies these days that do everything for us. It's sad that now we've consciously got to put an hour aside to move our bodies these days when, once upon a time, it was just part of the labour of everyday life. We now have little gadgets that count how many steps we take each day and have to schedule an hour out of our busy day to go and move our bodies, and most of us aren't even doing that! It should be part of our lifestyle. Our generation is so stagnant. We sit at desks staring at a screen, stiff all day, with all these expectations getting put on top of us. In a fast-paced world we are struggling to keep up. Then, we're coming home, we're grumpy, and we're tired, then sit on a couch staring at another screen all night. *What kind of life is that?* Include conscious movement into your lifestyle, do things you enjoy; run, walk, swim, dance, kick the footy, ride.

4) Love and invest in your relationships. Put in as often as you take away and get rid of the relationships that don't make you feel good. We have a lot of expectations on us, whether it's in business, maybe it's in friendship circles, or even in the dating world. I'm not sure what rings true for you, but if you've got a relationship you do not enjoy being in the company of, get rid of it. It's not rocket science, right? Yet so many of us are putting up with these people and these energies that literally drain that fun-loving energy out of us. I like to call them energy vampires! If you can't get rid of them, limit the time you spend with them.

5) Reflect. Just like Alcohol addiction, ask what role is technology having in your life? Use it as a tool, don't let it use you. Technology has awesome perks and has made life easier for us in so many ways that most of us take for granted. But just like alcohol, any substance or vice, people can become addicted to it. Ask yourself what kind of role technology is playing in your life. When you come home, are you having conversations with your roommate, your partner, your kids? When you're going out and you're with girlfriends or with your mates, are you there? I would love for you to use this time to have a conscious reflection and think, *what role is technology playing in my life?* If it is having a negative impact on your relationships, on your decisions, I suggest maybe it's time to put in some boundaries. I know a great one for me (because I'll admit, I'm the worst for it. I do most of my business via blogs, YouTube, Instagram, Facebook), is my phone doesn't come into the bedroom anymore. I don't pick it up until 8:00am, and it gets put away at 7:00pm. Then, after that, I'm turning off. I am enjoying time reconnecting with my partner after our days working on our separate projects, reading a book, writing, or sleeping. *Fancy that?!*

6) Practice Gratitude. Be thankful for your running, clean water, warm showers, our health care system, a roof over your head. When you come from a place of abundance, you attract abundance. It's not rocket science, right? Stop complicating health and just get back to basics. Move your body every day. Eat more whole foods, surround yourself with beautiful relationships that light you up, that inspire you, that help you be the best version of you. Drink more water. Technology and all these awesome gadgets meant to make our lives easier, don't. They seem to just put a lot more expectations on ourselves, and on others, and we're really struggling to keep our head above water. *That is not what we're here for.* Stop just surviving and start thriving! Get back to basics, I encourage you to not complicate things. Are you eating right? Are you feeling like shit? Are you feeling grumpy? Don't look for a diagnosis. Don't sit there and wonder, *what's wrong with me?* Go do some conscious movement. Go have a glass of water. Eat some food touched by the sun. Inhale abundance and exhale gratitude.

This is for you mammas - I see you!

Now, for all you mammas out there, I know, as women, it is in our nature to be givers and providers but first, you need to give to yourself. Looking after yourself – self-love, self-care, or whatever you want to label it, is not a "luxury," it's a necessity!

Self-love is not selfish, and if you think it is, fine. Then sometimes you need to be selfish to be selfless! You need to be the best version of you to be able to give the best version of you to your kids, partners, siblings, partners, colleagues, employers, and society.

You need to invest in your health (both physical and psychological) to continue to even be here to "give" to your loved ones. A great metaphor I love to use when explaining this is, when you're in an aeroplane and the air hostess explains the safety procedure, they always explain you first need to put your own oxygen mask before putting on anyone else's.

You're no help to anyone when you're stressed, out of breath, drowning, or dead! Sorry for being morbid, but I promised you no fluffy stuff here. I am all about getting rid of the sugarcoating!

Your universal assignment for today is to pop this book down and have a beautiful, simplified day, lovers! Get outside, do something for you, gain a bigger perspective. Make time for something that naturally excites you, something that purely the thought of it calms you and somehow magically grows a smile across your face. Whether it's going for a walk, feeling the sun kiss your skin, watching a movie with your partner, playing with your children, or dancing all night with your girlfriends. Embrace it.

Take the first step, do something for you, allow yourself some wind-down time because you cannot have success in life, relationships, or business, without your health.

Universal Assignment:

Do something for you.

Chapter Fifteen

Playing Above the Line

Before picking up this chapter, I hope you gave yourself permission to enjoy some downtime, appreciating all the small things around you. One day, you will look back and realise the small things were the big things!

What you have in front of you is nothing compared to what you have inside of you.

Everyone has their own story; everyone has their own demons. Stop letting the fear of other's opinions and your comparison game prevent you from going after what you want and what footprint you want to leave behind because you only have one life.

You have your own zone of genius and are here for a reason, so let's agree, no more wishing it away or wasting it. Let us all start walking passionately and fearlessly to the beat of our own drum with appreciation for other people's music. Agreed?

Are you starting to realise you have been playing small? Or have you not been playing at all? Are you giving 100% commitment and conviction to whatever is important to you at the moment?

There is this thing called "the responsibility game" that I love to do for myself and in my one-on-one coaching with some of the women I mentor in business. I would love to share it with you to help you see if maybe you have been playing small. Maybe you didn't realise you were playing small until this:

RESPONSIBILITY

BLAME
SHAME
JUSTIFY

If you are clear on your goal, you want to be playing above the line and be 100% responsible for it and 100% committed that you are all in. Taking 100% responsibility means you acknowledge and understand the goal will be a direct reflection of your efforts, of your mindset, of the action you take, and the faith you have.

Maybe you have to meditate on it to get in the right head space to truly hone in on it and become "successed" (my word for being obsessed with success!) So, 100% responsibility is your goal; whatever goal you're currently working towards at the moment. I would love for you to ask yourself, *are you taking 100% responsibility? Are you playing above the line?*

Lots of us, when we play this game, fall below the line when we blame others, shame, and justify. One excuse that falls below the responsibility line is blame. We say, "I so would have gone to the gym five days this week, but the kids are just crazy at the moment."

They're blaming it on others, or, "I would have started my business this year. I would have jumped out of my comfort zone. I would have done that, but I just didn't have the support from my partner." Or maybe it is a personal goal. Maybe, "I would have eaten really healthy this week, but when I went to Coles or Woolworths, they didn't have all the food I needed."

Instead of taking 100% responsibility for our goal, we make excuses to make ourselves feel better because it's not our fault. It's somebody else's. We blame others.

Another excuse that falls below the responsibility line is justify. Let's say, for example, you have a health goal. Maybe you say, "my goal is to eat really healthy and have no junk food from Monday to Friday, or no chocolate."

Then, you justify it and you say, "You know what? I had a really hard day on Wednesday so it's ok I had chocolate." Or let's say you're going for a business goal, and you justify saying something like, "I would have done

Universal Assignment:

If you're working on a goal at the moment — are you playing above the line?

Are you taking 100% responsibility for that?

Are you using blame, shame, or justifying why it can't happen?

that. I would have reached that goal this month but it's okay because I had other stuff going on. Yeah, it was Christmas and things just happened."

We justify why we didn't take 100% responsibility for our goal. I remember I had a business goal I was working towards that I had on my vision board, honestly, for eighteen months. The month came to play all out and execute my master plan, but I found myself playing below the line.

I kept putting it off and was umming and ahhing about whether I would go for it at all. I fell victim to shame. Shame is the third excuse that falls below the responsibility line. I let fear dictate me. Instead of playing 100% above the line and being like, *yep this is it. I'm all in. I'm 100% going for this. I will focus on it every day. I will work on my personal development and grow into a person who can achieve this goal*, I was letting shame rule me.

When I say shame, I'm talking about fear of failing. Fear of not being enough. Instead of me playing 100% above the line and saying, *yep, I got this!* I sounded more like, *yeah, maybe I won't just because I don't know if it's worth me putting myself out there. I don't know if it's worth me articulating, saying what I want and that goal, because if I say it out loud it means others will know my goal. That could be embarrassing because what if I fail? What if I put in all that effort and it is not enough, and I still fail?*

I share this with you because I want to let you know we have all been there and we all have that dark passenger or inner mean girl who taunts us. It is about having that awareness to catch yourself when you're playing below the line and calling yourself out on your bullshit, because those excuses aren't serving you. You are surrendering all your power and control in that situation and playing the victim. Ask yourself some better questions.

For the purpose of not glorifying or sugarcoating the story I will let you know I caught myself playing below the line. I cancelled my pity party and played all out that month for my business goal. I felt the fear and did it anyway! I honestly look back while self-reflecting and even asked for feedback from mentors to ensure I wasn't being biased and there was nothing I could have done more of or done better.

I gave it my all, and it wasn't enough and that is ok. I did it with integrity, pride and passion, and in alignment with my values and truth. However, with persistence, grit, and a growth mindset, I DID ACHIVE IT the following month!

"Criticism is something you can easily avoid. Easy. By doing nothing, saying nothing, and being nothing."

ANON

If you're unhappy with where you're at in life, relationships, finances, or career and you don't want to strive for any goals because you're scared of shame and you're scared of embarrassing yourself, that's cool. Stay where you're at and in thirty years' time let's see if your comfort zone was really worth that. Or if it could have been worth that five minutes of bravery or courage it took to step up and take 100% responsibility for your goals.

You can't have success and have someone putting you on a pedestal without another person trying to put you in a pit. You might have people who love you. They love your vibes. They love your mission. They love your values. They love what you stand for, but you'll also have people who are like, *"No, I hate that. I don't like it. You can't do this."* That's why I personally love *"haters"* because it means you're doing something. It means you're taking 100% responsibility and you're going for something that is important to you. I think that's something to be admired and be proud of.

> You can't have success and have someone putting you on a pedestal without another person trying to put you in a pit.

How you do something is how you do everything. You are here for a reason. You have a voice. You have so much power within you to create change and advocate for what is important to you. Whether it be with a simple smile to a stranger, asking how someone is AND LISTENING TO THEIR REPLY, encouraging a competitor, apologising when you're wrong, jumping at opportunities that come your way. Look for the lessons and live fearlessly and passionately.

So, who are you in the world?

For some of you, you may be a sister, a brother, a mother, a father, a teammate, a son, a daughter, a cousin, an aunty, an uncle, an employee, a boss, a mentor, a netball player, a soccer player, a dancer, a teacher. What about in the wider community?

You may be someone's inspiration. You may be someone's favourite

Universal Assignment:

Do you know who you are? Describe yourself in a paragraph.

social media profile to stalk for some encouragement and connection. You may have no idea, but you could be someone's secret crush. You may be the favourite part of someone's day. You may be someone's idol who they look up to in life, business, or relationship. Because of you, they took *that scary step* and made a change that changed the total trajectory of their life.

You may be the rising star or talent your boss or a coach has been secretly keeping their eye on because they see potential in you. You may be the reason your boss, mentor, or coach got out of bed today. They showed up despite the fact everything in their life was falling apart because they see so much in you and don't want to let you down.

How do you think people perceive you? If I then asked someone else in your family, friendship circle, place of work, or in the wider community who you are, would they agree with that description you wrote above? Or would they provide me with a different one?

You never know who is watching you whether it's online on Instagram or Facebook, on the basketball court, at a university, at work, out at a party, sitting on public transport, or walking down the street. (Especially these days with the number of websites tracking us online and government cameras!)

People will make judgments about you. We are human, that is our job as social beings. That is how our brains have evolved to keep us alive with mental shortcuts and heuristics to help us collate information quickly to make quick decisions and assumptions about our environment and the beings in it! Judging people is a protective mechanism.

For example, let's say you are alone and see someone walking down the street towards you who is dressed in dirty clothes that are torn and tattered. They smell like urine; they have a glass bottle in their hand and are yelling abusive words to themselves. *What do you instinctively feel like doing* (rational or not)?

I bet most of you (especially if you're a woman) would be compelled to look down, avoid eye contact, and even cross the road. Stereotypical of us, right, to think we may be harmed or harassed? Stereotypes and previous experiences have told us it might be safer to walk on the other side of the road as you have made the assumption they might be drunk or on drugs.

> Your charcter is defined by things we do when we think no one is watching.

"Integrity – choosing courage over comfort. Choosing right over what is fun, fast, or easy. Choosing to practice your values rather than simply professing them."

BRENÉ BROWN

Are we wrong to call on previous experience and knowledge to keep ourselves safe? Of course not. Sometimes the response is so innate you have already acted before your brain deciphered whether that judgement was rational.

On the weekend when you're at a party and talking to the opposite sex, how you treat an elder lady on the public bus, how you respond to a boss or college when they give you feedback, or even how you respond to an umpire when they make a bad call on the court, people are making judgements on how you hold yourself in any situation. How you act and respond speaks volumes about your character.

Your character is defined by the things we do when we think no one is watching. It is how you treat those who can do nothing for you. Ask yourself, who do I want to be? Who do you need to be to attain the life you want to live?

Do you want to have great relationships?
Do you want a successful career?
Do you want to own your own Business?
Do you want to be respected and admired by your peers?
Do you want to be wealthy and have unlimited opportunities, choices, and flexibility?
Do you want to be oozing gratitude, be bouncing around with vitality and radiating health?
Who do you need to become to attain those things?
Do you need to be kinder, more determined, more consistent, responsible, resilient, mature, dress well, humble, ambitious, hard-working, honest, fun-loving, energetic, educated? Different people want different things, which requires different skills, traits, and attributes.

All those things don't just depend on who you are today in this situation, but who you are in life.

All those things don't just depend on who you are today, in this situation, but who you are in life. It is about consistency, congruency, your character. Who you are in all contexts.

It's not just when people are watching. It's when you're at home, fighting with your partner or your kids, when you're playing sport, when you're out on the weekends, when you're online posting on Facebook or Instagram.

You don't know who is watching you, who is making judgments about you, and what doors that may open or close for you. Ones you may not even be aware of coming your way. But because of something you did that was incongruent with how you were showing up in other areas of your life, has now been consequently taken off the table.

You are your own person. Every decision you make you need to play above the line and take 100% responsibility for and be aware of the consequences it may have. That's not to say you can't make mistakes. No one is perfect. And if you were, trust me, people won't like you because they wouldn't be able to relate to you!

Who you are includes how you handle your mistakes, how you respond to your triumphs and fears; how you grow, and how you learn. Do you apologise when you are wrong or when you have hurt someone (intentionally or not)? Do you identify and accept it? Or do you deny and ignore it?

For an example, let's say in sport (I feel most people can relate to this analogy), you see Brad knock over Tom in football (pretty roughly, may I add). If Brad was to then keep running and leave Tom on the field injured without acknowledging he hurt him, what is your reaction or judgement as a spectator?

Maybe you think he is ruthless, rude, a thug, inconsiderate, doesn't care. Whether that is who he is in his personal life as a brother, as a son, you still rightly or wrongly judge him as a person, don't you? We all do! Like I explained, it is how our brains have evolved. Let's say the same incident happens but Brad takes five seconds to check if Tom is ok, apologises, and helps him back up before running to the other side of the field for the next mark.

Does your perception of Brad's character now change? Now, let's say Brad is dating Molly and is being introduced to Molly's parents that night for the first time. Do you think their opinion of the man dating their daughter will be different if they were in the crowd and saw one of the above scenarios?

Of course it does, because we, as humans, judge, and studies have found all it takes is a tenth of a second to form an impression of a stranger. And at our very base level, we know how you do something is how you do everything. How you play games is also how you play life.

This is just another example of life. Give your best and do your best at all times. Be human. Fall, fail, make mistakes, apologise, learn, endeavour to be better. Whatever you do, play 100% above the line and do the best with what you have got because life is happening for you, not to you.

If you're not taking ownership of your shit, where you are and where you're not showing up in the world, you then need to understand the implications and consequences of that. Recognise everything about you says something about you. This goes not only for you as an individual but businesses touch points, too.

Be the change you want to see in the world

This is important because I promise you, a sense of happiness, energy, confidence, and purpose comes when you know who you are. It's how you show up in every aspect of your life and you can honestly say you are proud of that person. Be someone you would like to meet! And if you're not that person, have the awareness to work on it.

If you are working on a relationship issue, be the change you want to see, give before you receive, show up before you expect. If you want to attract the perfect soulmate, work on being the person your soulmate would want to enjoy time with!

You need to be happy in yourself and enjoy your own company if you want them to, too. If you want a six to seven-figure-dollar business, and right now you're turning over a few thousand a month, roll up your sleeves, fire yourself and rehire yourself as the CEO of your multi-million dollar business.

You can't have a million-dollar dream with a minimum-wage work ethic. You need to show up for the game! You won't be given the opportunity to kick a goal if you're a spectator standing on the sideline, whining and yelling at the players and telling them how to play the game.

Likewise, you won't be given the ball if you're standing on the field throwing a tantrum because it isn't being given to you. Go get it. If you're honestly not sure how you're playing the game of life or how you're showing up, that is ok, too. Self-awareness is a skill, and you don't know what you don't know!

I want to introduce you to a communication tool called the Johari Window, which is also a strategy you can use to improve your emotional intelligence. We use it to improve the understanding of individuals. It is a great tool to help people build better, more trusting relationships with one another, solve issues, and work more effectively as a team (sport, business, or relationships).

You can build trust with others by disclosing information about yourself. And with the feedback from others, you can learn about yourself and come to terms with personal issues or things you may want to change that you weren't aware of. This way you can become a person you are proud of, or the person you need to become to attain the life you want to live.

It also is the opportunity to help team mates to understand the value of self-disclosure, encouraging to give, and accept constructive feedback.

1). OPEN AREA/ARENA: things you know about yourself, things others know about you, e.g. behaviour, knowledge, skills, and public history.
2). BLIND AREA/BLIND SPOT: things you aren't aware of but are known to others.
3). HIDDEN AREA/FAÇADE: things you know about self, but others don't know.
4). UNKNOWN AREA: unknown by you and others. E.g. your potential, how you will perform/respond under pressure.

The end goal is to enlarge the open area (self-disclosure). The more people know about each other, the more productive, co-operative, and effective they'll be in working together

As you share information, your open area will expand vertically, and your hidden area gets smaller. As people on your team provide feedback to you about what they know or see about you, your open area expands horizontally, your blind area gets smaller, too.

Universal Assignment:

The Johari Window. Complete this task with someone in a space you are striving to improve in, whether it is the workplace, a boss, mentor, a colleague, a teammate, a romantic partner, or friendship.

	Known to Self	Unknown to Self
Known to Others	**Open** (Public knowledge; what I show you)	**Blind** (Feedback - your gift to me)
Unknown to Others	**Hidden** (Private; mine to share if I trust)	**Unconscious** (Unknown; new awareness can emerge)

CHAPTER SIXTEEN

Your Personal Formula

How are you feeling at this point? I promised I would equip you with the practical skills and mindset. And I've backed this with the psychology, research, and statistics. I've also layered on some positive, warm vibes and sprinkled some tough love to help you unlock the code to success, not only in your lives, but relationships and careers.

I hope you're understanding by now that there isn't a one-size-fits-all. We are all on our own journey and some of us are further along than others. Living a Life Above Zero isn't a destination. It is not something you can tick off now you have finished the book as you never truly arrive at it.

It is a journey, and it is about having the awareness, the commitment to honour your soul's purpose. It's having the bravery to sit in discomfort and look at the not-so pretty parts of yourself, and the skills to redirect when you find yourself off track. Sometimes you may need to go back and revisit a chapter or an activity to help you navigate road blocks, because I promise you, you will stumble along some on your journey. Others will fall on your head with no warning or justification.

Pick bits and pieces of this book that call to you or align with where you are right now in your journey to help you live your own Life Above Zero. Keep it in a safe place for when you feel called to it again. I promise you, each time you read it or turn to a different chapter, you will pick up something new, depending what chapter of life you are in or what current goals you're pursuing (or lack of).

This book is honestly collated from millions of years and tens of thousands of dollars of knowledge, from all the amazing and inspiring people I have met. Also from what I learned from in my business ventures, university degrees, lecturers and research, books, courses, mentors, and relationships with others and myself. I honestly learn something from every person who crosses my path.

I truly believe life is our biggest teacher of all, if you commit to being a student. I catch myself sometimes when coaching others or presenting seminars and workshops thinking I am a fraud. The problems and feelings people come to me with are ones I still feel and experience today. Yet, they pay me for advice to make those struggles go away or get resolved. But that is the funny thing, they aren't paying us to do that.

What Psychologists, Life Coaches, and Business Coaches do is, essentially, just ask great quality questions and do years of training to get better at mastering the skills of active listening. They listen to not only what you say, but how you say it with your tone, your body language, and taking notes, even more so of the things you don't say.

Our job is to make you feel heard, make you feel loved, connected, and like you're not alone, because you're not. It is not in our job descriptions to give you advice. To be honest, you don't need it! With some strategic paraphrasing and parroting, a good coach will make you realise you have all the answers you need within you.

We are just over-paid master-askers who most of us need at one point or another to remind us "you are worthy, you are not alone, you are human, you are loved, you have all the skills you need. You know where to find the resources." We all need connection, we all need to be validated, acknowledged, and encouraged. You matter. You are enough.

Man, you are more than enough. There is Life Above Zero, and you, my friend, deserve to live it! You have all you need to live your own Life Above Zero. I hope this book has proved that to you; whether you are someone who needed my hippy positive vibes, my tough love, or the hard-stone facts and research to believe it yourself!

We all have shitty days, days where we don't feel enough, lost, or just blughhh. I hope, with this book, you now have the resources, skills, tips, personal experience, research, and recommendations for further exploration of books or podcasts. You pick what works for you and what doesn't; we all have our own formula.

My Personal Formula for Success

I have a distinct memory of me telling my partner the exciting news work had offered me a position I really wanted. His response was, "Of course you did, Lauren. It wouldn't be like you to not get what you wanted."

I remember then, calling my Dad to tell him the same good news, his response was similar. "Of course you did, you're Lauren. Everything always works out for you." At first, these remarks from the two men in my life from who I seek approval and attention offended me.

What they said sounded to me like I was a spoiled brat who gets whatever they want handed to them on a silver platter. I know that was not their intention. I know, and they know (*and anyone else who witnesses how hard I work, consistently, and wholeheartedly knows*) that is not the case.

But yes, they are right, in some way or another, I do always get what I want. There is a process to my thinking surrounding these things. This is my formula for success and happiness. To me, they are the same thing. I hope you can see and draw the parallels from earlier chapters to see why it has worked so far for me.

Feel free to steal bits and pieces of my recipe when you put together your own. You know what they say, success leaves clues. First, I have a hard think about what I truly, deeply want/need to be a happy and healthy human. I question what receiving or gaining that would give me or change in my life. I allocate my time and energies accordingly.

I guess this is why I am a Life and Wellness coach. I wholeheartedly want to teach others how they can get what they want, how to live the life they want, and how to be the person they want to be. If you won't go out and get it, no one else will give it to you.

Have a Vision

First, I ask, what is success to me? Is it a personal vision, a feeling, way of life, a position? Is it wisdom, ownership of materialistic possessions? I realise my goals, my passions, and my purpose, then I set and achieve goals in accordance to them.

My favourite ways to set goals or cast visions in my head is by creating a vision board or writing a letter from my future self. It sounds corny, but just try it. From there, work backwards and celebrate the small wins along the way!

Acceptance

When I don't get what I want, I don't stomp my feet and chuck a tantrum. Although I am sure there are occasions growing up my Dad would probably disagree with that. In the real "adult" world, I handle closed doors and disappointments very differently.

This is why people may have the "illusion" I always get what I want because I practice acceptance. I say, if I had always got what I wanted, I would be one unhappy girl today. I have learned to be thankful for closed doors, detours, and roadblocks, because they protect me from paths and places not meant for me.

==I shift my motivation and commitment to an alternative route and keep moving forward with even more enthusiasm.==

Sure, I have thrown a little pity party for myself, but have learned to free myself from them as I gain emotional intelligence and maturity. You need to identify your feelings. Recognise them and give yourself space to allow them.

Experience those feelings, otherwise they don't go away, they just get suppressed. However, I don't let my pity party turn into a pity bender. I shift my thought patterns (or call someone in my trusty circle to help me). I shift my motivation and commitment to an alternate route and keep moving forward with even more enthusiasm.

When I get knocked down, I get back up again, trusting the universe has bigger better plans for me. This is where religion may play a role for some. For me, it is faith in the universe and its laws.

Be Kind

I am kind to everyone I meet. Everyone. Whether they be in my professional or personal world, I am always kind. This can be challenging sometimes, especially when I was working in Child Protection. Nonetheless, I do it anyway. When you are kind and help others, most people are kind in return, and are happy to help you on your road to success.

If you need something, whether it be help, advice, or to be introduced to someone who can help, usually, a person you have been kind to will be more than willing to help. Don't have ulterior motives. Help others and be kind to every soul you meet. It's called "Karma" and it will return the favour someday.

Be Genuine

When I say I am kind, that does not mean I am fake or sugarcoat my words. I don't beat around the bush or just tell people what they want to hear. (This would definitely not work in Child Protection). Sometimes, if I have something I need to say that may offend someone, I will say it anyway (nicely).

I can explain my intentions. If I have to say something that might hurt someone's feelings I explain I've said it in the best interest of that person. Check back in with yourself, reflect, and question yourself to ensure it really is. How will this person benefit from hearing what it is you have to say? Does it really need to be said if it is at the risk of hurting their feelings or beating their self-esteem?

I explain to them I am telling them this because I care for them and want to be transparent with them.

Work hard

I identify my end goal and I ask myself; *how badly do I really want it? What am I willing to sacrifice for it?* It is true, if it was easy we would all have it or all do it. Sometimes it is easier to whine and moan, to blame it on bad luck and on others, than it is to take ownership, to take accountability, and to step up and make changes.

If I want to lose weight but I am not willing to eat a balanced diet or get my body moving, then I obviously don't want to lose the weight bad enough. If I want an A on my next exam but I want to keep watching that

> *"There is a big difference between working hard and hard work."*
>
> **LAUREN KERR**

TV series instead, it's obvious I don't want those grades bad enough.

If I want true, committed love, yet I am not willing to suck up my pride and have the uncomfortable discussions with my partner to work out our issues, then guess what? I don't want the relationship bad enough. Working hard isn't about instant gratification, either. If I want something, I work at it. I do not give up.

It's about persistence. It's making sacrifices today for something I might not necessarily see tomorrow or the next day but trust I will reap the benefits in a month or years' time. This is how university works!

I am sure a few of you reading this are just like me and juggled three to four part-time/casual jobs while studying at uni, knowing in four to five years' time it would all be worth it. Same as going for a run although you get an instant release of endorphins. You cannot expect to drop weight after one run. It comes back to consistent work.

If the end goal is truly something I madly, deeply want, something my heart is longing for, then the hard/persistent work won't discourage me as I will be in "flow." I will go to bed dreaming about it and wake up excited about it! And if I don't, I revisit my goal and ask myself; *do I truly want it?* This is leads me to:

Reflection

This is a biggie for me. I frequently reflect to ensure the life I am living is in accordance with my values, things I believe are important. This is how I decide and weigh up what sacrifices are worth making, or if I am sacrificing too much.

A way I keep this in check is by using my "mission statement." It is a little piece of paper I have written and keep in my diary and in the notes section of my phone. I have identified my top five values and articulated how the person I aspire to be would ideally incorporate these into my life accordingly.

> This is how I decide and weigh up what sacrifices are worth making, or if I am sacrificing too much.

Universal Assignment:

What bits and pieces from this book will you incorporate in your life? What is your success formula?

By reflecting, I ensure I align my behaviour with my values, essentially making sure I am walking my talk. I reflect the purity of my intentions. And I ensure they are not manipulated by society, status, fashion, or money, as these are things I have identified in my mission statement are not values of mine I want to be controlled or dictated by.

Forgiveness

In life, you must have emotional balance, just like you need a healthy dose of work and play, veggies and sweets, sun and rain. There is happiness and sadness. It is inevitable you'll get hurt. Don't let the world make you hard. Love and live wholeheartedly. Forgive. Don't hold on to negative energy, hating, bitching, or stalking someone's Instagram/Facebook pages.

All that does is make you spiteful and heavy. It takes way more energy to hate than it does to love, so forgive. It's like my favourite saying. *"Resentment is like drinking poison and hoping it will kill your enemies"* – Nelson Mandela.

Forgiveness, however, does not necessarily mean to forget. I make an executive decision. I am my own boss. Do I want this person in my life? If I do, fair enough. I acknowledge what they did was wrong. I also realise they can do it again, and I love and accept them anyway by planning for it or not allowing them to be in the position to hurt me again.

> *I am motivated, yet, also at peace with where I am.*

> *I happily achieve not achieve to be happy.*

I consciously decide to be a lover not a fighter and know better for next time. If I decided, no, I don't want that person in my life anymore, then that's also fair enough. I respect myself enough to walk away from anyone or anything that no longer enriches or grows me.

I appreciate that lesson and let it go. I don't waste energy ruminating over it; I forgive them and use that energy to be constructive, move forward, and closer to my success and happiness.

This is my personal formula. It may not work for everyone, but that's the whole point of this book. Identifying what is important to you, the individual, and living your life accordingly.

By practicing these seven things in my life, I am a happier person. People often describe me as "happy–go-lucky" and a "go-getter." I am motivated, yet, also at peace with where I am. I happily achieve not achieve to be happy. I get to live life light with no baggage, no regrets, nor hatred.

I can look at myself in the mirror and be proud of who I am, because I treat everyone the same regardless of what they offer me. Like everything in life, it comes down to balance. Be a nice human but don't expect things to be passed to you because of it. You still have to get up and chase those big dreams yourself, but that's where the fun begins!

CHAPTER SEVENTEEN

Do the Best You Can, with What You Can, as Long as You Can

It wouldn't be a book on life without also talking about death. As you have learned by now, everything comes in duality. I promised I wouldn't sugarcoat this for you, so I want to create the space to talk about death, rather than uncomfortably skimming over it.

The question is, will you wait until the last moment to let death be your teacher? I see it happen all the time in my job. People often have to lose something before they appreciate what they have. People often lose a loved one, a job, a spouse, become disabled or ill before they look for another source of income or invest in their health.

The mere possibility of death has the power to teach us at any moment. I love Michael Singer's perspective that he shares in his book *The Untethered Soul: The Journey Beyond Yourself.* A wise person realises at any moment they might breathe out and the breath might not come back in. It could happen any time in any place and your last breath is gone. Learn from this. A wise being completely and totally embraces the reality, the inevitability, and the unpredictability of death.

Any time you're having trouble with something, think of death. Let's say you were the jealous type and you can't stand anyone being close to your friend or partner. Think about what will happen when you are no longer here. Is it really all that romantic your loved one should live all alone with no one to care for them with no support networks to lean on?

If you can get passed your personal issues, you will realise you want the person you are with to be happy and have a long and beautiful life.

Since that is what you want for them, why bother them or waste your energy making yourself feel heavy for just talking to someone?

Or, let's say you work in the health and wellness field and you see somebody else use similar content and concepts in their business. Is it really worth the energy despising or hating them for it or accusing them of "copying" when they are just trying to help share the mission and message. You help more people sharing content together than you do alone, which is the real reason you do what you do in the larger scale of things.

Another example I know comes up for a lot of women. I will sheepishly admit I have been there, too. Let's say you have been with your partner for years and secretly can't wait to get married. You see your friends around you getting engaged and they haven't even been together half the time you have with your partner. Do you waste your energy feeling resentful and jealous?

Does their love subtract or take anything away from yours? In the larger scheme of things, you would hate for them to go through life without love. Aren't you grateful your friend has found someone in this lifetime who makes them that happy? It shouldn't take death to challenge you to live at your highest level. Why wait until everything is taken from you before you learn to dig down deep inside yourself and reach your highest potential?

This is the consciousness needed for deep and meaningful relationships. We take it for granted our loved ones are there and will continue to be there for us. What if they die? What if you die? What if you knew this evening will be the last one you get to see them?

How would you feel? How would you interact with them? Would you even bother with the little grudges and complaints you have been carrying around? How much love would you give to your loved ones? How much would you be loved in return?

Think about what it would be like if you lived like that every moment with everyone? Your life would be really different. Death is not a morbid thought. It is the greatest teacher in all of life.

Look at how much time and energy you put into various things.

Imagine if you knew you'd die within a week or a month.

How would you change things?

"We're all gonna die. We don't get much say over how or when. But we get to decide how we're going to live. So, do it. Decide. Is this the life you wanna live? Is this the person you want to love? Is this the best you can be? Can you be stronger? Kinder? More compassionate? Decide.
Breathe in. Breathe out and decide."

RICHARD WEBBER

Take a moment to look at the things you think you need. Look at how much time and energy you put into various things. Imagine if you knew you'd die within a week or a month. How would that change things? How would your priorities change? How would your thoughts change? Think, honestly, about what you would do in the last week. What a wonderful thought to contemplate.

What are you doing with your time now? *Throwing it away? Wasting it? Treating it as if it's not precious?* What are you doing with this life you were gifted? That is what death asks you. If I was to tell you you only have one week left to live, *do you feel like you need more?* That is a good indicator you've been playing below that responsibility line.

God gave you the last fifty-two weeks, why do you need an extra one? What have you done with the rest? Were you not paying attention? Did you not think it mattered? That is a telltale sign of what you think of your life. God doesn't give you a warning, you are living on borrowed time. Why not be bold enough to regularly reflect on how you want to spend your week?

Enlightened and awakened people wouldn't change the way they live, think, or behave. They are living their lives fully and in alignment with their values. They are not playing the responsibility game with themselves, settling for mediocrity, or letting the fear of what others think cheat them out of the best experiences and decisions of their life.

For you to do the same, you need to be living Life Above Zero as if death is staring you straight in the face and then, come to peace with yourself. It doesn't matter whether it is, or it is not. Instead of letting this chapter scare you, let it liberate you to live your life fully. Don't feel uncomfortable or be scared to talk about death.

Why are you not living this way? You will die. You know that. You just don't know when. Death will take every single thing from you. You will leave behind your possessions, loved ones, and all your hopes and dreams. All that will be left is your footprint. *What footprint are you leaving behind if you die today? What will you be remembered for?*

Some of us fear death; not the fear of dying itself, but the fear of losing a loved one and wanting to be selfish and enjoy them longer. This, too, is inevitable and for the vast majority of us, unpredictable. Like all emotions, the pain demands to be felt. You can try to shrug it off, deny it, and even

"The reality is you will grieve forever. You will not "get over" the loss of a loved one; you will learn to live with it. You will heal and you will rebuild yourself around the loss you have suffered. You will be whole again, but you will never be the same. Nor should you be the same,
nor would you want to."

ELIZABETH KUBLER

suppress it, but it will just continue to pop up in other areas of your life until you give yourself permission to feel it.

Death sometimes can leave a bigger imprint and make a bigger positive impact than one person's life could have done alone. How often do we hear someone's spirit, their attitude, their ambitions, their passions, and legacy continuing to live on after their death because their life was a testament to their mission?

They left unfinished business behind or they lived so fiercely with the days they had left, those they left behind felt inspired and compelled to step up into greatness so their legacy lived on. Sometimes it may be in the form of a charity with the suffering of one saving the many, rallying, or fighting to raise awareness for a greater population. Or even inspiring those who are left behind to become a better person, parent, daughter, or sister.

Death is our biggest teacher, but you decide whether you will be the student and look for the lessons and the gratitude. *How lucky are we to have loved someone so much it makes saying goodbye hurt so much?*

There are moments in life that stop and make you think. These moments make you realise the small, insignificant problems in your life aren't as nearly as important or dramatic as you think. It is called perspective. Perspective is life's way of telling you you aren't the centre of the universe. Look around and appreciate what you have, not what you don't have.

Celebrate your Birthdays!

Personally, this is why I love celebrating birthdays because you're celebrating another year you were gifted with. I get so frustrated when people say it is just another year or they don't want to celebrate the fact they are getting older. Damn right, it was another year!

Another year so many people were not gifted with, so jump up and down with gratitude and excitement for life! I am not saying you need to throw a massive party. What I *am* saying is take the time and make the space to reflect on your last twelve months. *What did you learn? What did you get to see, experience, feel, or achieve?*

Don't live the next year in vain and ignorantly assume you will see

Universal Assignment:

On a spare piece of paper, draw seventy squares (ten lines going one way and seven going the other). Then, cross out a box for every year you have lived. There are seventy because the average life expectancy in the world is seventy years.

How many squares have you crossed out?

Have you spent them wisely?

How many squares do you have left?

What do you want to do with the remaining ones?

your next birthday. *How will you be a better person, a wiser person, a happier and healthier person or help more people and make the world a better place because of what the last twelve months has taught you?*

If you are gifted with another twelve months, will you spend it wisely or waste it repeating the same mistakes or moaning about the same petty shit? You know if it is your birthday, I will always ask you, "What was your biggest lesson this year? What do you know now that you didn't on your birthday last year?"

> If you are gifted with another twelve months, will you spend it wisely or waste it repeating the same mistakes or moaning about the same petty shit?

I encourage you to ask yourself and your loved ones this every year, too! Not just because it stops them going through the motions unconsciously and forces them to think if they are living their own Life Above Zero, but you can also learn from them.

I am a massive believer the universe will tell you what you need to hear when you need to hear it. You have no control where it will come from though. Insanity is the definition of doing the same things repeatedly and expecting a different result. Why not save yourself the time, energy, pain, and money and learn from your loved ones' mistakes? And be open to the universe's feedback. When you're looking for advice, it may surprise you with what methods it uses to communicate it to you.

You don't have to change your whole life; you just have to change how you are living it. It is not what you're doing, it's how much of you is doing it!

When was the last time you were grateful for your sight, hearing, legs, fingers, food, a roof over your head?

When was the last time you got up early just to watch the sunrise, laid on the grass to look up at stars, or really treasured the moment of an embrace with a loved one and took it all in? Their smell, their warmth, the way their body fits so snug like a puzzle piece next to yours?

Everybody dies but not everybody lives

Since you know you'll die, be willing to say what needs to be said. Let go of what you have no control over and do what needs to be done. Be willing to be fully present without being depressed over what has happened in the past, or anxious or afraid of what will happen in the next moment. Be grateful you have *now*. Only then, will you have fully experienced life and released the part of you that is afraid of living.

The only thing to gain from life is the growth that comes from experiencing it. So dream big, set goals that align with your values, play above the line and enjoy the journey, the lessons, the people you meet along the way, and most importantly, the person you grow into!

Life itself is your career and the interaction with life is your most meaningful relationship. What gives life meaning is your willingness to live it. There was an anonymous quote I stumbled across online a few years ago from an eighty-year-old woman the week before she died, where she spoke about the rocking chair test. This is a little question I now use and ask myself when I find myself conflicted to make sure I continue to live my Life Above Zero!

It could be as simple as me pondering on whether I should pay a little extra money to fly down and visit family in peak season. Or maybe get up a little earlier to watch the sunrise, or not get my to-do list done so I can enjoy dinner with my partner instead.

When death is around the corner, it is you who changes, not life. Life exists with or without you. It's been going on for billions of years, you just get to experience a tiny slice of it. Life would not be precious without the awareness of death. You would waste every second of it because of the assumption you would always have it.

> When death is around the corner,
>
> it is you who changes, not life.
>
> Life exists with or without you.

"I think the best thing we can do is just constantly imagine yourself being eighty, sitting in a rocking chair, and looking back on your life. Think about all the opportunities you're presented with every day and ask yourself; would my eighty-year-old self be happy with this? Like, say your dad wakes you up at eight in the morning and asks if you want to go out for breakfast. Right now, as a young adult or teenager, you would probably just roll over in your bed and refuse because you're too tired or can't be bothered. But as an eighty-year-old looking back, you would jump out of bed and go have breakfast without any second thought.
It is just the little things, you know."

ANON

People fear death because they think it is taking something away from them, but it's constantly giving life meaning. Death gives meaning to life; you are the one who throws life away. You really don't need any more time before death, you just need more awareness of death while you are living.

Death is the landlord and you are the tenant. I work hard and consistently pursuing my goals, not only because of my awareness of death, but the awareness if I don't. I am also mourning the death of what could have been. The lives I could have touched, the opportunities I could have created, the things I could have seen. And the magical moments and experiences I could have enjoyed with loved ones, purely from just consciously deciding to live Life Above Zero rather than settling for a mediocre one.

It doesn't mean I don't get scared, have moments of doubt or insecurity. I hope you are learning by now we are ALL human. We ALL feel those things. But I feel the fear and do it anyway for that exact reason. Because we are human, which means we are not immortal.

> You really don't need any more time before death, you just need more awareness of death while you are living.

I don't want to look back and wonder "what if?" I could live a different life if I didn't constantly reflect and put myself in check to ensure I am living in alignment with my values and challenge myself.

This is the same way I look at my health. I move my body and come from a place of love and gratitude that I can. I don't need to lose something or have a health crisis for me to count my blessings. Likewise, I don't look in the mirror and shred myself to pieces because I ate that piece of pudding (who am I kidding; I ate three!) and wish my stomach was flatter, my belly button was a cute little innie, or my nose wasn't so damn wonky! I know when I am on my deathbed those things won't matter. It will honestly come down to: H*ow well did I live and how much did I love?*

I have the same approach in business. In my early twenties, without kids, my partner and I don't need to go down to one income or wait for a crisis before we think about other ways of making an income or creating multiple income streams. We only have one life, so I am deliberate and proactive in creating income streams that allow me to spend mine the way I want to live it. Is this the way you want to spend yours? *Really?*

I'm not a millionaire, nor do I want to be. I just want the lifestyle and freedom to enjoy life instead of working fifty hours a week during the best years of my life in hope I'll enjoy it in the last years of my life. Life is happening now. Are you getting the time to enjoy it? Or have you bought into the rat race epidemic, too, where you seem to spend every waking hour working, yet still can't seem to get more than a week ahead?

Instead of trading your time for money, have you looked into other ways and options of creating an income? Have you even looked into Babes in Business to see to see if it could be something for you? I am a massive believer that we can divide passions into two categories; you can pursue a passion and it generates an income for you or you generate an income so you can pursue a passion.

Sadly, what I have found is most people are doing neither. They're going through the motions of life like it is groundhog day without experiencing much fulfilment, purpose, inspiration, or passion. Trust me, I have been there. I get it! But I got out of my way and made a conscious decision I wanted more for my life. I committed to playing above the responsibility line to create a life I love. And stopped taking advice from broke, overworked, unhappy, and unhealthy people along the way who had not achieved what I wanted.

I love that I now have the freedom to work on my own terms, and in my own time from wherever I want to work. Some weeks I work between beach swims, yoga classes, and lunch dates with girlfriends. While other weeks I work between road trips, visiting family interstate, and adventuring other countries. Work to live, don't live to work.

My girlfriend, Emily, was in a freak accident a few years ago when she was having the time of her life travelling the world and fell through a roof in a hostel in Peru. She is an incomplete paraplegic and has spent the last few years teaching herself how to walk, live, and love again.

Being able to watch her healing journey has been nothing short of inspiring and a constant reminder of our blessings. It truly is the awareness of death and tragedies while you're living that give life so much meaning. I

"Oh my God, what if you wake up someday and you're sixty or seventy-five and you never got your memoir or novel written; or you didn't go swimming in the warm pools and oceans all those years because your thighs were jiggly and you had a nice, big, comfortable tummy; or you were so strung out on perfectionism and people-pleasing that you forgot to have a big, juicy, creative life of imagination and radical silliness and staring off into space like when you were a kid? It's going to break your heart. Don't let this happen."

ANNE LAMOTT

cannot imagine what Em has been through and continues to go through.

Getting better is a full-time job for her, but I don't believe you need to personally break every bone from your neck down to be reminded how fragile life is. I would love for you to learn from Emily's experiences and here are some of her reflections for you to ponder on before you embark on a new week:

"2.5 years ago, if in a single moment, I wanted to get up, leave work in the middle of my shift without telling anyone, and go learn to surf. Well, I could have! Might have lost my job – but I could have. 2.5 years ago, if in a single moment I decided I wanted to do a salsa dancing class (FUN) well, I could have changed my plans and gone dancing. 2.5 years ago, if in a single moment I felt the urge to be somewhere I've never been, see people and sights I'd never met or seen – grow; expand my mind; expand my horizons; live on my own time; travel – well, I could have scraped together my pennies, packed my bags, and flown high! When you're attached to a drip and literally can't move as loss of antibiotics could equal loss of foot, amputation. Well, to go Travelling?

I cannot. When you are NOT allowed to stand on your feet due to recent surgery, well, dancing?

I cannot. What are your excuses? Let them go.

Do it for all those in hospital beds. I wanna see you living. Your job is NOT stopping you, your financial situation is not stopping you.

And if your HEALTH is not stopping you, then, only YOU are stopping you.

If you want to make something happen, you totally can; if I can make my legs work, you can use yours for whatever you want to. They and health can take you anywhere. The truth is, if you're going to quit anything – quit waiting for the right moment.

The moment is now. Like I always say, it's NOW, sometimes tomorrow does not come quite as expected.

Trust me on that one."

– Emily Wornes

My wish for you after reading this book is that you embrace each day with a new zest and enthusiasm for life. Stop dying for weekends or holidays or settling for jobs, lifestyles, or relationships less than the ones you can have and pursue.

Universal Assignment:

The rocking chair test. Let's imagine you're eighty and sitting in your rocking chair. What is an opportunity that is presenting itself to you right now you would regret not pursuing and giving 100%?

Like Steve Jobs says, *"If today were the last day of my life, would I want to do what I am about to do today? And whenever the answer has been 'No' for too many days in a row, I know I need to change something."*

Today is the first day of the rest of your life

Live each day with passion and pride and to your very fullest because you're able to! Every day you wake up is a day longer than you can expect. You're living on borrowed time. Tomorrow is a gift. It is not promised. Everything you assume you build your foundation upon like times with family, the embrace of your partner, kids, the sunrise on your face, may not be yours to feel any longer, so pay attention to it.

Take the time to enjoy it. Appreciate it and stop sweating all the small stuff! What will you do or say or feel when you're told your time is up? If not the time of your life, the time when you had it easy? Don't wait to lose a job, a loved one, or your health before you start build a life of health, wealth, and abundance.

Because the things you are whining and moaning about now, once upon a time you prayed for them, and someone, somewhere in the world, has it so much worse. So acknowledge your feelings (all feelings deserve to be validated) but don't wallow in that pity party for too long.

Life is too damn short to not be living Above Zero. MAN, THE FUCK UP! Don't be so quick to give up and throw in the towel when things don't go your way or throw a tantrum when they are more challenging than you initially thought. Your dreams and goals are worth so much more than a stable pay check or group of people's approvals.

Be resilient. Persevere. Don't wish it was easier. Wish you were better! Some days you thrive with leaps and bounds, while other days, it is just about taking each day a step at a time. Focus on *now*, appreciate the journey, and find the bits of light in the darkness.

Don't spend time feeling sorry for people whose situations you cannot change, there is no point in that. What you really need to do is be grateful for the people in your life and the ability you have to live life. There is no excuse for you to not live life fully. You owe it to the people who are unable to; you owe them that service, to go out there and do your best.

By living your Life Above Zero, you vibrate at that higher frequency,

"We have calcium in our bones, iron in our veins, carbon in
our souls, and nitrogen in our brains.
93% stardust with souls made of flames,
we are all just stars that have people's names."

ANON

which naturally raises others up with you. Remember the universal laws. We are all just energy and you can control the energy you're radiating at which gives others permission to do the same. It assures those who don't know how they can, too, because what is in you is also in them.

We are all so lucky to live in a time where the world is smaller, and our minds are bigger. Strangers are friends we haven't met yet. There are so many fruits you haven't tasted, so many beautiful songs you haven't discovered, spices you've never heard of, and intriguing conversations you haven't had.

> There is no excuse for you not to live life fully.
>
> You owe it to people who are unable to;
>
> you owe them that service, to go out there and do your best.

There are oceans you have not felt and plants you haven't seen. Books you've never read and souls your heart has not touched. The Earth is incredible, and it's only one of the billions of planets out there! Few of us stop every now and then to take a step back and think of the big picture.

Earth is one of the smaller of the one hundred billion planets in our solar system with only one moon. Jupiter and Saturn have sixty-two moons each. Our star, the Sun, is huge compared to the size of Earth. About one million (1,000,000) Earths would fit inside the sun.

Our galaxy, the Milky Way, which includes our solar system is comprised of at least two hundred billion stars like our sun. More recent estimates put the number close to four hundred billion. Our entire solar system is 1/200 billionth of our galaxy. Our sun cannot be seen when looking at the Milky Way.

The universe has one hundred billion galaxies. Our galaxy is 1/100 billionth of the universe. If we would look at the universe, each galaxy would look like a small, bright object. The estimated number of stars in the universe would be twenty billion-trillion (or twenty sextillion) stars.

Where we fit into this equation: if our sun represents 1/20 sextillion, we can estimate that planet Earth would be 1/millions of that, which would make our share of the universe to b... drum roll

0.000000000000000000000000005%.

In effect from the universe perspective, Earth almost amounts to nothing. Each human being is 1/6 billion of this nothing! How does that help put your problems into perspective in the larger scheme of things? The universe does not revolve around us. We are only a small, invisible, almost non-existent blip on the radar of the universe.

We are here for a brief moment in time and space in this form. All that matters is that we do our best, enjoy the ride, and let the rest unfold in due course. We are nothing yet everything all at once. We are all energy; we never truly die. We just transmute into and out of form.

We are one. Everything in existence, as we know it, originated from the same source of energy. Everything just is. This unifying view can help us in leading lives with understanding and appreciation, no judgment or use of force against anything or anyone. Life still goes on as intended.

The universe goes on with or without you, so lighten up and don't take things too seriously. We are fortunate to experience and participate in this magnificent cosmic dance.

Be empowered and reminded to choose thoughts that are flexible, not rigid; soft, not hard. Think with humility, not arrogance; with detachment, not attachment. Practice thinking big and accomplishing small wins at a time and thinking in harmony with nature, rather than with your ego.

Prefer peaceful solutions and using the universe's flow to gain momentum rather than fighting against currents to solve disputes. Know in the darkest hours, you are not alone. You are always connected to a higher source, whoever you perceive that to be.

Don't believe me? Tell yourself to stop thinking, *who is that rude person ignoring my instructions and still chatting away in my head?* When you go to sleep, who is responsible for what happens the eight hours when you clock off? Who dreams those dreams? Who keeps your heartbeat moving? Who pulls up the blankets when you're cold, or turns over in the middle of the night when you're uncomfortable?

Do you think it placed you here on Earth to crawl and struggle through life?

When you are trying to sleep and sit there restless for hours, but you have a voice in your head yelling back at you when you're not even talking. Who is that? You are being guided. The universe is magical, powerful; it has created billions of planets, and it has also created you.

You are not in the universe; the universe is in you. So when you're doubting your ability to do something, you're really doubting the source, and do you honestly think it doesn't know what it is doing? Do you honestly think it placed you here on Earth to crawl and struggle through life?

If you can believe in Santa for fifteen years, then you can believe in yourself for two minutes! And if that is too hard for you right now, why not believe in something bigger than you and trust you are here for a reason and trust that pull in your gut? Intuition is real. Vibes are real. Energy doesn't lie. Tune in rather than drowning it out with excuses, noise, drugs, pharmaceuticals and petty bullshit.

You're way too smart to be the only thing standing in your own way. You have got this. There is a divine knowing inside of you. Pretend you're in an airplane and you're learning to fly. You're full of nerves, you're pressing buttons and trying to implement what you learn as you go. But in the seat next to you, you have a pilot who has been flying for years who will ensure you don't fall.

> You do the best you can, with what you can,
>
> as long as you can.
>
> You're living Life Above Zero.

It is doing all the small things in the background to keep the airplane in the air which you aren't even aware of yet, let alone grateful for. Oh, God bless you, thinking you're doing it all by yourself. You're so cute! This is how life works. You have your conscious brain, but you also have your unconscious brain, the habitual brain, which is working in the background full-time, every single day. It's consistently communicating and interacting with the universe and its laws.

If you can practice with the skills provided in this book to calm your conscious brain, make room to quiet it every now and then. Tune in, listen and align with your inner knowing, it knows what to do. It always has. An amazing thing happens when you get honest with yourself and start doing what you love, what makes you happy.

Your life literally slows down. You stop wishing for the weekend. You stop merely looking forward to special events. You live in each moment, and you feel like a human being rather than a human constantly doing. You just ride the wave that is life with this feeling of contentment and joy.

You move fluidly, steadily, calm, and grateful. A new veil is lifted, a new perspective is born. You appreciate mortality, growth, and every person who is part of your journey. Acknowledge that, even though they may not be there to stay, you are grateful the universe allowed their soul to drop by. You do the best you can, with what you can, as long as you can. You're living Life Above Zero.

"In the end, I've come to believe in something I call 'the physics quest', a force in nature governed by the laws of gravity. The rules of quest physics go something like this: If you're brave enough to leave behind everything familiar and comforting and set out on a truth-seeking journey, whether internally or externally, and if you are truly willing to regard everything that happens to you on that journey as a clue, and if you accept everyone you meet along the way as a teacher, and if you are prepared most of all to face and forgive some of the most difficult realities about yourself, then the truth will not be withheld from you."

EAT, PRAY, LOVE

www.ingramcontent.com/pod-product-compliance
Lightning Source LLC
Chambersburg PA
CBHW061205070526
44583CB00025B/3123